ADVENTURES
ON A MOTORCYCLE
gearing up for touring & camping

Richard Mawson

Adventures on a Motorcycle

First Edition 2013

Photographs

Front Cover © David Carson
Back Cover © Richard Mawson

all others © respective owners
all maps produced using Google Maps

www.2bikes1mission.co.uk/books

"A desk is a dangerous place from which to watch the world"

-John le Carré

Contents

Preface 11

Introduction 12

What the guide does not cover or have 12

What the guide does cover 12

BIKES 14

Choosing a Motorbike 14

Luggage 34

Soft Luggage 34

Throw Overs 34

Soft Bags on Frames 35

Ventura Bike Packs 36

Hard Luggage 37

Plastic 37

Aluminium 39

Other Luggage 49

Tank Bags 49

Top Boxes 50

Roll Bags 51

Tail Bags or Tail Packs 52

A Little Bit of Everything 54

Tank Panniers or Crash bar Bags 55

Waist Packs/Bum Bags 56

Backpacks/Rucksacks 57

Luggage Extras 57

Pannier Lid Bags 57

Pannier Net Pockets 58

Bike Modifications 60

Screen 60

Manufacturers Adjustable Screens 61

After Market Screens & Spoilers/Laminar Lips 61

Winglets 62

Seats 62

Heated Grips 64

Hand Guards 65

Bar Risers 66

Engine/Bike Protection 67

Engine Bars or Crash Bars 67

Crash Mushrooms/Crash Bobbins 68

Radiator Guards 70

Headlight Protectors 70

Lighting 72

HID 73

Auxiliary Lights 74

12v Take Off 79

Liquid Transportation 80

Clothing 82

Helmet 82

Flip fronts 83

Motorcross /Duel Sport Style 83

Sun Visors 84

Pinlock 84

Chin Fasteners 84

Gloves 85

Boots 86

Waterproof Over boots 88

Jacket/Trousers 89

Socks 91

Layering System 92

Base Layer 92

Mid Layer 93

Outer Layer 93

Extreme Layer 93

Neck Tube 94

Heated 94

Packing the Bike...96
Pre Trip Bike Maintenance... 101
  Tyres 101
    Types & Tread..101
  Battery 103
  Coolant 103
  Oil 104
  Oiling and Adjusting...104
  Hydraulic Levels 104
  Suspension..104
  Tool Kit...105
  Food & Drink..109
CAMPING...119
  Tents...119
    Single/Double Skin Tents 120
    Ventilation 121
    Styles 122
    Fly Sheet/Outer Tent/Hydrostatic Head..124
    Ground Sheets/Footprints 125
    Porch/Vestibule..126
    Seasons of a Tent..126
    Doors 127
    Poles 127
    Pegs 128
    Overall Pack Weight..128
    Example Tents...128
  Sleeping 144
    Sleeping Bags..144
    Sleeping Bag Liner...153
    Sleeping Mat...153
  Other Items To Pack...156
    Stuff bags 156
    Bin Liners 156
    First Aid kit/First Aid 156

ICE – In Case of Emergency 159

   ICE Information 159

   Whistle 159

   112 160

   Footware 162

Wash kit 164

   Towels 165

Campsite tools 167

   Multi Tool 167

   Paracord 167

   Tent Kit 168

Setting Up Camp 168

   Choosing A Spot 168

   Making Camp 169

   Sleeping Kit 172

   Moving In 172

Maintaining Camp 173

   Lighting 173

   Seating 174

Cooking 175

   Kit 176

   Stoves & Pan Sets 176

Striking Camp 189

Camp Sites 190

ELECTRICALS 191

Bike charging 191

Solar chargers 191

Power Banks 192

BEFORE LEAVING HOME 194

Planning and Prep 194

   Overall Planning 194

   Riding Buddies or Solo 195

    Riding Solo 195

Route Planning 197
Documentation 197
One or Two Months Before 198
Routines 198
Test pitch tent 198
Shakedown trip 198
Check docs 198
Bike Service 199
Day Before 199
Fill Up 199
Pack 199
CHECKLIST EXAMPLE 200
SECURITY 203
PAPERWORK & DOCUMENTS 204
NAVIGATION 207
Maps 207
Map Scale 208
Sat Nav/GPS 209
Brackets 211
Non Bike Specific Sat Nav 213
Bluetooth Earpiece 214
Analogue Sat Nav 215
RIDING IN EUROPE 216
Kit 216
GB Sticker 216
Spare Bulbs 216
Headlight Beam Deflectors 217
Breath Test Kit 218
Hazard Warning Triangle 218
Money 219
Riding 223
Roundabouts 224
Priorité à droite 225

Speeds/Speeding 226
Styles of Local Driving.. 227
Drink Driving 227
Petrol Stations.. 228
   Pumps.. 228
   Belgium 229
Motorways 229
   Toll Plaza Routine 229
   Vignettes 231
   Tolls 231
   Riding.. 232
Off the Motorway 232
General 233
Tunnels & Passes... 233
Border Crossings.. 235
112 236

TOP TIPS... 239
ROUTE IDEAS.. 243
AUTHORS KIT AND PERSONAL VIEWS 252
LIFE ON THE ROAD 261
Acknowledgements & Thanks 272
EXTRAS 273
DIRECTORY... 274
RESOURCES... 275

Preface

I've always been an outdoors type of person. I've been camping since I was a boy and mistakenly took it as the norm that everyone would know how to pack for a camp, pitch a tent, cook at the side of a tent etc. Joining camping and motorbike riding together just always makes me smile.

For me one of the great things about motorcycle touring is riding all day on roads or tracks I've not ridden on before, then finding a spot to camp for the evening, cooking up some food, maybe finding a pub and having some time to chill knowing that the next day is going to be more of the same.

Over the years I've done quite a bit of touring. Not always to the same place and not always using the same roads, but nearly always camping. I've not managed to get out of Europe on the bike yet, but there is always time.

A few years ago a friend of mine who was new(ish) to riding an adventure style motorbike decided he wanted to take the next step and start looking at camping and touring. This was when it dawned on me that not everyone does know about camping and route planning and so on. That was what made me think about writing this book.

I've tried to look at things from a total newcomer to motorcycle touring. So I'm sure there will be some sections that people feel don't need so much explaining, but listening and chatting to some fellow bikers who are starting out with touring, it's always good to know a little extra, or a handy tip.

Things Change

Every effort has been made to make sure the information within the book is as up to date as possible (see French breathalyser for an example!); but things do change. If you know of anything that has changed please contact the author and it will be included in the next updated edition. update@2bikes1mission.co.uk

Introduction

Over the last few years 'adventure' biking has grown in popularity to become one of the largest motorcycle markets. Most riders have aspirations of riding off over the horizon, with dust and stones flying up behind them. Alas, we don't all either get the chance nor have the ability to ride the dunes of North Africa, or the fire roads and tracks of Europe or the tough tracks of the Australian outback.

This guide is aimed at the newer adventure bike rider, who has either moved over from sports bikes or someone who now wants to do more than a 50 mile ride on a sunny Sunday afternoon and wants to start touring and camping.

A bike trip/adventure does not have to be about packing in your job, letting out your house for six years while you ride round the world (nice as it would be). You can have an adventure trip in your own country over a few days (it's what you make of it that counts). This guide is here to help you get out there and enjoy it after giving you some basic pointers and advice.

Throughout the book you will be reminded that it's NOT the bike that is an adventure bike – it's the trip, the ride, the overnighting and the destination that's the adventure.

Any bike is an adventure bike while ever you have an adventure on it!

What the guide does not cover or have

This guide does not cover round the world routes, or Australia to the UK via Asia and Russia as these are for the future of your motorcycle touring career.

If nice big full page photos of 'blinged' up bikes touring are your thing, then this book will disappoint as there are none; but there are some really great small pictures.

What the guide does cover

It covers some basics like, styles of bike, preparation (both you and the bike), clothing, luggage choice and packing, as well as camping equipment, camp craft, navigation, and current European laws for the biker on the continent and a few route ideas.

Preparation and planning is the key to most things in life, but it's a fine balance between over planning and no planning. If you want to do something well, there has to be some element of preparation involved. Taking the first steps to motorcycle camping is no different. See Before Leaving Home/Planning section.

Before setting out, you need to purchase the right kit that suits your needs and budget, (your choice, not some author of a book or the salesman at the shop – but definitely use them for advice and pointers), be able to plan a trip, pack it all onto your bike in the best and safest way and also be able to use it all correctly.

The book is not really designed to be read from front to back, it's for reading up on a specific section and then working with the information.

BIKES

This is a large section covering everything from the bikes themselves, luggage options, bike touring clothing and even a few bike modifications.

Choosing a Motorbike

Just because this is an adventure motorbike guide it does not stop anyone doing a trip on a VanVan, scooter or big easy rider cruiser – an adventure bike is what you make of it. If it starts when you press the button or kick the kickstart, then you are on the way to touring and camping with it

As mentioned in the introduction the adventure bike sector of motorbike sales as been on the up over the last few years. Because of this the sector has quite a range of bikes to choose from. But if you already have a bike, then work with it to turn it into a bike for adventure and camping.

Firstly do you want to be heading down the larger adventure bike route like the BMW1200GS or maybe the lighter trail style bike or maybe even look to more of a tourer like the Triumph Sprint for example? The choice is yours – you can work with any bike to make it suitable for touring and camping. An adventure bike is what you make of it.

The following pages have a brief overview of some of the bikes available at the moment. It is not an exhaustive list by a long way. It's been broken down into a few categories – Adventure style bikes first and then the more road based tourers, and then others.

| MAKE: Aprilia | MODEL: Caponord ETV1000 |

Introduced onto the market in 2001 it has been one of the most under stated bikes in its class.

It's been through 2 phase upgrades and had a couple of 'special' versions (The Rally Raid and the Base Camp)

It's a big-off road style machine that works superbly on the Tarmac. Aprilia's excellent 1000cc V-twin engine combined with a high-tech aluminium beam frame should have made it a class leader but it was marred by soft forks and poor build quality. The Caponord is well spec'd as standard. Ambient air temperature, remote shock adjuster, accessory socket, fuel gauge, mirrors that work and headlights among the best in biking are handy.

The ETV1000 Caponord Rally Raid is amore off-road orientated model with adjustable front suspension, lower gearing, aluminium panniers centre stand and a few more extras. Along with its load carrying abilities; rider comfort and all round wind protection makes it a highly versatile bike.

Top speed: 140mph	Engine size: 998cc
Power: 98bhp	Engine: 8v V-twin, 6 gears
Torque: 72ftlb	Frame: Aluminium beam
Weight: 215kg	Front suspension adjustment None (available on the Rally Raid)
Seat height: 820mm	Rear suspension adjustment Preload
Fuel capacity: 25 litres	Front brakes: Twin 300mm discs
Average fuel consumption: 43mpg	Rear brake: 272mm disc
Tank range: 230 miles	Front tyre size: 110/90 x 19
Drive: Chain	Rear tyre size: 150/70 x 17

MAKE: BMW	MODEL: R1200GS

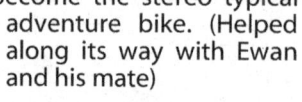

No list these days would be complete without the inclusion of the BMW GS range. The GS Adventure has become the stereo typical

adventure bike. (Helped along its way with Ewan and his mate)

On paper at least this bike shouldn't work at all. It weighs 223kg, the suspension is three inches taller than the standard R1200GS and with a 33-litre tank full of fuel its a heavy beast. But in reality it's one of the best mile-eating bikes money can buy and one of the quirkiest. For 2010 the BMW R1200 GS Adventure gets even better with a touch more torque at 88ftlb, a new twin cam 110bhp motor and the addition of the updated BMW ESA II suspension system and a clever exhaust valve which passes noise tests but opens up as revs increase.

More accessories than you can shake a stick at are available for the whole GS range, so if you want it – it's made for it.

Now the latest water cooled version of the 1200GS is about to hit the trails in 2013, it looks like this marque will carry on for a while to come.

Top speed: 130mph	Engine size: 1170cc
Power: 88ftlb	Engine: 8v Boxer twin, 6 gears
Torque: 72ftlb	Frame: Tubular steel trellis
Weight: 223kg	Front suspension adjustment Preload
Seat height: 890mm	Rear suspension adjustment Preload, rebound
Fuel capacity: 33 litres	Front brakes: Twin 300mm discs
Average fuel consumption: 41mpg	Rear brake: Single Disc, ABS Optional
Tank range: 300 miles	Front tyre size: 120/70 x 17
Crive: Shaft	Rear tyre size: 180/55 x 17

| MAKE: Honda | MODEL: Varadero 1000 |

In theory: the Honda XL1000V Varadero is a great idea; take the funky Firestorm motor and put it inside an adventure touring chassis. But the result didn't live up to that and the Honda XL1000V Varadero hasn't

matched the success of the BMW.

The Honda XL1000V Varadero comes with the Combined Braking System which links both front and rear discs, splitting the braking force between them.

This is more a road bike bias bike wearing adventure clothes

While it has bags of comfort, luggage capacity and grunt, its thirsty engine, top heavy handling and plain Jane looks haven't helped it win friends. More recent models have had sump guards added.

Top speed: 125mph	Engine size: 996cc
Power: 93bhp	Engine: 8v V-twin, 6 gears
Torque: 72ftlb	Frame: Steel tubular type
Weight: 241kg	Front suspension adjustment Preload
Seat height: 843mm	Rear suspension adjustment Preload, rebound
Fuel capacity: 25 litres	Front brakes: Twin 296mm discs
Average fuel consumption: 35mpg	Rear brake: 256mm disc
Tank range: 180 miles	Front tyre size: 110/80 x 19
Drive: Chain	Rear tyre size: 150/70 x 17

| MAKE: Honda | MODEL: XRV 750 Africa Twin |

It's been around since 1989 now, but Honda's Africa Twin is still very much a cult bike, with owners travelling the world on what has become one of the best loved Honda machines of recent years. Production stopped in 2003.

This is a big trail bike you really can take off road. The Honda XRV750 Africa Twin is one of the best Japanese trail/desert rally bikes. Power output is much lower than the latest machines but the slimmer seat makes it easier to manage once you leave the Tarmac. It's not light though.

Its getting a little long in the tooth now, but still a very capable machine with a strong following.

Top speed: 110mph	Engine size: 742cc
Power: 61bhp	Engine: 6v V-twin, 5 gears
Torque: 46ftlb	Frame: Steel perimeter
Weight: 202kg	Front suspension adjustment Preload
Seat height: 860mm	Rear suspension adjustment Preload, rebound
Fuel capacity: 23 litres	Front brakes: Twin 276mm discs
Average fuel consumption: 38mpg	Rear brake: 256mm disc
Tank range: 190 miles	Front tyre size: 90/90 R21
Drive: Chain	Rear tyre size: 140/80 R17

MAKE: Kawasaki	MODEL: KLR650

The Kawasaki KLR650 is a comfortable, grunty, quiet and reliable bike. Forget your Mr. Fancy-pants BMW R1200GS' - providing you can live

with lots of adjusting and lubing of a chain the Kawasaki KLR650 is at least as good at overlanding and a mere fraction of the price.

The Kawasaki KLR650 has been on the market since 1987 and underplays its hand as a round-the-world contender with no centre stand, fixed rubber blocks on the footpegs and no official hard luggage. All of which can be fixed with aftermarket options. The Kawasaki KLR650's charging system is a bit on the mean side, apparently throwing out around 12 amps, which will limit your ability to plumb in heated vests and a GPS and the like.

It has fantastic off road poise, but can also sit on a motorway allowing for long distance travel.

Top speed: 94mph	Engine size: 651cc
Power: 42bhp	Engine: 4v single, 6 gears
Torque: 45ftlb	Frame: Tubular steel cradle
Weight: 168kg	Front suspension adjustment None
Seat height: 870mm	Rear suspension adjustment Preload
Fuel capacity: 14 litres	Front brakes: Twin discs
Average fuel consumption: 53mpg	Rear brake: 220mm disc
Tank range: 160 miles	Front tyre size: 120/70 x 218
Drive: Chain	Rear tyre size: 180/55 x 18

MAKE: KTM	**MODEL:** 990 Adventure

The original KTM 990 Adventure was already a brilliant adventure trail bike, but the 2009 version adds a little bit more refinement and power. A new crank has smoothed vibes, and touch extra power is not instantly noticeable but welcome all the same. Without the celebrity cachet of Ewan and his mate on to push sales along, the KTM is capable of staying the distance.

The off-road sized rims and heavily-treaded tyres should spell vague handling, but largely they don't. The quality WP suspension offers a plush ride. Feedback is enough to inspire confidence, and it rarely gets flustered.

A digital dash, ok rider comfort and a protective fairing make for a happy riding experience. The twin fuel tanks require filling individually, which is a minor inconvenience but helps keep the bike slim-line.

Top speed: 130mph	Engine size: 999cc
Power: 106bhp	Engine: 6v 75° liquid-cooled v-twin, six gears
Torque: 73.8ftlb	Frame: Tubular steel
Weight: 209kg	Front suspension adjustment Preload, compression and rebound
Seat height: 860mm	Rear suspension adjustment Preload, compression and rebound
Fuel capacity: 19.5 litres	Front brakes: Twin 300mm discs
Average fuel consumption: mpg	Rear brake: 240mm disc
Tank range: 203 miles	Front tyre size: 90/90 x21
Drive: Chain	Rear tyre size: 150/70x18

| **MAKE:** Moto Guzzi | **MODEL:** Stelvio NTX |

This is not the first time that the name 'NTX' has been used on a Moto Guzzi. In 1986, in the heyday of long distance African races such as the Paris-Dakar and the Rally of the Pharaohs, the Mandello del Lario based marque used this moniker to distinguish its extreme adventure models.

Phase2 of the NTX was released in 2011. Which had many technical & functional upgrades, such as the enlarged petrol tank that now holds 32ltrs of petrol, with an additional 6ltrs on reserve, ABS that can be turned off, Automatic Traction Control, heated grips, roomy aluminium panniers, spoked wheels, on board computer and spot lights to name a few.

It's not as focussed as the BMW R1200GS Adventure off road perhaps, but it's easy to ride and it comes with an air of exclusivity. To top it all, it's cheaper than an equivalent-spec'd BMW too. Definitely worth a look if you're after something a bit different.

Top speed: 130mph	Engine size: 1151cc
Power: 105HP	Engine: 90° V-twin engine, 6 gears
Torque: 83.3 FtLbs	Frame: Tubular steel
Weight: 272Kg	Front suspension adjustment Completely adjustable USD fork
Seat height: 820-840mm	Rear suspension adjustment Preload, compression and rebound
Fuel capacity: 32 litres	Front brakes: Twin 320 mm discs
Average fuel consumption: mpg	Rear brake: 282 mm disc
Tank range: 203 miles	Front tyre size: 110/80 R19
Drive: Shaft	Rear tyre size: 150/70 R17

MAKE: Suzuki	MODEL: DL 650 V-Strom XP

The 650 V-Strom has been around for a few years now, available as a basic model through to the GT and DLX and finally the XP version.

The Suzuki DL650 V-Strom is a tourer, a sportsbike and a commuter all wrapped together in one. Against other, trail-style middleweights, the Suzuki DL650 V-Strom has a very competitive price tag and you're really getting a top all-rounder for your money.

The Suzuki DL 650 Xpedition is based on the long-serving and successful 650 V-Strom, but kitted out with a few extras to give it a new look and role. (panniers, centre stand, hand guards, engine bars, abs and alloy sump guard). With these extras you really can pickup and go with this bike. Its off road capabilities are probably limited, but would be fun trying. There is absolutely nothing bad to say about the bike (apart from it's not the sweetest looker from the front).

The MK2 has a lot to live up to when it replaced the MK1 in 2011.

Top speed: 124mph	Engine size: 645cc
Power: 65bhp	Engine: 8v DOHC four-stroke 90° V-twin 6 gears
Torque: 44.3ftlb	Frame: Cast aluminium trellis frame
Weight: 199kg	Front suspension adjustment Preload
Seat height: 775mm	Rear suspension adjustment Rebound damping and preload
Fuel capacity: 22 litres	Front brakes: Twin 310 front discs
Average fuel consumption: 47mpg	Rear brake: 260mm disc
Tank range: 227 miles	Front tyre size: 110/80 R19
Drive: Chain	Rear tyre size: 150/70 R17

MAKE: Suzuki	MODEL: DL 1000 V-Strom

The DL1000 V-Strom is no longer in the Suzuki range due to European emissions tests. Although it's rumoured a new redesigned 1000 V-Strom is on the way.

Again not the prettiest bike in the garage, but since 2002 the V-Strom 1000 has been showing it is a far better bike than its looks suggests. Its engine is the excellent V-twin motor from the TL series. Detuned for greater low-down grunt the Suzuki DL1000 V-Strom will drive hard out of corners or past lines of caravans on long distance trips. Oh and it sounds good too. The chassis is top notch road-trailie, it's comfortable, brisk and excellent value.

The Suzuki DL1000 V-Strom GT, introduced in 2006 with heated grips, centre stand and luggage pack as standard fitments helped it become a get on and tour bike.

Its not as off road biased as some bikes, but should cope with smooth fire tracks ok.

Top speed: 130mph	Engine size: 996cc
Power: 105bhp	Engine: 90-degree 4v V-twin, 6 gears
Torque: 68ftlb	Frame: Aluminium twin spar
Weight: 207kg	Front suspension adjustment Preload
Seat height: 875mm	Rear suspension Preload, compression, rebound
Fuel capacity: 22 litres	Front brakes: Twin 310mm discs
Average fuel consumption: 39mpg	Rear brake: 265mm disc
Tank range: 185 miles	Front tyre size: 110/90 R19
Drive: Chain	Rear tyre size: 150/70 R17

MAKE: Triumph	**MODEL:** Tiger 800XC

The 800 XC is very much the bigger, brother of Triumph's standard 800. From the moment you swing your leg on board it's clearly a taller, seemingly more substantial machine. The combination of 21-inch

wire front wheel (the standard 800 is cast 19"), longer travel (by 40mm) 45mm forks (the 800's are 43mm) and slightly wider (by 32mm), higher, wider and further back bars make the XC seem a much more 'full-size', and full-on, proper, adventure bike where the 800 is the more novice-friendly middleweight.

The Triumph Tiger 800XC's modern switchgear, thorough clocks, tapered bars, mirrors and screen are all a level above the offerings of its BMW rival.

Lots of after market accessories are now available for the 800XC & 800 from lights and aluminium luggage to radiator guards and engine bars.

But for many, the full-sized XC looks better, due to its size and stature and with genuine off-road ability, has more tricks up its sleeve.

Top speed: 130mph	Engine size: 799cc
Power: 94bhp	Engine: 12v transverse triple, 6 gears
Torque: 58ftlb	Frame: Cast Tubular steel
Weight: 215kg	Front suspension adjustment none
Seat height: 845mm	Rear suspension adjustment Preload
Fuel capacity: 19 litres	Front brakes: Twin 308mm discs
Average fuel consumption:	Rear brake: 255mm disc
Tank range: 230 miles	Front tyre size: 90/90 R21
Drive: Chain	Rear tyre size: 150/70 R17

MAKE: Triumph	**MODEL:** Tiger Explorer XC

Triumph has announced an addition to their Adventure Touring range with the launch of the new Tiger Explorer XC. Based on the standard explorer, but clearly taking it's styling from the Tiger 800 XC variant, the new Tiger Explorer XC gets several enhancements that add to its adventure touring appeal. The bike will be available in Khaki Green complemented by new aluminium rimmed, steel spoked wheels. The bike also comes equipped with adventure hand guards, high performance 55W dual fog lights, tough 22mm steel tube engine protection bars, and an aluminium sump guard.

The XC is still powered by the same shaft-driven 1215cc triple in the standard bike. Producing 135bhp with 89ft.lbs of torque, the engine offers all the power a rider could need. Add into the equation cruise and traction control, switchable ABS and a virtually maintenance-free shaft drive, and you have the perfect combination for long distance adventure touring.

It's expected to be available in the spring of 2013

Top speed: 130mph	Engine size: 1215cc
Power: 135bhp	Engine: Four stroke, three cylinder.
Torque: 89ft.lbs	Frame: Tubular steel trellis frame
Weight: 244.5Kg	Front suspension adjustment none
Seat height: 837mm to 857mm	Rear suspension adjustment Preload
Fuel capacity: 20 litres	Front brakes: Twin 305mm discs
Average fuel consumption: 48 mpg	Rear brake: 282mm disc
Tank range: 190 miles	Front tyre size: 110/80 R19
Drive: Shaft	Rear tyre size: 150/70 R17

MAKE: Yamaha	**MODEL:** Tenere xt660z

The Yamaha XT660Z Tenere is a great value, superbly capable adventure bike with real off road capability. Useful touches such as the durable crash panels and front towing hoop put it in a class of it's own.

Again not the 'looker' in the garage (it looks like a grasshopper). But it's a style you either love or hate.

Despite the relatively heavy weight and tall seat height the Tenere's wide bars and good balance gives slow speed confidence. Like most motorcycles with off road abilities the forks dive under braking. Off road, the chassis will cope with all but the severest conditions.

Durable panels are fixed to vulnerable areas on the Tenere's fuel tank and engine and are designed to prevent excessive damage in a fall. The small fairing is surprisingly effective even without the optional taller screen. Yamaha accessories will kit it out (at a cost), but a wide choice of aftermarket accessories are available.

The Yamaha XT660Z Tenere has an impressive blend of on and off road ability with some neat and well thought out design touches.

Top speed: 120mph	Engine size: 660cc
Power: 46bhp	Engine: 4V single cylinder, SOHC, five gears
Torque: 43ftlb	Frame: Tubular steel, semi-double cradle frame
Weight: 183kg	Front suspension adjustment none
Seat height: 895mm	Rear suspension adjustment Preload
Fuel capacity: 22 litres	Front brakes: Twin 298mmdiscs
Average fuel consumption: 44mpg	Rear brake: 245mm disc
Tank range: 200 miles	Front tyre size: 90/90 R21
Drive: Chain	Rear tyre size: 130/80 R17

MAKE: Yamaha	**MODEL:** Super Tenere xt1200z

The introduction of the XT1200Z Super Tenere in 2010 helped continue Yamaha's adventure bike pedigree.

A 1199cc liquid-cooled parallel twin that is just as at home at autobahn

speeds as it is lugging rider, pillion and luggage. Performance isn't ground-breaking but the engine is smooth and there are minimal vibes.

Power delivery can be tamed by switching to touring mode via a bar-mounted button. It has a traction control system that is hardly noticeable when it cuts in and can be turned off for off-road use and a clever ABS and linked brake system. Maintenance free shaft drive, adds to the appeal.

Yamaha have got the weight distribution spot on. The only time weight is a problem is backing it out of the garage or picking it up.

Top speed: 120mph	Engine size: 1199cc
Power: 109bhp	Engine: DOHC, 4v four-stroke parallel twin, six gears
Torque: 84ftlb	Frame: Tubular steel backbone frame. Cast alloy swingarm
Weight: 261kg	Front suspension adjustment Fully
Seat height: 845mm	Rear suspension adjustment Preload
Fuel capacity: 23 litres	Front brakes: Twin 310mm discs
Average fuel consumption: 48 mpg	Rear brake: 282mmdisc
Tank range: 200 miles	Front tyre size: 110/80 R19
Drive: Shaft	Rear tyre size: 150/70 R17

MAKE: BMW	MODEL: K1200GT

2006 saw the release of the K1200GT which uses BMW's latest frame

and across the frame four cylinder engine which is a much faster, more stable motorcycle with more luxury than the original offering.

The BMW's riding position is comfy for both rider and pillion, the electrically adjustable screen is useful, shaft drive effective and maintenance free, panniers useful and instruments comprehensive. There is a huge range of extras available for this bike, including heated seats.

In a sentence – a lot of bike for your money that is capable of getting you from A to B fast.

Top speed: 165mph	Engine size: 1157cc
Power: 152bhp	Engine: 16v in-line four, 6 gears
Torque: 96ftlb	Frame: Aluminium twin spar
Weight: 249kg	Front suspension adjustment none
Seat height: 800mm	Rear suspension adjustment Preload, rebound
Fuel capacity: 22 litres	Front brakes: Twin 320mm discs
Average fuel consumption: 47mpg	Rear brake: 294mm disc
Tank range: 245 miles	Front tyre size: 120/70 R17
Drive: Shaft	Rear tyre size: 180/55 R17

MAKE: Suzuki	**MODEL:** Bandit 1250

2007 saw the revised 1250 Bandit on the market, with the GT option coming soon after.

The GT is basically a Bandit 1250, but with a selection of options aimed at turning the all-rounder into a proper touring bike. By adding a full fairing, Suzuki has given the Bandit much improved wind protection for long-distance riding, while panniers and a topbox mean it's gained the luggage capacity to rival purpose-designed touring bikes. At the end of the day, it's a Bandit, and as such it's an upright seating position, nice seat and perfectly placed footpegs and handlebars. Suzuki haven't changed the chassis too much from the old model, just beefed up the GSF1250 Bandit's frame rails and revised the suspension damping and springs.

The dashboard is a nice combination of analogue and digital displays..

Top speed: 145mph	Engine size: 1255cc
Power: 97bhp	Engine: 16v liquid-cooled in-line four, 6 gears
Torque: 79.6ftlb	Frame: Tubular steel double cradle
Weight: 229kg	Front suspension adjustment Preload
Seat height: 785mm	Rear suspension adjustment Preload and rebound
Fuel capacity: 19 litres	Front brakes: Twin 310mmdiscs
Average fuel consumption: 42mpg	Rear brake: 240mm disc
Tank range: 150 miles	Front tyre size: 120/70 R17
Drive: Chain	Rear tyre size: 180/55 R17

| **MAKE:** Triumph | **MODEL:** Sprint GT |

Take the Sprint ST sports tourer, add greater practicality and more emphasis on the 'touring' aspect of 'sports touring' and out comes the Triumph Sprint GT.

As you would expect from a British machine wearing the famous Grand Tourer tag, the Sprint GT delivers outstanding real world performance in a practical and stylish package. With 130bhp on hand and an updated version of Triumph's 1050cc triple, the Sprint GT offers excellent real world performance. With no fancy power mode settings and no traction control, it does have ABS though.

The GT is practical; with 31 litre panniers, ABS brakes as standard, built in rack with grab rail, 200 mile fuel range and an optional top box with a 12 volt power supply to allow 'on the go' charging of electrical items.

A bike that is capable of all-day riding comfort and taking on the twisties is the Triumph Sprint GT.

Top speed: 160mph	Engine size: 1050cc
Power: 128bhp	Engine: Liquid-cooled, DOHC, 12v four-stroke triple. Six gears
Torque: 80ftlb	Frame: Aluminium dual beam frame. Cast ally single-sided swingarm
Weight: 268kg	Front suspension adjustment Preload
Seat height: 815mm	Rear suspension adjustment Preload and rebound
Fuel capacity: 20 litres	Front brakes: Twin 320mm discs
Average fuel consumption: mpg	Rear brake: 255mm disc
Tank range: 200 miles	Front tyre size: 120/70 R17
Drive: Chain	Rear tyre size: 180/55 R17

| **MAKE:** Yamaha | **MODEL:** Fazer 600 |

The Yamaha FZ6 Fazer looks sharp, has a brilliant motor, excellent handling and offers huge versatility. Towns, twisties and longer trips, it can do it all. A great all-rounder.

The Yamaha FZ6 handling is spot on due to a new chassis, fat tyres, wide bars and good suspension (despite limited adjustment potential), giving the rider loads of feedback. The brakes work well too. A heavy clutch, considerable play on the throttle and a need to work the gearbox endlessly are a few niggles. The seat could also be comfier, which will probably require gell pads or an Airhawk if touring.

Attach a set of Givi rails (and the panniers) to the bike and straight forward no fuss touring is waiting.

On the dash there's a digital speedo/rev counter (depending on version) plus a fuel gauge. The double under seat exhaust really sets the bike off.

Top speed: 140mph	Engine size: 600cc
Power: 90bhp	Engine: 16v inline four. Six gears
Torque: 42ftlb	Frame: Aluminium dual beam
Weight: 186kg	Front suspension none
Seat height: 795mm	Rear suspension Preload
Fuel capacity: 19.4 litres	Front brakes: Twin 289mm discs
Average fuel consumption: 42mpg	Rear brake: 245mm disc
Tank range: 180 miles	Front tyre size: 120/70 x 17
Drive: Chain	Rear tyre size: 180/55 x 17

MAKE: Moto Guzzi	MODEL: Norge GT 8V

Moto Guzzi's Norge tourer got a makeover for 2011. Now called the Norge GT 8V, it got a new chassis, body panels and the latest evolution of the Italian firm's eight valve engine, replacing the old two-valve motor.

It's as comfortable as ever with a plush ride, but Guzzi have stiffened up the suspension to help its composure on fast motorway bends.

Producing 102bhp the Norge GT 8V is powered by an air-cooled 1151cc, 90° V-twin motor with fuel injection and shaft drive. In typical Guzzi style the motor is mounted long-ways in the chassis, with a cylinder head poking out each side of the bike.

There are a decent amount of goodies as standard, like ABS, heated grips, sat nav, panniers and an on-board computer. It also has an electrically-adjustable screen.

If you're after a relaxed, comfortable tourer with bags of character and lots of toys, the Norge GT 8V is superb value for money.

Top speed: 135mph	Engine size: 1151cc
Power: 102bhp	Engine: 8v, V-twin. Six gears
Torque: 104ftlb	Frame: Tubular steel double cradle with single sided swingarm
Weight: 257kg	Front suspension: none
Seat height: 810mm	Rear suspension: preload & rebound
Fuel capacity: 23 litres	Front brakes: Twin 320mm discs
Average fuel consumption: 42mpg	Rear brake: 282mm single disc
Tank range: 215 miles	Front tyre size: 120/70 x 17
Drive: Shaft	Rear tyre size: 180/55 x 17

MAKE: Derbi	**MODEL:** Terra Adventure

Take a BMW R1200GS, shrink it in the wash, fit a revvy four-stroke single, top-notch brakes and forks – and you get Derbi's Terra

Adventure 125. If you're looking for adventure on a budget or just a small capacity bike to have some fun on you won't be disappointed.

The styling is well thought out, and even has a bash plate to protect that vulnerable engine. So, not only does the Derbi do the job, on or off road but it also looks the part and gives the appearance of a larger capacity bike.

The Terra Adventure 125 comes with dirt tires, optional aluminium panniers, hand guards, bigger windscreen, larger bash plate and bigger wheels. Its cool-looking dash with analogue rev counter and digital speedo finish off the bike

With the optional panniers or some soft luggage thrown over, you will have hours of touring fun – albeit at a slower speed.

Top speed: 70mph	Engine size: 124cc
Power: 15bhp	Engine: Air-cooled, four-stroke single, six gears.
Torque:	Frame: Double steel beam
Weight: 117kg	Front suspension adjustment none
Seat height: 850mm	Rear suspension adjustment Preload
Fuel capacity: 11 litres	Front brakes: 300mm disc
Average fuel consumption: 70 mpg	Rear brake: 220mm disc
Tank range: 181 miles	Front tyre size: 90/90 R21
Drive: Chain	Rear tyre size: 130/90 R17

Luggage

You now have a bike, and as you know bikes don't have nice big boots to throw everything into. So some form of luggage system is required (unless you are the type of rider that just packs a toothbrush and a credit card in their wallet and heads off!)

As luck would have it, gone are the days when all you had to choose from were the manufactures offering, which were probably ok at best, or a sports bag bungeed onto the back seat.

The range of third party luggage options now is overwhelming, but you need to look at all the options carefully. After all, you have to live out of your luggage, even on short trips, so you want to get it right.. Also think about how secure your luggage is going to be – could you happily walk away leaving it mounted to the bike?

For pannier options there are basically two choices – hard or soft. Riders debate the pros and cons of both for hours at a time (sometimes over a beer or two). But at the end of the day its down to personal preference/requirements/fitting.

Soft Luggage

Throw Overs

Soft luggage for quite some time basically meant some form of throw over setup where the two fabric (usually cordura) bags were connected under the rear seat via some form of strap, most popular being Velcro.

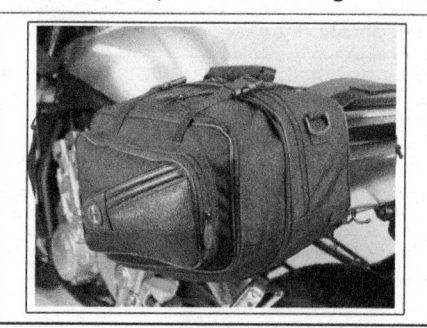

The nice thing about this setup is it's usually a cheaper option than hard luggage, and does not require any rack to be fitted to the bike. Although they do need to be bungeed or tied to the bike frame as well.

The down side to soft panniers is that they are usually are smaller in capacity. But, saying that this makes them lighter overall. However, from a security point of view they can be cut open to get at you goodies inside. And they are not usually waterproof (though some do come with plastic over covers)

A different take on the traditional soft panniers is for manufacturers to use a fully waterproof rollbag for the storage units. Companies like Enduristan who make the Monsoon soft panniers, Ortliebs MOTO Saddle-Bag, Wolfmans Teton bags and Oxford with their AquaBags really are bringing soft luggage up-to-date and making it practical.

Soft Bags on Frames

This type of luggage is a little like the best of both worlds and seem to be gaining popularity with riders. It's basically a waterproof rollbag fitted onto a frame, allowing for heaver loads and added peace of mind knowing that they are attached to the bike better than a throw over setup.

The ones illustrated here are by Kreiga. The packs are 100% water, dust and sandproof. Constructed from double-stitched 1000D Cordura with reinforced sides and twin straps, which compress the load, whatever the terrain. 60L of storage (4 x 15L, 2 per side). This style of soft pack offers a great solution for off road riding,

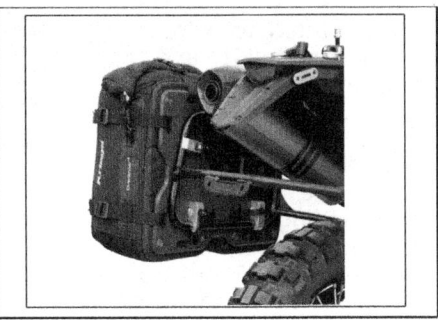

with adjustable pack size and flexibility on impact.

The platform is made of tough low-density polyethylene, and accept Overlander bags or Rotopax fuel/water containers.

The kit consists of 2 x ADV. platforms, 4 x 15L packs and all mounting hardware to connect to 18mm pannier frames (These can be bought from the likes of Touratech, Metal Mule etc.) They are good, but they do come at cost compared to traditional throw overs.

Other manufactures of similar types of bags are AdventureSpec & Touratech

Ventura Bike Packs

This system could have gone here in the soft luggage section or in the tail bag/tail pack section. So to avoid repeating things also consider this system when looking at tail bags.

Ventura originate from New Zealand, and this style of packing, high at the back of the bike is popular within Australia and New Zealand.

Ventura started way back in the 70's to give motorcyclists the opportunity of having a luggage system that was individually designed and custom-made for their bike.

They now cover a large range of bikes from cruisers, sports bikes and everything in between.

Right – The Ventura system fitted to a Harley Dyna Superglide and a Keeway 250 cruiser.

The recommended way is to have the pack overhanging the rear seat putting the weight near the rear wheel; but you can also fit it the other way around hanging over the rack. With a heavy bag, that would make the bike quite tail heavy and the weight high.

Hard Luggage

Over the past few years hard luggage has started to become the standard for all type of overlanders, be it for a weekend away or a two or three week trip round Europe or beyond. Many motorcycle manufacturers offer their own hard luggage options for their bikes. These are mainly based on plastic panniers. Thirt party hard panniers are now widely available from the likes of Hepco & Becker, Givi, Touratech, Metal Mule and many more.

Hard luggage does offer a better level of security and waterproofing than traditional soft luggage, but like most things in life this does come at a cost.

Like soft luggage, hard luggage can be broken down into two categories - plastic and metal (usually aluminium). There is also another option to throw into the mix here, and that's top loading or side loading. Side loading is usually more common on the plastic style panniers and again think about how they will be used and how you would live with them. A friend of mine always had side loading panniers and said they worked great for him.

Plastic

Depending on your requirements and financial status, plastic may be the way to go for hard panniers as they tend to be cheaper than aluminium. But at over £400 for a set of H&B Gobi panniers, some of them are still not that cheap.

Traditional styled plastic panniers from the likes of Givi and Hepco & Becker have always done what it said on the tin (or pannier in this

case), but have been styled more to the road bike.

Options like the Givi E36/E45 (shown left on a Yamaha Fazer) have been around for years and have earned their spurs as a good all-rounder and starter pannier, though some riders buy them once and have them for life. One of the down sides to this type of pannier is that they are side opening. This can lead to some amusing situations when they are opened and half your stuff falls out. They do have straps inside, but they are not always that strong.

Over the last few years a couple of manufactures have developed adventure style plastic panniers. These have a more 'rugged' look to them. Givi have come up with the Trekker, which is plastic with a thin aluminium 'veneer' over the top. They are also both a top loader and a side loader!

They look tough, and come in 46l and 33l options, so can easily be used to balance up a bike with only one exhaust pipe.

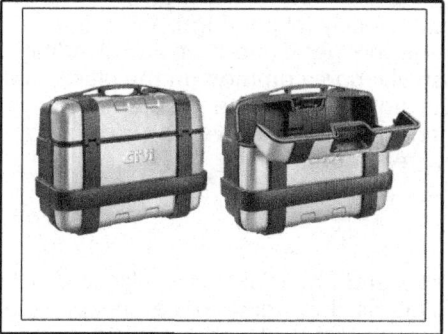

Hepco & Becker are another manufacturer who have looked at the growing adventure market and produced the Gobi panniers. They are extremely durable and close to unbreakable in normal use. They come with a 100% water resistance guarantee and are top loading similar to aluminium panniers.

In short these are aluminium panniers made out of plastic.

They also have a little trick up their sleeve.... Each pannier has a

double outer skin which allows for the storage of about 3.5ltrs of liquid. On paper this is quite a clever idea, but it does add to the overall width and weight of the panniers.

Gobi panniers were standard equipment on KTMs for some years, so they must have thought they were good.

Overall the Gobis are a good bit of kit, but given they only offer 37ltrs of space, they do stick out quite a way which may be a concern for some.

Right & above- Hepco & Becker Gobi panniers fitter to an Aprilia Caponord Rally Raid

If you already have your bike and rails, but are struggling to find panniers to fit, have a look at fabricating your own using Peli-cases or similar. As with anything DIY make sure it is thoroughly tested and checked before taking on the road.

Aluminium

Panniers made from aluminium have become the 'de rigueur' of the biking and adventure sector over the last few years, with the likes of Touratech, Metal Mule, Stahlkoffer and others all producing them. More recently even Givi have moved into the metal pannier game and are releasing their Trekker-Overland aluminium pannier set. (Release date 2013). They all have different designs and styles, but in their most basic form they are metal boxes.

What you basically get is an aluminium pannier with a lid. Some come complete with locks and fittings; others come as a basic pannier with locks as an extra. Why that is the case who knows! Isn't that the advantage of them, to be locked?

Even some bike manufacturers offer their own range of aluminium panniers as can be seen here on Phil Gough's BMW GSA fitted with BMW panniers.

On average a typical metal pannier can hold between 30 and 40lts of luggage. But always have in the back of your mind that all the extra weight you are carrying has to go somewhere and that's the frame of the bike and the pannier rack. It will also affect the overall handling of the bike particularly over rougher terrain. (Or the normal roads in Sheffield).

Moto Guzzi and Suzuki have teamed up with SWMotech to provide their 'boxes'. So here you are getting the skill of a pannier manufacturer teamed up with a bike manufacturer to produce a great end result and an all in one package.

The flat tops of aluminium panniers also provide a great place to sit extra bits and bobs that don't fit. Pannier top bags are easy to fit and usually start at about 10lts, or use a small 15ltr dry bag available from outdoor/camping shops and use shock cord or rock straps to attach it to the pannier. But remember, this again may alter the handling of the bike and might make it a little tricky to get into the panniers.

Unlike most other bits of motorcycling kit such as boots, helmets, and other luggage, aluminium panniers can be a little hard to source. There are now quite a few brands available, but there are few retail outlets that stock a range, so you might need to spend some time travelling round to see all the ones you're interested in. (or the internet is your friend)

If you don't have the time, then the following overview of aluminium panniers might just point you in the right direction.

The following pages contain extracts from a review of aluminium panniers by Adventure Bike Rider Magazine (Issue 3 2011). The criteria used for the rating was: water and dust proofing; robustness, strength and build quality; ease of fitting and detaching; value for money; weight and size; looks and style; security; additional features such as carry handles and attachment points. (Prices correct at time of publication in ABR Magazine)

Brand: Touratech
Model: Zega Pro Size: 38ltr, 45ltr
Price: Single panniers from £369; Rack and two pannier set from £825
Contact: www.touratech.co.uk

German company Touratech has played a leading role in the popularity of adventure motorcycles by offering a huge range of aftermarket products including the Zega range of aluminium panniers.

ABR RATING 8 out of 10

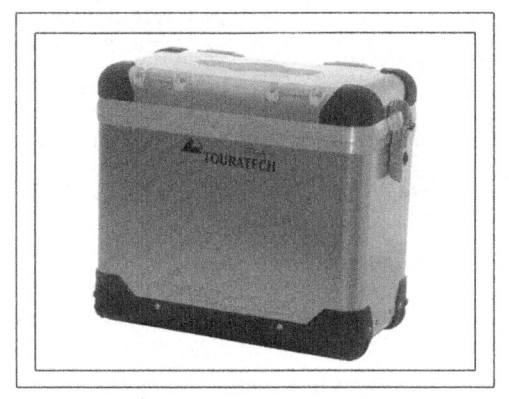

Fitting the frames to the bike was stress free, despite the basic and poorly translated instruction sheet. If you are paying good money for a product you at least expect better fitting instructions.

Security and stability on the bike is very good, though access to the panniers and ease of mounting/dismounting is not the most user friendly. You have to buy four padlocks to secure the lids or the optional locks – why they don't come with lock as standard, who knows.

The lids are detachable for versatility and the four offset attachment loops are spot on for stashing additional gear on top of the pannier.

Price-wise they are near the top end of the scale, but the professional look and feel of the panniers is up there too.

In a line

Look great and perform just as well

Brand: Metal Mule
Model: Max Pannier Size: 31ltr 38ltr, 45ltr
Price: Single panniers from £352; Rack and two pannier set from £1199
Contact: www.metalmule.com

There is no getting away from it, that these British made panniers are expensive. But the attention to detail, engineering, components and workmanship are as near to faultless as you're going to get. Look at these as an investment that's going to last a lifetime.

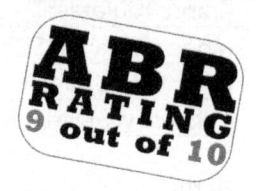

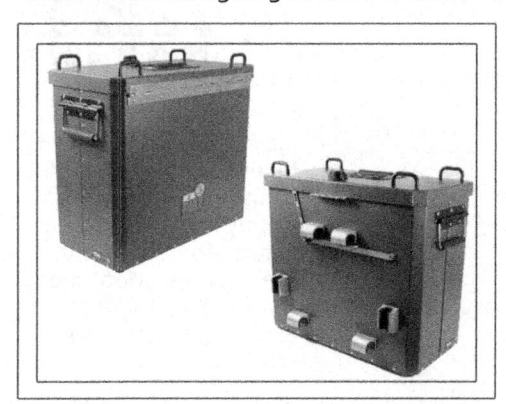

Fitting the Metal Mule frame to the bike was exact and simple and attaching the panniers to the frame has to be the most user friendly.

The built in lid lock continues the no fuss theme, making them the easiest storage boxes to live with on a day-to-day basis.

The panniers are taller and narrower than most, making for a slimmer profile, but non intrusive if you are carrying a pillion.

The twin grab handles make carrying the pannier from the bike a breeze and although the top handle is a nice touch, is it really required. Four tie-down loops on the lid are included for lashing on additional gear.

In a line

A work of pannier art

Side note:

Metal Mule have just released the Ute pannier system. The system (two panniers plus the rails) is currently available at £600

Brand: Hepco & Becker	
Model: Alu Standard **Size:** 38ltr, 45ltr	
Price: Single panniers from £230; Rack and two pannier set from £658	
Contact: www.motobins.co.uk http://www.hepco-and-becker-luggage.co.uk/	

These are not the toughest or best panniers in the overview, but they are fantastic value if you are looking for a quality product that'll enhance the look of your bike. Added to that, they are practical and easy to live with, plus most riders

will find them robust enough to cope with their needs.

The frames are of a smaller diameter than the more expensive brands, but they fit on the bike with ease and are as stable as any others. The mounting mechanism which attaches the boxes to the frame is secure and a no fuss operation via a single lock. (Accessible without having to open the lid).

The lid comes with two big grab-handles, which help if you need to carry them any distance, plus they also act as tie-down points. The lid is secured by a single integral lock with a fixed hinge at the other end. This means the lid is not fully removable, but opens wide enough for unrestricted access.

The Hepco and Becker panniers in test were fully water and dustproof, thanks to a well thought-out foam gasket design which sits in the outer lid lip.

In a line

Great value, professionally made and finished

Brand: Jesse	
Model: Safari **Size:** 45ltr, 55ltr	
Price: Rack and two pannier set from £814	
Contact: www.twowheeltrekkers.co.uk	

Jesse is a US company, but are distributed in the UK by Two Wheel Trekkers.

These panniers split opinions more than any other; on the one hand there's the bombproof construction and slim profile, while on the

other, there is the non standard looks and they're less user friendly than others.

The rack system is more complex than others and you may need an exhaust adaptor for fitting.

The hinged lid does not detach, which some people like and some don't. It also holds a claimed 10ltrs of luggage, secured in place by a spring loaded lid packer. The lid is secured by two integral locks and while the panniers were watertight there are concerns about the long term robustness of the rubber seal. Also, there are no tie-down points.

The shape of Jesse boxes are not the normal 90 degree edges; they are cut folded and tapered, to reduce the severity of the leading edges, which, in the event of a fall is said to lessen the impact and resistance.

There is little doubt that the Jesses are built with the RTW tourer in mind rather than the occasional tourer who likes his niceties. They are global touring storage facilities rather than an all-frills motorcycle accessory.

In a line

In the event of nuclear war, climb in a Jesse

Brand: Alpos
Model: Alpos **Size:** 32ltr, 36ltr, 41ltr
Price: Single pannier from £91; SWMotech frame, adaptor kit and two pannier set from £430
Contact: www.bykebitz.co.uk

These are budget boxes compared to most other panniers on test. They look and feel cheap: Think oversized biscuit tins and you've got it. That said, there is nothing to stop you setting off on a RTW trip with a set of Alpos on

your bike and the odds are they will survive.

You get what you pay for with the Alpos, though they do come with a surprisingly good finish, better than some of the more expensive panniers.

The lid locking/catch mechanism is simple and crude and you will need a padlock to secure it. The lid is hinged and non detachable with no attachment points but a single grab handle for carrying is handy.

On first inspection the water tightness of the Alpos was dubious, but after attacking it with a power-washer it remained dry as a bone. However a waterproof inner bag would be recommended for a long arduous journey.

Alpos do not make dedicated frames or frame mounting kits and the boxes can be adapted to fit a number of frames from different manufacturers.

If you have a tight budget then the Alpos panniers will do the job.

In a line

Cheap and cheerful but does the job

Brand: G+G Panniers
Model: Premium Pannier Set Size: 41ltr
Price: Two pannier set from €340 (£285) mounting kit from €70 (£59)
Contact: www.aluminium-panniers.co.uk

The quality of materials is high for a budget pannier, the polished finish is attractive and is better than some of the more expensive on test – plus from 2011 they come anodised as standard.

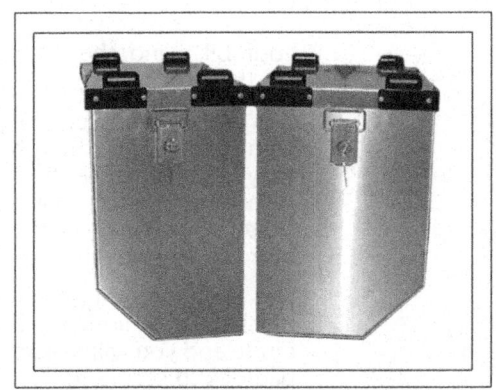

Water and dust will be no problem as a well positioned and constructed gasket is bonded to the box, and the detachable lid fits neatly. The riveted construction is improved by neatly applied silicon sealant.

The system for fitting them to the frame is similar to that used by Touratech – functional and secure, if a little fiddly. They can also me modified to fit other racks like Hepco & Becker.

As value goes this is on of the surprises; the product is simply better than the price would suggest. At 6.3kg, the weight is above average, but the overall dimensions are big and offer plenty of space for gear.

With an integrated lock there is no need for separate padlocks. They also have tie down loops built into the lid.

In a line

You get a lot of pannier for your money

Brand: Stahlkoffer	
Model: Premium Pannier Set **Size:** 33ltr, 35ltr	
Price: Frame and two pannier set from £475	
Contact: www.aluminium-panniers.co.uk	

British made panniers from the Black Country. The Stahlkoffer panniers have that hard-as-nails ammo box look and cheap in price at the side of others.

ABR RATING 8 out of 10

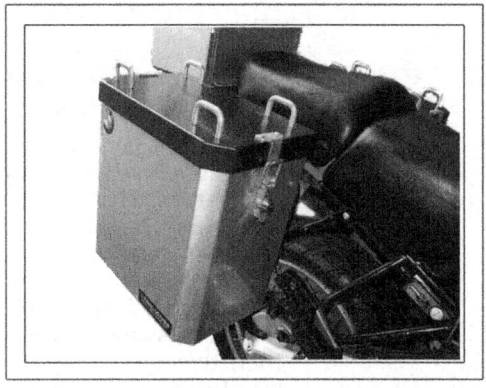

The company supplies a dedicated rack to fit most BMW's, Yamaha Tenere and the KTM 990, and the mounting mechanism fits the rack, which means you'll need to do a bit of DIY if you want these panniers and you own anything but the above.

The rack and mount supplied is effective and secure, but the locking mechanism is fiddly when compared to others.

From the top there is a fully detachable lid, which comes with four attachment loops. The lid is secured to the main body by two latches which include integral locks. Water and dust is kept out via a foam rand stuck to the inner of the lid; while its been fine while on test, it has the potential to be a weak spot over time.

The main box is welded with not a rivet in sight. It was found to be exceptionally sturdy and robust and at the price quoted these are looking very good value. The finishing is not as pretty as, say, Touratech or Metal Mules.

In a line

The looks and performance of panniers twice the price

Brand: Heavy Duties
Model: Heavy Duties **Size:** 39ltr, 48ltr
Price: Single pannier from €90 (£76) Frame and two pannier set from €330 (£280)
Contact: www.heavyduties.ro

Heavy Duties are made by a couple of Romanian brothers with a passion for motorbikes and travel. They began making panniers four years ago, for their own needs, but encouraged by others they now offer them

on a commercial basis at great value for money.

It's fair to say that the look and finish of these panniers is homemade and would be difficult to see them sitting on the shelf of a highly polished dealership. That said, if function is your priority then these are a serious bit of heavy duty kit at a cracking price that will

stay with you on a RTW trip.

The boxes are constructed using rivets, seam sealer and 2mm aluminium. The panniers come fully lined with isoprene insulation and reflective stickers on the outer edges – nice touch. The frame mounting system is very secure, though not the easiest panniers to detach and attach.

From the top down you get a hinged lid, which is non detachable and secured by a couple of latches, plus an integral top mounted lock for security. You also get four substantial loops for lashing down overflow gear. The panniers passed the pressure water test, but would recommend waterproof bag liners for peace of mind.

There's no doubting the robust nature of the Heavy Duties and at these sorts of prices we'd be getting picky pointing out faults.

In a line - Not pretty, but robust, cheap and have that instant rugged look. **Note:** Just released a revised design which has smoother lines.

Pannier Racks

So you have decided on your type/style/manufacture of pannier, now you need to attach it to the bike. Soft throw overs are not usually an issue as they are designed to be used without any form of rack. But hard luggage really does need some sort of rack system (or rails) to attach them to the bike sub-frame.

Most makers of panniers also make their own racks for a range of bikes. Right is a Hepco and Becker rack system for an Aprilia Rally Raid. For strength there are four points of contact to the bikes sub-frame.

This is the nice, easy straightforward option as panniers and rails are all designed to fit and work with your specific bike.

If on the other hand you have a bike that's not supported by the pannier manufacturer, you have a couple of options open to you. Firstly look again at your choice of luggage and see if there is a company that does racks for your bike, and reconsider your pannier choice, or consider the DIY route.

For the DIY option, you either need the required skills, tools and time to design and build a good strong rack or you need to talk to one of the companies that offer one off rack builds, but as always with bespoke items these may come at a cost.

The rack choice should be capable of easily carrying the panniers fully loaded. This weight should really not exceed about 10/15Kg

Other Luggage

If you are planning something more than a quick few days away and overnighting in a B&B or motel, then other storage options may be required for the extra kit that will be carried, so a re-think on packing will be needed.

Tank Bags

These (as the name suggests) fit over the tank of the bike in front of the rider. Some people swear by them and others just hate them. Some of the larger bags can make riding a chore especially when you are struggling to see the dials or keep the bike steady in slow control.

They do offer a convenient place to store items that may be needed throughout the day (cash, phone, map, waterproofs etc) and some have a clear plastic section where you can put your map for the day.

Fixing is usually either via magnets or straps. Firstly check to see if your tank is magnetic if you are thinking of getting a magnetic tank bag! It sounds daft, but some tanks are plastic, and if that's the case then you are limited to straps.

Whichever fixing system you are using always make sure your tank is

clean before fitting to reduce the chances of scratching the paint work, or place a non-slip cloth between the tank and the bag.

Some tank bags are designed for a particular make and model of bike tank to have a nice snug fit, whereas the majority tend to be generic styles. Always have a look to see if anyone makes a bag to fit your bike first.

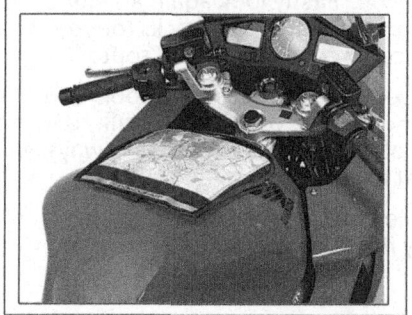

After starting small (some are designed to be just map pockets so are quite thin - but handy), they get larger and larger to the point where an expandable tank bag can rival a small roll bag in size. Because of this it's easy to get a bag that's too big or interferes with your comfort or ability to operate your motorbike.

If possible, it's a good idea to test-fit your bag of choice on your motorcycle before you buy it.

Top Boxes

These fit on the rack behind the pillion seat and are usually attached via a bespoke plate that is available from the manufacturer. Again people either love or hate them.

From a negative point of view they do put a lot of weight high up and affect the bikes centre of gravity, so never over load them. They can also catch any cross winds.

From a positive point of view they do provide easily accessed secure storage.

Roll Bags

These are a good way of adding carrying capacity as they keep weight

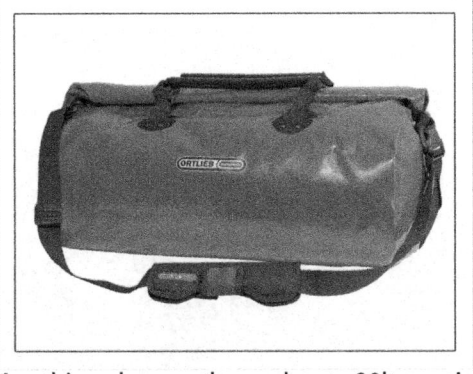

within the bikes centre of gravity.

They are tough bags made from either a fully bonded thick PVC, or have internal PVC tarpaulin bonded to an outer nylon cotton shell and either open at the end or along the length.

Forms of roll bag are usually available from 15ltrs up to 100ltrs. Anything larger than about 80ltrs might be on the large side. (Remember to try and pack light). The smaller ones don't matter too much if they are end opening, but for the larger versions try and look for a lengthways opening one. That way you can get to your kit easier.

Roll bags (or duffels) as their name suggests are a) a roll in shape and b) roll over and over at the opening to seal. This is a proven method of sealing and really does make them watertight.

Compression straps to pack the size of the bag down even further are always good along with carry/shoulder straps.

If you use a smaller bag and no top box then you could attach it to the bike on the tail behind the pillion seat, but again think about the weight distribution. Ideally it's best to have them fastened to the bike lengthways over the pillion seat onto the tail, or crossways over the seat and maybe just resting on the panniers.

Fixing a roll bag to a bike depends quite a lot on the type of seat you have got and if the bag is going to go 'in line' or across the bike. Bikes with a split seat can have lightweight cam buckle straps/Arno straps running easily under the pillion seat for either choice.

Some bikes that have split seats also have a converter which allows you to remove the pillion seat and have a nice flat surface to put a roll bag on.

Right – Two bikes packed with roll bags. One in line and one across the pillion seat.

Manufacturers to look at include: Ortlieb, Lomo, Overboard, Touratech and others.

Good reports have been heard about Crane Sports roll bag from Aldi even though its end opening; but cost substantially less.

Tail Bags or Tail Packs

These are a good way of adding a small storage bag to the back of the bike. Ideally if the bike has a rear luggage rack then they fit great with

the built in bag straps. The plus point of these over plastic or aluminium top boxes is the weight and size. Weight, as they are usually made of fabric (cordura) and size because they are much smaller (usually 10 to 20ltrs), which make them great for day to day items like maps, sunglasses, visor cleaner etc.

Try to avoid putting large heavy tail packs on the luggage rack, as it could make the bike unwieldy or difficult to steer -- especially if the bag sits too far back on the motorcycle's luggage rack.

If you are looking at a solo touring setup and are not looking at a roll bag, then larger tail packs that sit in line on the pillion seat are an option. These are larger than the above type of tail pack and have capacities up to about 30/40ltrs

These larger style tail bags or packs usually sit fully on the pillion seat and attach to the bike using straps and bungee cords.

Many motorcycle riders prefer using a compact tail bag rather than a tank bag because a tail bag sits out of your way when you're riding. Also it keeps the added weight of your gear close to your bike's rear suspension. You can quickly attach or remove a motorcycle tail bag, and you needn't move a tail bag aside when its time to fill up as you must with a tank bag.

This Oxford X40 Tail pack has elastic netting for stowing lightweight items such as gloves, has a quick release base which doubles as a mini tail pack, converts to a backpack, has self-sealing zips and has a 40ltr capacity.

A few things to keep in mind when looking at tail packs or any luggage for that matter.

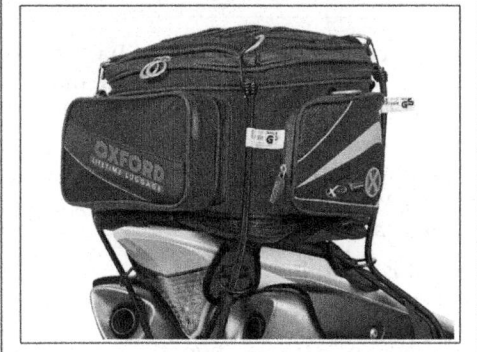

- The type of motorcycle you ride (not all luggage suites all bikes).
- Weather conditions in which you ride (is the item waterproof?).
- How often you ride.
- Seasons in which you ride.

A Little Bit of Everything

For shorter trips the roll bag with built in small saddle bag from the likes of Jofama might be worth looking at. The largest size from

Jofama is 52 ltrs. Practical luggage roll suitable for most bikes. Having one central compartment, smaller, separate compartments on each side and three other external pockets, with options to fasten using elastic straps. Ideal as a weekend bag if camping is not involved, or very light weight camping.

In short, a small roll bag with a couple of small saddle bags to add to the storage in one piece of kit. One downside to this style of luggage is that the weight is quite high with no low down weight as with panniers.

These are becoming quite popular and there are designs from companies like, SW-Motech Bags Connection - Speedpack goes up to 90ltrs, Wolfman Beta Plus Seat Bag is another alternative, but only has 45ltrs capacity.

Right is the offering from Italian company Givi, the XS305. Features include: adjustable straps, two pockets an external elastic net, two extendible side compartments, water-resistant zips, reflective inserts, rain cover stored in a dedicated pocket, handle and shoulder-strap for easier transportation, four

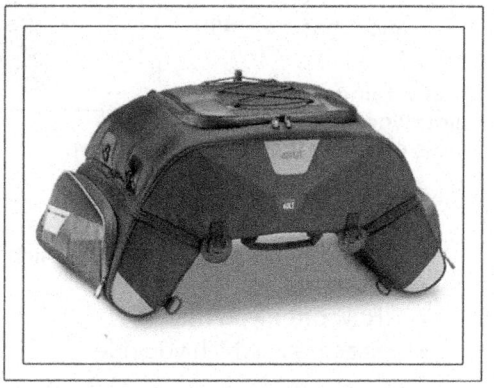

straps to secure the bag to the seat with an additional safety strap on the base, to fit under the seat or tail. And its 60ltr storage

Available February 2013 from Givi, it's a good example of how with a little bit of lateral thinking you can get suitable luggage for any type of bike and go touring and camping.

It's not the bike that has to be 'an adventure bike' to go touring and camping – any bike is the 'right' bike

Tank Panniers or Crash bar Bags

Tank panniers are not overly popular with UK bikers. Usually they form

part of a tank bag/pannier set. The side panniers usually add an extra 10ltrs or so to the front of the bike. Famsa and Touratech are two companies that produce this arrangement. Wolfman produce a 'stand alone' option that does not require a tank bag

Crash bar bags are an alternative to the full over tank pannier sets. If you own a BMW GS then Touratech do a set that will just fix right on. But at nearly £100 you have to start thinking if they are worth it.

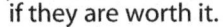

Another company that makes specific crash bar bags for the BMW and KTM is Black Dog Cycle Works. And Storm Industries will custom make crash bags for any bike.

Both companies are US based.

If you like the idea of crash bar bags and BMW and KTM are not your 'bag', and you don't want custom made bags, then start to think a little bit laterally.

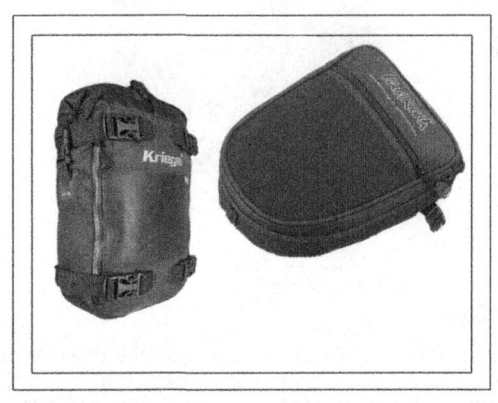

Look at the bars and look at what's available that will fit with a little farkling. Kreiga US10's are an option or perhaps a pair of Hein Gericke Tuareg Rack packs – at about £20 might be worth thinking about.

These are handy bags to store some of the less fragile bits of luggage like tools etc. as its moving some weight low and forward. But not the best place if you drop the bike, or are involved in an accident.

Waist Packs/Bum Bags

Depending on how you travel and pack these can be a great addition for the motorcycle tourer. If you look at the ones designed for bikers,

they have wide belts and big secure clips, are made of tough durable materials and have a good attempt at being waterproof (unlike the ones designed for walkers which are thinner and lightweight).

Again a lot is down to personal preference and choice, but these are great for keeping everything you need to survive while on a trip all in one place (and that's the key to them – all in one place, so you will always know where things are) – spare bike keys, house keys, money/wallet, passport, ferry/tunnel tickets, breakdown card, phone, smokes (if you do), etc. Then all that is required is to pick it up and you have everything

Kriega make a couple of great waist packs, and Hein Gericke Tuareg waist pack is good option.

Backpacks/Rucksacks

In a word – DON'T

Yes, motorcycle backpacks are made and sold, but only think about backpacks for touring as a total last resort. They put strain on your back and shoulders and at worst can move about and change the whole balance of you and the bike.

Luggage Extras

This section is really for expanding on what luggage you already have and how to fine tune for maybe additional storage.

Pannier Lid Bags

These, as their name suggests, fit on the lid of the panniers. This is an easy way to expand the carrying capacity of a pannier. They normally

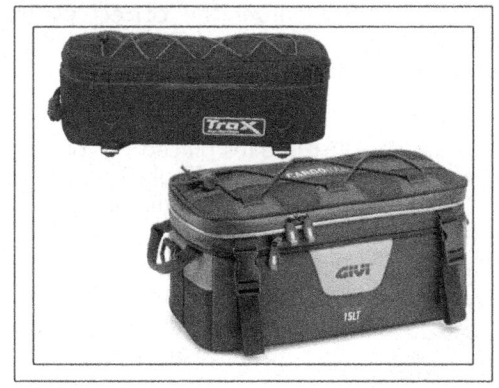

come with straps and fit on top of the pannier using four tie down points on the lid (see aluminium pannier review). These bags are usually made from tough cordura or similar material, so always think about using a bin bag or similar inside them just in case. They also carry a hefty price tag for what they are.

Several companies produce these handy bags in a variety of sizes from 6ltrs to about 18ltrs, like, Touratech, SW Motech, and more recently Givi with their 15ltr Trekker-Outback bag

As an alternative try a small watertight roll bag (about 10/15ltrs) securely fastened with shock cord.

Either way they can make access into the panniers fiddly at best.

If you are looking for a small tail pack, then don't rule these out, as they make great little tail packs as well – Might need to do a little farkling to get it to fit just right.

Pannier Net Pockets

These are little flat nets that can be fixed to the front or rear of hard panniers. They are great for storing items like maps, routes, cereal bars/chocolate, small purchases bought along the way not worth

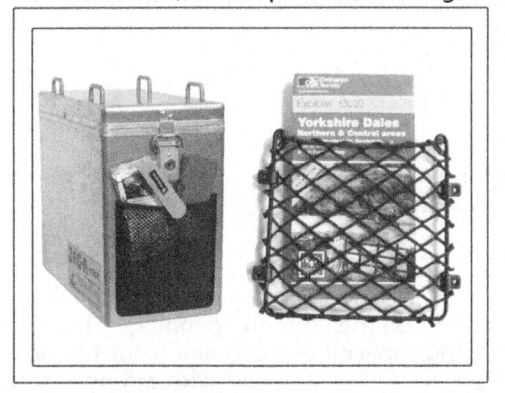

opening the panniers for. But don't put anything in here that can't get wet!

Available from the likes of Touratech for about £22. As an alternative look at Mud Stuff, they have a range of nets designed for Land Rovers which will do the job starting from about £7. Make sure you measure the pannier space to order the correct width.

The external net pockets can be simply screwed on or fixed with rivets and suitable waterproofing.

Smuggler Box/Raid Box

As their name suggests, these are small(ish) boxes placed out of easy sight to carry small items like puncture kit, a simple tool kit, maybe a

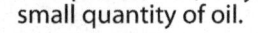

small quantity of oil.

Normally some form of farkling has to be undertaken, but commercial options are now also available.

One option is a small peli case behind the number plate. Needs to be lockable and waterproof. Another is a box between the pannier frame and the bike.

Other luggage additions include; alloy tables that fit between the two panniers at camp, nets to fit inside the pannier lids and other farkles.

Soft Luggage Pros	Soft Luggage Cons
Light	Not as secure as hard luggage
Inexpensive (in general)	May not be waterproof
Helps make you travel light	Easy to tear (once torn hard to repair)
Majority don't require a rack	Heat from the exhaust can be an issue
Better anti vibration qualities	
Fits a greater range of bikes	

Hard Luggage Pros	Hard Luggage Cons
Strong	Expensive
Waterproof (usually)	Heavier
Secure	Rack required
Can be used as a seat	Can make the bike quite wide
In a light fall can act as a buffer to the bike	Not suited to heavy off road riding
Easier to clean	

Bike Modifications

Any bike modification is a personal choice, it's usually to enhance comfort, or fine tune the protection that the bike already has. Occasionally, a bike modification is there to just add a little bit of lipstick to the old girl. (ie. cosmetic).

Again, as this book is not initially aimed at RTW travellers some areas in this topic won't be touched on in great depth, or at all, like fitting a super long range fuel tank, or even building your own! – If you are staying within Europe your existing tank will be fine, so no worries there.

As good as some bike manufacturers are they still get it slightly wrong sometimes, and that's where third party kit comes in. For example, the Suzuki V-Strom is said to suffer from a badly designed screen and mirrors, so if you have a problem, look at changing items. Don't change them because everyone says so. Take advice and see for yourself.

Screen

This has to be one of the most talked about pieces of equipment on a bike. Two riders can have identical bikes and one rider hates it and the other cant praise it enough.

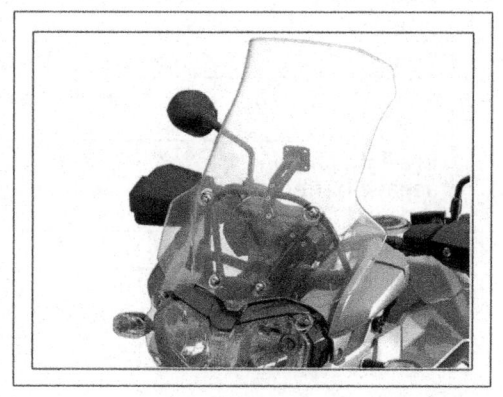

When bikes are designed, they are generally designed for 'Mr Average' (whether he exists or not). Most people probably don't fit this category, which is why there are so many different opinions about screens.

A good screen will, dramatically reduce wind fatigue on your body, improve wind resistance so less engine power and fuel needed, improve the bike's stability especially when overtaking traffic since your body will not be blown all over the place, protect you from most of the rain, insects and cold in winter and reduce wind noise in your helmet.

Obviously the screen is there to protect the rider from the elements, but in doing this can create buffeting and noise behind it. The strength of wind and duration of riding is the main cause of fatigue on your body, head and ears if the screen is not working.

If this is the case then try ducking down behind the screen to find the still air pocket, and then sit very straight, or stand a little on the pegs to find clear air. Then sit back to the normal riding position. Probably the wind and noise is right in your face/neck if you have an issue. Use your hand to deflect air up from the top of the screen to see if a taller screen would help. – Do this on a very quiet straight road and under control.

Also talk to other riders with similar bikes and see if they have an issue and what they did to resolve it.

Manufacturers Adjustable Screens

Some bikes come with adjustable screens as standard, (some are simple thumb screws and others require tools to adjust), so try moving the screen up, then go out and test again. Even try lowering the screen as this sometimes makes a difference. But any adjustment should help.

After Market Screens & Spoilers/Laminar Lips

Some after market screens are actually quite subtle with just maybe an inch taller, but with a steeper angle towards the top of the screen. Some are classed as touring screens and can be up to about 10cm taller.

Spoilers or Laminar lips fit on the top of the screen. They are designed to deflect the airflow around the rider. They can be purchased as a stand alone addition that just bolts on to your existing screen.

Left is a screen by MRA which incorporates an adjustable spoiler and also opens the bottom of the screen to allow air to enter the air pocket behind the screen to reduce the vacuum, which also assists with buffeting and noise.

Givi and Puig also make similar designs. If you combine this with a bracket from the likes of

Magstad, you can have a fully adjustable screen - vertically, through angles both front to back and left to right.

Winglets

These are small additional spoilers, usually mounted near the lower part of the screen and upper fairing. The idea behind them is to disrupt the airflow further from the screen or body. Usually designed from clear plastic they can be available as OEM parts, after market accessories, or some riders make their own.

Seats

Riders spend most of the day on the seat, if road touring, so the seat really needs to be comfy. Standard manufacturer seats vary quite considerably in quality, width (nice and wide or quite thin) and type - a sit on (where the seat stops flat against the tank) or sit in (where the

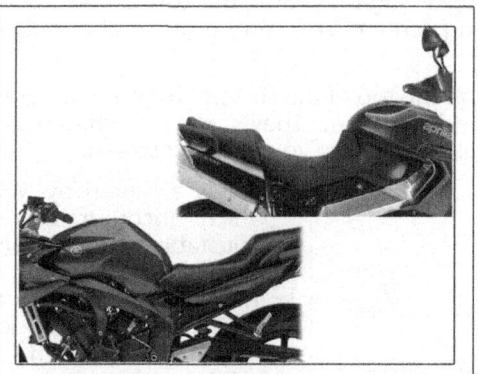

seat is sculptured a little more like a horse saddle). If you can only manage about 70-100 miles before you start to fidget and the sitting position becomes intolerable; there is a problem with the seat.

Some riders will find that they get used to their seat, so the initial pain factor lowers. Others will get to a stage where they just can't get on the bike! Before setting off on a long bike trip, make sure the seat is comfy.

There are quite a few options to look at here to make the riding day more pleasurable, and people have come up with several of their own options that work for them.

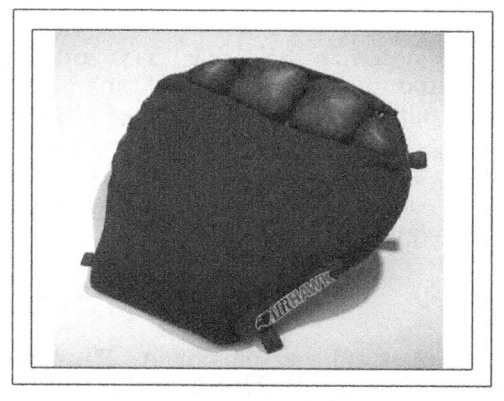

Firstly, there is the well heard of and talked about Airhawk system. These are inflatable cushions made up of small pockets which fit into a cover with a non slip base which is then fastened under the bike seat. The idea here is to spread the load of your bum over a greater area. These have sorted many seat issues, but some people say it's a bit like sitting on a 'squidgy' cushion of air and that they don't feel as though they are 'sat' on the bike. Genuine Airhawk systems can be in the region of £160+ for the premium options.

Something very similar is a stadium seat. Not initially designed for motorbikes but at about £10 might be worth trying before an Airhawk

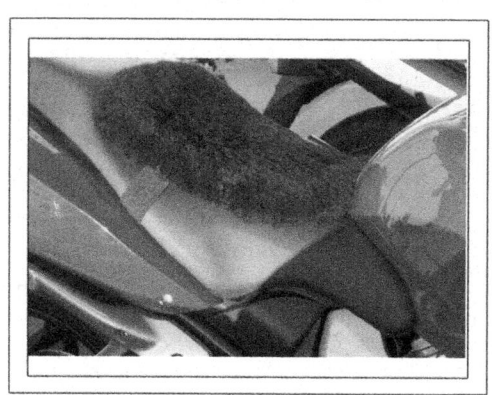

If you are new to bike touring you have probably seen at least one bike with what looks like half a dead sheep on it! And wondered what that's all about. The idea behind this is similar to the Airhawk; it's to help spread the weight of the bum, but it also allows air to circulate underneath, thus stopping sweaty bum issues when you get off the bike. These range from the full on shaggy un-trimmed hides through to tailored purpose made ones like above.

Again its all down to personal choice, as some people just can't bring themselves to have a soggy ruminant mammal under their bum.

Top Tip

If this is the option for you, try to get hold of a part treated skin that's not had all the lanolin washed out of it. Lanolin's waterproofing property aids sheep in shedding water from their coats, so will add to the waterproofing of your sheepskin

Gel Inserts & Resculpture

Having the seat resculptured and perhaps having gel pads added is another option. This is a no return option; as if you still can't get on with the seat then a new seat is required or a return to the upholsterer.

After a quick chat about the issues and what you require, a specialist upholsterer will be able to re-profile seat foams lower or higher, softer or firmer, add gel inserts, and even add colour coded piping, and a new covering of your choice if required.

Heated Grips

Now to some people heated grips are the soft option. But some people just can't stand having cold hands, or have cold hand related problems and thicker gloves don't always do the trick. Heated grips sometimes work best with thinner gloves to allow the heat through.

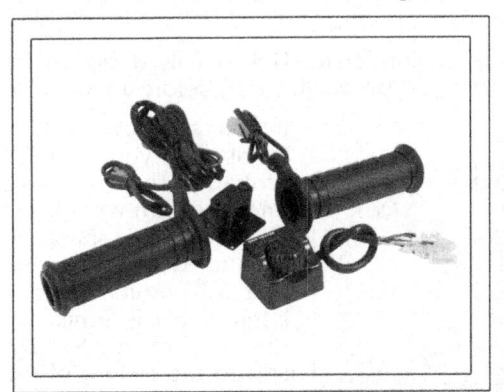

Originally they were only found on top of the range bikes, but have been filtering down the ranges and with the aftermarket explosion they have also become a popular retro fit. These are available in three main types: Whole grip replacements, under grip elements, and over grip wraps.

Over grip wraps are the simplest to fit as they just slip over the existing grips and once they are wired in to the supply they are up and running. About 20minutes should see them fitted. The downside is that they increase the diameter of the bike grips, which may cause issues. Those supplied by Oxford come with plenty of wire (almost too much) to fit any bike. There is no thermostat supplied so a lot of switching on and off is involved.

Whole grip replacements

This style of fitting requires the replacement of the whole grip with the ones supplied in the package. This can make for a very tricky installation, but fitted correctly can offer a very robust and professional end result. This type of grip usually comes with some form of heat control, from a basic high/low option through the fully variable settings via a thumb wheel of similar.

Under grip elements

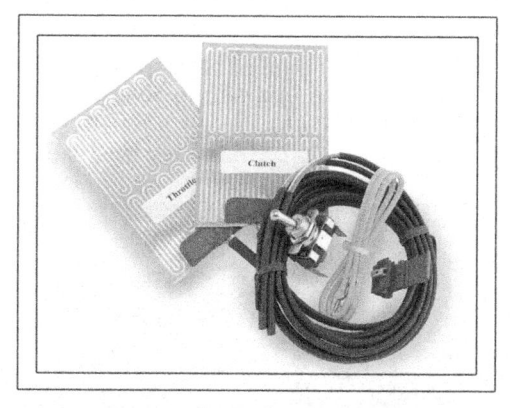

As the name suggests, these are thin heating elements on flexible mylar tape that fit under the existing grips via permanent adhesive on the back. Once wired into a supply the original grips are refitted. A simple toggle switch is included for off/high/low settings.

Hand Guards

These can be fitted to almost any bike from adventure style to a standard street bike. Originally produced to keep brush and scrub off the hands of trial riders, they are also great at keeping the weather elements away from the hands and also offering a little protection for the bikes levers if the worst happens.

Guards range in size from the simple metal lever protectors right through to plastic guards with added wind deflectors. How good added deflectors are is debatable. (A great addition or just another marketing ploy?)

If the guards have some form of metal strip running through them, then this really will help protect the leavers in a fall. A broken leaver really can ruin a trip. When it comes to weather protection a good hand guard really can keep the wind and rain away from the hands.

OE guards are probably the easiest to fit as they have been designed for the bike, so should just fix straight on, but are not always the best.

Third party guards designed to fit specific bikes usually have a bit more structure to them than OE ones, and again should fit straight on. Touratech is one manufacturer.

Generic guards can be bought for quite a range of bikes from the likes of Barkbusters, Acerbis and others, where one set of guards will fit several bikes with the addition of adaptors.

Right – a set of generic Acerbis guards fitted to a Yamaha Fazer.

Again talk with other riders of the bike model and see what they fitted and how easy/hard it was. A good example is the Moto Guzzi Stelvio guards which are a one for one replacement for the Aprilia Caponord guards, and much better the OE ones.

What ever choice is made, make sure that none of the cables catch the guards to avoid chafeing; and that a full lock can be achieved without touching the tank or the screen. If full lock can't be achieved then you are in danger of cracking the screen in a fall or even failing the next MOT test.

Bar Risers

As the name suggests, these raise the handle bars on the bike by adding either a fixed spacer or a universal adjustable riser. They are available in many forms and from many manufacturers.

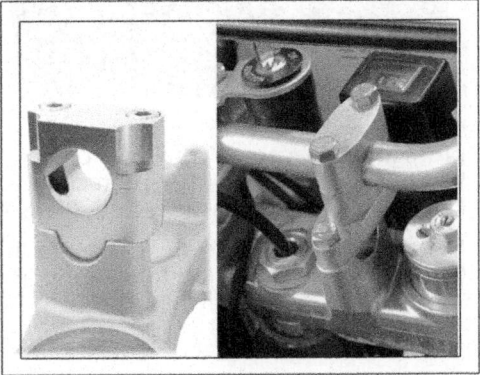

Bikes that have a lower riding position are not always the best ergonomically to go touring on, as the angle of the hands and wrists can start to cause pains. The raised handlebar position is designed to give a much more upright riding posture, thereby relieving the wrists of body weight and straightening the back and neck which could greatly improve distance riding.

With any raising of the bars special attention needs to be given to the cables, and any risers higher than about 20/30mm may require longer cables.

Risers on the more adventure styled bike can also aide with riding over tricky ground whilst standing on the foot pegs

Engine/Bike Protection

It's a fact of motorcycling life that at some point almost all bikes will either simply fall over when stationary, or will be involved in an accident with the bike sliding down the road or track.

Bike protection is often an overlooked option for the more road biased rider, but on the larger 'Adventure' styles bikes its common practice to try to protect vulnerable areas of the bike. But some people do get carried away.

The longer any trip, the better it is to protect the bike from minor tumbles, stones/rocks, bottoming out etc

Engine Bars or Crash Bars

These have one purpose and that is to protect the engine and surrounding body work in a fall. They are usually made from high quality steel tubing which attaches onto the chassis to provide a secure cage around the bike.

Design and fitment is a personal choice; some bars are designed to fit low down to protect only the engine, others go higher to protect the side panels as well. BMWs with their sticking out opposed cylinders are a prime candidate for some type of protection.

The photo above shows an Aprilia Caponord with both lower and upper engine bars and a Yamaha Super Tenere with Altrider engine bars fitted.

Initially, the purpose of engine bars may appear to be just for looks and to make a bike look more rugged than it really is, but if fitted in the right place they can be very effective. *(See Authors Notes & Views for more information)*.

Manufacturers of adventure style bikes often fit them as standard or they can be bought as an OE extra. There is also a growing market for third party crash bars from the likes of Touratech, Hepco & Becker, Altrider, SW Motech and others. They are not necessarily a cheap item to buy, but far cheaper than having to replace plastics or engine parts after a tumble, or if on the continent having to be repatriated.

Crash Mushrooms/Crash Bobbins

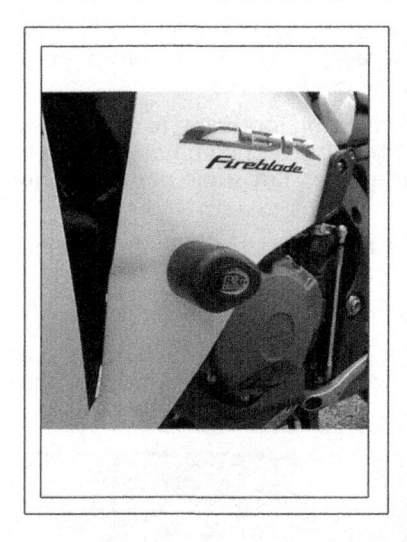

For the more road bias bikes these are a great alternative to engine bars. Crash bobbins or crash protectors, are designed to minimise the amount of damage to your bike's bodywork in the unfortunate event of it being dropped.

They are fitted to the bike where the frame meets the engine (the strongest part of the bike) and are designed to stand out from the bike so in the event of a tumble it's the bobbin that hits the floor not the bike.

Available from most bike shops and dealers from the likes of R&G, Bike Design and others.

Sump Guards/Bash Plates/ Belly Pans

Call them what you want, the purpose of them is to protect the engine from at the least, road grime and stones, and at the worst rocks and bottoming out when travelling on unmetalled roads.

Some OE parts that manufacturers fit as standard are made of plastic which will offer limited protection to the sump of the engine.

Others and third party designs are made from aluminium of about 4mm thick and designed to cover the whole of the sump and a little up the sides.

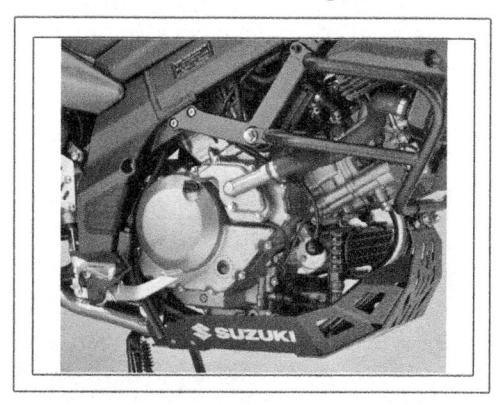

If you already have lower engine bars from a third party make sure the sump guard will fit if it's from another supplier.

Manufacturers include Altrider, Touratech, Cymarc, Guard IT Technology, SW Motech.

Sump guard tool boxes are a neat little idea, but how useful they are and how close they go to the wheel may be an issue. They allow for the safe storage of articles such as tools etc and keeps them locked away down low.

For the full bespoke option go to a fabricator who will be able to design and construct a bespoke guard.

For the more road bias bike there is the belly pan option. Usually made out of tough plastic, so not as strong as aluminium (but more in keeping with the bikes styling) it is plenty to protect the lower engine and pipes from stones and road grime.

Radiator Guards

As the name says these are guards which fit over the front of the bikes radiator. As seen below on a Triumph Tiger, they are designed to stop

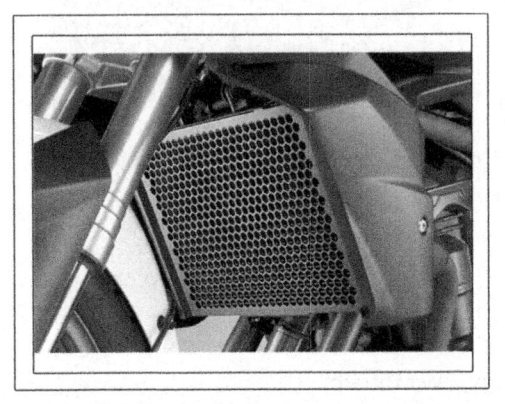

damage from stones, twigs and anything that can get blown or kicked up onto the radiator.

Bike specific guards can be bought from SW Motech, Wunderlich, R&G, Beowulf and many others.

Top Tip

If you want a radiator guard and no one makes one for your bike, or you don't want to spend upwards of £30, look into some strong, fine mesh chicken wire, paint it and farkle a guard.

Headlight Protectors

The headlight unit on any bike can be expensive to replace if it gets hit by a flying stone or other debris.

There are two types of protector – wire mesh and perspex. Perspex has better coverage over the whole of the light and should stop even the smallest of stones. When washing the bike remember to clean the wrong side of the plastic as well otherwise the light beam may get distorted or look weak.

Mesh guards by their nature should be stronger, but the smaller stones and debris will still get through.

Other Protection

There are many other areas on a motorcycle that some people have a need to protect. For example on the market there are brake master cylinder guards, pipe guards, rear brake reservoir guards, aluminium chain guards, fork protectors, front brake reservoir guards. There is even an aluminium guard for the horn switch!

Protection is better than having a broken bike, but at the same time does the horn switch really need protecting?

Side Stand Footprint Extender

Known by various names – Camel Toe, side stand extender, side stand pads, side stand big foot. They are all names given to a device which

fits on the bottom of the side stand to make its 'footprint' larger.

The idea behind it is to stop the stand sinking into soft ground (at a camp site for example) or soft tar etc. and thus stopping the bike toppling over. They are designed to slide over the small standard base and then clamp over it. Custom designed for different makes/models of bike from the likes of Adventure Parts (who make the original Camel Toe), Touratech, AMC, Altrider and many others.

These little modifications can make life on the road a little easier, but are not essential as in its most basic form it's a plastic 'puck' that can be bought for a pound or so from the local bike shop that's put down before the side stand. (Or even a flattened tin can will do the trick!)

Top Tip

Make a small hole in the puck, and then thread some string through the hole and tie it to the puck - needs to be long enough to reach the handlebars. Tie knots in the string at intervals. (This aids with grip when wet). Now when you stop put the puck down, rest stand on the puck and tie the string to the handle bar. When you are ready to go and sat on the bike, untie the string from handlebar, pull up the puck and put it in your pocket until you are on firmer ground when you can stash it away.

Lighting

It's a fact of life that for many years the OE headlights fitted by motorcycle manufacturers were passable at best. In order to save money most manufacturers only fitted basic bulbs to the bikes. Saying that, some stock bulbs/lenses are considerably better than others.

Listen to most bikers talking about their lights and most will have done something to them.

Headlight upgrade options include either replacement of stock bulbs with higher output units, fitting a HID conversion kit, or adding additional lighting with the installation of auxiliary lights (either standard or LED).

Even if there are no plans to ride at night, lights are there to light the road for the rider at night and also to help others can you, both at night and during the day.

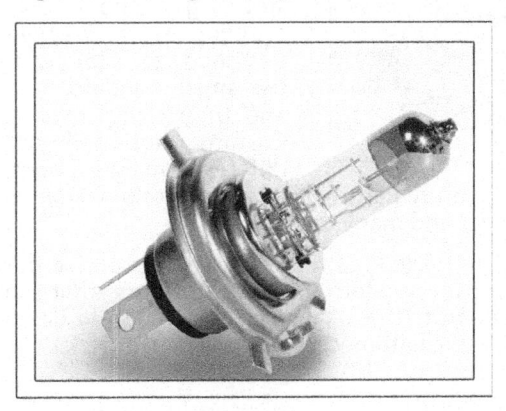

The most straight forward option is to change the stock bulbs for a 'better quality' bulb. Seeing what a bulb change can actually do is quite impressive.

In this case a Philips XTreme Vision bulb which claims to provide up to 100% more light than standard halogen bulbs in both dip and main beam.

The bike was a Suzuki V-Strom and had stock bulbs fitted. The owner then changed one bulb to a Philips Xtreme Vision and left the other as standard for a comparison. The difference was amazing. The standard bulb looked very weak and yellow at the side of the Phillips Xtreme which was a crisp white and much brighter light.

I'd guess the beam was at least half as bight again over the stock Suzuki fitted bulb.

This performance gain is achieved through a new filament design, a quartz burner and high pressure gas filling to deliver maximum light output and longer life expectancy.

As a side note; make sure any bulbs fitted don't use an illegal increase in wattage to produce more light, (X-Treme Visions are designed around the standard 55/60w output) and are safe to use with plastic lenses.

Other types of bulb are available from the likes of Osram, Ring and others in the Philips range.

HID

This is another option that has become popular over the last few years. HID or High Intensity Discharge, (sometimes known as Xenon) is a technology that relies on an electrical charge to ignite xenon gas in sealed bulbs. This system does not have a filament like normal bulbs, but instead creates light by igniting an electrical discharge between two 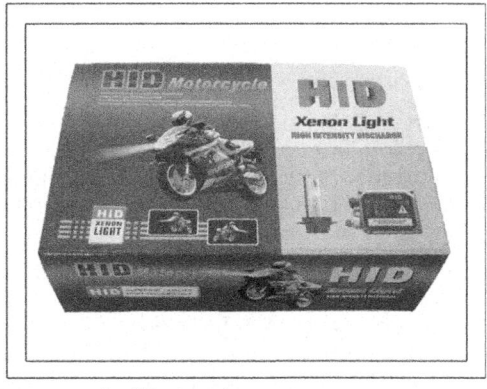 electrodes in an air tight quartz capsule filled with xenon gas.

In a similar way that florescent lamps work, HID lamps need a ballast to start and maintain their arcs. This method varies from make to make, for example using a third electrode or by using pulses of high voltage.

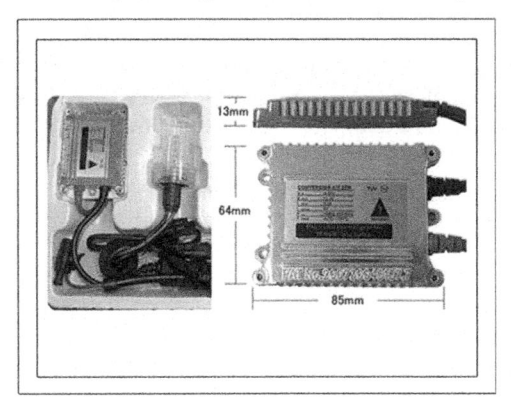

There are numerous advantages of HID headlights. Brightness, efficiency (the light output from a 35W 4300K HID Xenon lamp can be up to 300% more visible light than a 55W halogen bulb), and looks are the most notable advantages of HID conversion kits.

There are however a couple of downsides to this system. Firstly they require quite a high current to start, which may be more than the standard bike loom can handle, so a relay switched supply will need to be fitted. Then there is the issue of where to fit the ballast box. Originally these were quite bulky, but are getting smaller. They can also take a second to light, so not so good for full beam.

Buying a HID upgrade for motorcycles can be a bit of a minefield, with so many types and makes, all of differing price and quality.

As a side note:

Most HID lamps produce significant UV radiation, and require UV-blocking filters to prevent UV-induced degradation of lamp fixture components. Exposure to cheap HID lamps operating with faulty or absent UV-blocking filters can cause injury to humans such as sunburn and arc eye.

Also there is a legal issue at the moment as to whether they are legal or not in the UK. The latest directive from VOSA includes their view that unless strict criteria are met, after-market HID kits may not be legal. There is some confusion regarding the change in legislation towards HID kits. So if you are thinking of converting to HID light check with VOSA or a friendly MOT tester first.

Auxiliary Lights

One piece of information someone once gave me was to ride as though no one else could see me. Then you will always ride safer, pause a little longer at junctions, and look at other vehicle drivers faces at side junctions. Adding auxiliary lights to a motorcycle can help minimize the chances of other road users not seeing you, both at night and during the day.

How many times have you been driving in a car on a motorway and spotted the motorcycle with its aux lights on from miles away? A motorcycle with a headlight and a pair of driving lights mounted high or low makes an unusual triangle of light that catches more attention than just a headlight

Below is an article from the Motorcycle Safety Group by James Davis, they ran a study into the best ways to make bikes more visible and the best places to mount aux/running lights.

"We have all heard and lament that car drivers inevitably argue that they didn't see the motorcycle before the collision occurred. Certain that the real problem is that they were otherwise busy talking on their

cell phones or simply not paying attention, we do not credit that excuse other than with a "Yeah, sure". But what if it's true?

Most motorcyclists have heard the word 'conspicuity'. It means conspicuousness or obviousness. It is a ten-dollar word that turns off most people who hear it, but there is substance behind it. It certainly

helps your ability to be seen if you are conspicuous or obvious, though that person on the cell phone still might not notice you, and even if they do, they may not be able to recognize what they are seeing.

When you hear the word 'conspicuity' you probably think 'light colored clothes'. Yep, that can certainly help - when the sun is shining. But I suggest that at night/dull weather you are FAR better off having reflective strips of some kind on your jacket/helmet/motorcycle than if you are wearing a light colored jacket as opposed to black. Those reflective strips or patches should be across your upper back and on your shoulders (facing to either side) for best effect.

And why is it that we tend to think of the person who is ahead of us needing to see us more than the person behind or from the side? The truth is, it doesn't matter where 'they' are, they MUST be able to see you and recognize you for what you are.

Curiously, despite the natural desire to be seen by drivers coming toward us, when motorcyclists think about adding some lights to their rigs they think about rear facing lights first. They add bigger, brighter, brake lights and even modulated lights to aid those who are behind them. I say curiously because most threats to a motorcyclist are in front of your motorcycle, not behind.

Many years ago the railroad industry determined that the most conspicuous lighting arrangement, and safest, was to have a triangle of forward facing lights, the largest, brightest light at the top and two slightly smaller/dimmer lights mounted horizontally below it. This configuration had benefits that might not be immediately obvious. Most notably, when a train is moving toward you the two bottom lights appear to get farther apart. Thus, you not only recognize the lights as coming from a train, but you can tell if it is moving toward you, and you can even estimate at what speed.

A motorcycle can have exactly the same lighting advantage. If you mount running lights below your headlight you have created that magic triangle. When seen from the front you no longer look like a far distant car. Since nobody expects to see a train coming toward them on a public road, you are recognized for being 'something else' - indeed, almost certainly a motorcycle."

Well yes it's a longish article and yes some people out there will disagree totally to the triangle of light, but just think how many other road vehicles will look like a triangle of light, so the driver instinctively takes a better longer look at what's coming towards him.

Halogen bulbs - Auxiliary lights come in either driving or fog style lights. Driving lights are spotlights designed to light up the road a good distance ahead. The lens on a fog light is designed to give a wide, low beam to light more of the road close to the vehicle.

One thing to think about when fitting extra electrical kit to the bike is; will the generator produce enough power to keep it all going? Most auxiliary lights take about 55w per light, so 110w in total for a pair. If this is too much draw on the generator, look at stepping down to 35W bulbs.

Options here are split into motorcycle specific from the likes of Touratech, Givi, SW Motech etc or car based ones with a little farkling to get them to fit from the likes of Hella, Ring, etc.

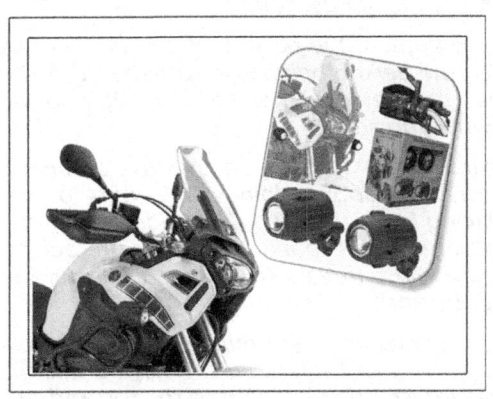

Lights designed for motorcycles usually come with a bracket that will fit round a crash bar or from the likes of Touratech who design their own bike specific mounts and guards.

Left shows a set of Givi S310 Trekker lights. For around £140 for the set, they are ideal for providing extra light in bad weather or low light situations. The Trakker lights have 12v/55w halogen bulbs fitted, which are controlled by a remote handle bar switch.

Right is Touratech's offering fitted using a bike specific mount; in this case to a Yamaha Super Tenere. If you have a bike they support then this can be a neater option than generic fittings, but at just under £300 for a pair of fog lights or £400 for one spotlight, one has to think twice sometimes.

As always it can pay to think laterally sometimes. If you have the time and the skill, car based lights can sometimes be farkled to fit a motorcycle with the use of fabricated brackets etc, and as they don't have the term 'motorcycle' in the description are usually much cheaper.

Ring Luminator Fog Lights are a great set of lights to fit to a motorcycle. And many have.

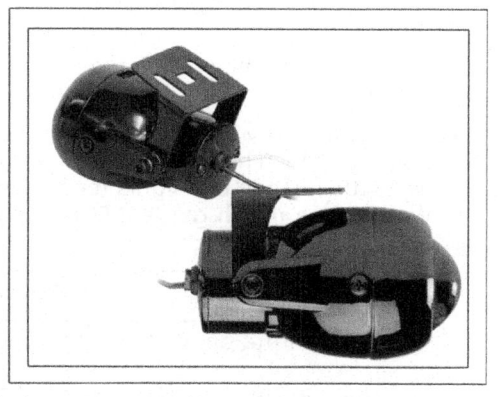

They are constructed from a solid metal alloy and have a precision beam pattern for improved visibility during adverse weather conditions. They also come with a flat base plate which is ideal for modifying for motorcycle fitting. At around £30 they are not going to break the bank.

Hella Mico DE lights are another set that can be made to fit a motorbike. With H3 12V/55W, they are noted for their ruggedness and reliability. In fact these are the light bodies that Touratech use in their lights. Again if you are prepared to farkle, a pair can be picked up for about £150.

LED (Light Emitting Diode) is the latest in lighting technology and is considered the light source of the future. LED lighting is the most effective of all lighting technologies available right now. The technology is now being deployed in many different applications. In the automotive world, the incredible durability and sturdiness, combined with the superior lighting quality makes it a logical choice. . So why not use them for lighting on a motorcycle.

LED Lights – Over the last couple of years LED lighting has taken leaps forward with reliability and light power. So, what's the advantage of LED lights?

What makes LED lights stand out is their incredibly low power consumption, and their high efficient light output and low heat.

LED lights require only a fraction of the power used by normal Halogen, or HID lights. LEDs are extremely sturdy, and can handle shock and vibration much better and for much longer. They also last at least 250 times longer than Halogen, and at least 20 times longer than HID lights. LED motorcycle/car lights are extremely compact, so in turn allow for smaller packaging when compared to most bulb type assemblies.

On top of all that they require very little power compared to other light sources.

If LED is the auxiliary light of choice aim to go for a CREE LED package as these are a much higher output than standard LEDs. Just to confuse things a little further, LED lights tend to me measured in Lumens and not Watts. As a rough guide a 60W tungsten bulb has an output of about 700 to 750 lumens.

	10W LED	Halogen Bulb
Light output per Watt	80 Lumen	12 Lumen
Light output per Amp	1067 Lumen	144 Lumen
Amp draw @ 12V	0.75 Amp	8.3 Amp
Bulb Life	50,000 Hours	200 Hours

Left - A set of 800lm LED lights. These are drawing about 12W at 1000mA.

LED lights are available from the likes of BikeVis who are now producing 10 Watt 900 Lumen Cree LED lamps which are low power and just 0.66 Amps per light.

Rigid Industries also produce a range of LED lights suitable for motorcycles like the SRM2 single row mini. Available from ZenOverland in the UK. There is also a reputable seller on ebay who several ABR forum members have used with good service and delivery times.

The VisionX Solstice Solo is available through several suppliers including Adventure Spec for about £100.

There are now quite a few to choose from to give you that extra LED lighting option and to build a triangle of light.

LED white light really does get you noticed on murky dull days.

LED Bulbs – As an option for normal lamp bodies LED bulb replacements are now available. These give you the best of both worlds if you have already got a set of 55w lights fitted. As an example a H3 foglight LED replacement bulb gives a super daylight white light. They draw about 150mA at 2W giving 160LM.

As a side note: Check that the bulb conversion purchased is road legal.

12v Take Off

As people now carry with them so many electrical items, there needs to be a way to power them or recharge them whilst touring (also see Electricals section).

Most bike manufacturers are finally realising that people have items that need powering so are starting to fit 12v take off points as standard. Most are in sensible places, but for reasons only known to themselves, Aprilia decided to fit the 12v take off on the Caponord just below the seat where the leg is when riding. So fitting an additional point 'up front' is required.

Waterproof 12v sockets can be purchased from most boating or caravanning stores for a few pounds. Fitting them is fairly straight forward, by either using their own fused loom straight from the battery, or by connecting into the AUX loom from the fuse box, again fit another inline fuse to protect both the bike and the kit being powered. Another  consideration to think about is whether the supply is to be switched (goes off with the ignition) or unswitched.

CAN-bus bikes may not be so straight forward as they can get upset with non compliant accessories.

Top Tip

When wiring the socket the pin is the positive and the outer is the ground.

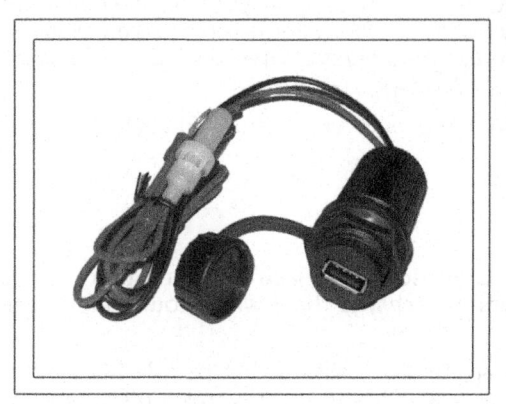

As an alternative to the standard 'cigarette' style socket, and as more devices are becoming USB powered, perhaps look at a waterproof USB powered socket.

Liquid Transportation

We have all seen them – aluminium panniers with brackets on the back and a 2ltr bottle, or a couple of 1ltr Sigg style bottles.

These black 2ltr plastic jerry cans are really for carrying a little extra petrol, or oil. Within the normal riding of most bikers on a trip within Europe they are not really necessary. As long as you know your bike

and fuel gauge, then you can always find a filling station before its too late. (Unless you are in Italy and it's a Sunday – most fuel stations away from the AutoStrada close on Sundays). They are available from the likes of Adventure Parts and Touratech and made from stainless steel. Trips further afield may need you to re-think fuel carrying capacity.

Carrying water in Sigg style bottles or Meths/Petrol in fuel bottles opens up a few more options.

The Adventure Parts chassis can be used for either the 2ltr black petrol canister or (if you re-thread the straps) 2x1ltr Sigg style bottles. If you go down the Touratech route then a different chassis is needed.

A soft holder made from heavy duty Ballistic Nylon is also available from Wolfman. The adaptor kit will be needed if fastening onto hard luggage.

Recently, 'tool tubes' have been making their mark for transporting fluids. These are originally designed for instruction manuals for farm machinery, but make a great way of securing a 1ltr bottle to the bike. Seen left on a Super Tenere.

Some people have even used simple pedal bike bottle cages bolted onto the pannier. Always remember to secure the bottles to the cage so they can't vibrate out.

All these methods provide quick and easy access to either water, a reserve of petrol or meths for cooking. When fitting this type of storage, always remember that the lower down and closer to the bikes centre of gravity, the better.

As a safety note: Only use marked up bottles for fuel/petrol and don't over fill as petrol expands. MRS, Primus, Trangia and Optimis bottles are widely available.

Sigg stopped producing fuel bottles a few years ago. Their markings were not always the best and could rub off; they also had some issues with the stoppers. But as a rule, if it's a black washer then its fuel, if it's a white washer then it's anything BUT fuel.

Clothing

What to wear when on the bike, like lots of things where the human body is involved, is down to personal choice. Some people feel the cold more than others; some handle heat better than others. But whichever type of person you are there are some basics that are always required.

Helmet

It is law within the whole of Europe that if riding a bike you must wear a helmet. There are many designs, colours and makes out there these days. There are arguments about which colours are easier for other drivers to see (or do you want it to match the bike?), and also about

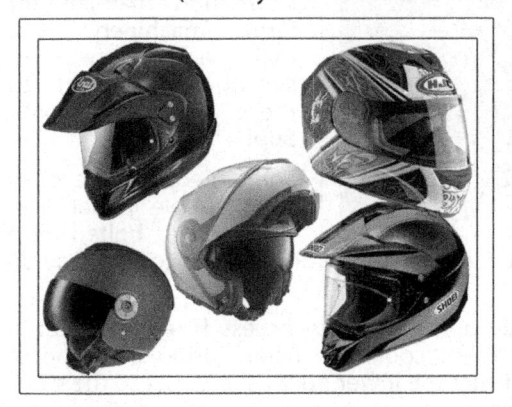

which style motorcycle helmet is safer. But most of all be sure to get one that fits properly (no tight pressure points round the ears and forehead) and is comfortable; don't just surf the internet and buy from a website, go and try them on and get advice from an experienced fitter. Some good advice often heard is to buy the best quality motorcycle helmet you can reasonably afford or budget will allow.

So take a look around and find one that suits you, your bike and requirements and fits correctly.

Whatever helmet you have, always look after it properly. Depending on the type of finish clean it with a soft clean cloth with a spray of MucOff Optic cleaner (always check with the instructions first). Store away from direct sunlight in a soft helmet bag.

If you are a naturally warm person, or planning on riding to warmer parts, don't forget about good ventilation.

Flip fronts

These are recommended by many riders as they allow easier interaction with people without having to shout or remove your helmet. And at toll stations on the continent you can flip the lid, grab

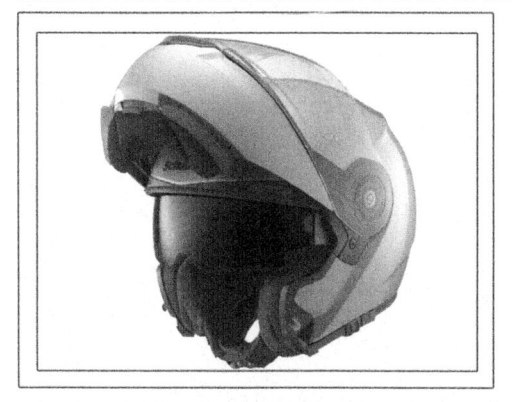

the toll ticket and hold it with your teeth while you ride to the side before stashing it in a pocket!

Some of the typical drawbacks of this type of helmet (generally): Extra weight due to the mechanics of the hinging feature (although they are getting lighter) and extra wind noise due to the seams at the hinged feature.

If you are on a very tight budget then the Nitro F341 is a good starting point with offers from £60. At the other end of the scale is the Schuberth C3 at around £500 (which is said to be one of the worlds quietest helmet, and used by many Police forces); as always there is everything in between.

Brands include Shark, Shoei, Caberg, Schuberth, Nitro HJC and many others. Most motorcycle shops will have a selection available.

Motorcross /Duel Sport Style

A popular style of helmet for the adventure bike rider is the motorcross or duel sport style. These are good for riding in bright sunshine especially if the sun is low in the sky due to the in built peak.

Some models allow the visor and peak to be removed, thus giving three helmets in one: Peak and visor, Peak no visor and goggles, or no peak and visor.

Arai are one of the more popular brands with the Tour X range. Not the cheapest, coming in at £500 with a design or less in a single colour. They come with fully washable and removable Dry Cool® interior, Emergency release tab cheekpads, Visor Pinlock® ready and Pinlock® insert included and the ventilation is spot on.

Other brands on the market include Shoei hornet range, AGV, Duchinni D311 (with built in sun visor), Wolf Prima, Airoh S4, HJC, Acerbis Active, plus others.

As a word of caution: Unless you are used to riding at speed in this style of helmet, be careful, as the peak can easily catch the wind at motorway speeds.

Sun Visors

Many helmets are now coming with built in internal sun visors that flip down, using a slider. This really adds to the practicality of the helmet. If it's warm, have the visor open and the sun visor down to allow air onto the face. As the sun goes down, just flip the sun visor back. No more swapping tinted for clear visors.

Pinlock

The Pinlock system is essentially a means of double glazing the visor to prevent it fogging up. The airtight pocket between the Pinlock insert

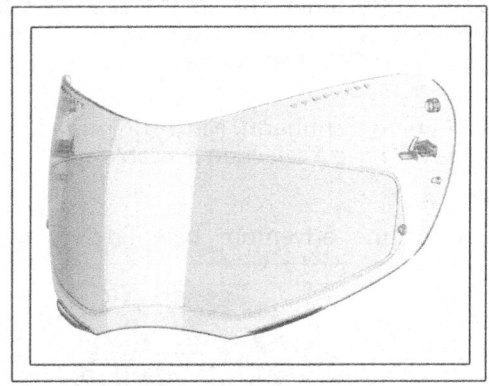

and the visor creates an extra insulation layer, further increasing the anti fogging properties of the total system.

Pinlock is so effective that manufacturers like Shoei, Arai, HJC, Schuberth and many more are supplying their helmets as standard with the Pinlock Original.

Chin Fasteners

Basically there are two types, the double D-Ring and clip buckles (of various styles). Some riders really struggle with the double D-Ring fastener, but with a little time it's really straight forward (through both, back through the first and press stud down - have a play in a shop and see what you think).

Gloves

There are many materials, designs and styles available in the gloves section. The final choice is down to you the rider as no one style will suit all.

Gloves are worn to protect the hands from the elements and (should the need arise) in an accident. Wearing the right type of glove for the riding conditions always helps. The gloves should keep your hand warm without it becoming sweaty – If it does then a slightly thinner glove is required and the opposite applies.

For long days on an adventure style bike a thinner MX style glove works well. The padded palms and slightly tacky material really allows you to feel the handlebars. As seen above the Spada MX1 has a good level of protection over the knuckles and fingers, a strong Velcro wrist band, sure-grip palm and fingers while being a light glove option. Give them an occasional spray with Nikwax to keep the worst of the weather out.

Thicker waterproof gloves again should offer good levels of protection over the knuckles and fingers. They should fit snug, but at the same as they are bulkier should not hinder movement of the fingers to get to the controls. And being thicker they will be warmer, so if you are touring in the summer months your hands may get sweaty. Many different styles and materials are available ranging from leather to technical textile fabrics and are available from the likes of Spada, Rukka, Alpine stars, Frank Thomas and many others. Try different makes on to see which feel right and are not so thick you can't move your fingers to the clutch and break!

As an alternative to 'traditional' brands, SealSkinz motorcycle gloves are highly protective, totally waterproof, breathable and thermally lined. Available in thicker or lightweight designs.

For breathable waterproof materials look for trade names Gore-tex, Sympatex, eVent, D-Dry and similar.

For warmth look for Thinsulate, Thermolite, Polar Fleece, Dexfil insulation and see what the label says about the lining.

Also see the Heated Clothing section.

Top Tip

Two are warmer than one thick one

If you feel the cold then look at how skiers keep their hands warm; a thin pair of silk glove liners and then the main glove over the top. The layering system really can add extra warmth to the hands.

If your gloves leak or your hands sweat in them, a pair of tight fitting surgical style gloves under the main glove should stop the water making your hands cold and pruney and help stop the lining pulling out when you take them off.

Always take at least two pairs of gloves if touring. Basically if one pair gets a soaking they need to be allowed to dry. And some days are warmer than others so a change to lighter gloves is always nice.

Boots

As with all motorcycle outer gear, go for the best you can afford in the style you want as this kit is there to protect you.

After a good helmet, boots are next in terms of importance, but are so often either overlooked or skimped on. First and foremost, don't think wearing a pair of hiking boots will do the trick. Boots that protect the feet, ankles and lower legs are required.

The feet and lower legs are susceptible to stones flying up from the road and front wheel, or they may get dragged under a pannier in a tumble. The more that can be done to protect the legs the better.

Some makes of bike boots even have metal

shafts running along the sole for strength and heat shields on the inner side to protect the leg if it's trapped under the bike in a tumble.

So if you were thinking of touring in a pair of hiking boots, please reconsider.

Don't go out and buy a new pair of new boots the day before setting off on a bike tour. Like any boot, they do need to be broken in. This will make for a comfier time on the bike, and if sightseeing is involved make sure they are easy to walk in as well.

An ideal boot would have protective panels both front and back, a steel shaft in the sole, heatproof panels on the inside leg, have a good non slip sole (Vibram), and be comfy to walk in.

Most intermediate boots of the higher style have cam buckles for adjustment, make sure the buckles are easy to clip open and shut, and are easy to adjust. Make running adjustments as you go along as your feet and ankles will need more room on hotter days.

Try several pairs of boot on in the shop and

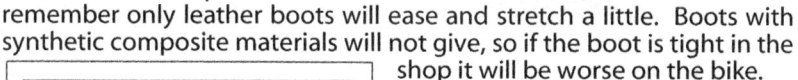

remember only leather boots will ease and stretch a little. Boots with synthetic composite materials will not give, so if the boot is tight in the

shop it will be worse on the bike.

Many manufacturers claim their boots are waterproof, some are better than others. Look for a Gore-tex (or similar) lining to the boot. This will keep your foot dry, but allow it to breath.

Some good examples of a cross boot style are W2 4 Adventure boot, waterproof, with a vibram sole, at about £149 these boots keep winning recommendations all over. Oxtar Dunes, comfy and have plenty of protection, a heat guard, but are not waterproof. TCX Desert, a touring boot with an adventure look and feel. Tall leather uppers with a Gore-tex liner, heat guard on the calf, a grippy sole and three adjustable buckles. At £260 some may say a bit pricey, but the Sidi Adventure Gore come in at over £300. The Altberg Clubman Classic boots feature Anfibio water repellent leather, Sympatex waterproof lining, Skywalk chunky sole, four wide Velcro fasteners and are they are based in Yorkshire.

One more reminder that this style of boot will be stiff when new and will require breaking in over time before riding off.

Waterproof Over boots

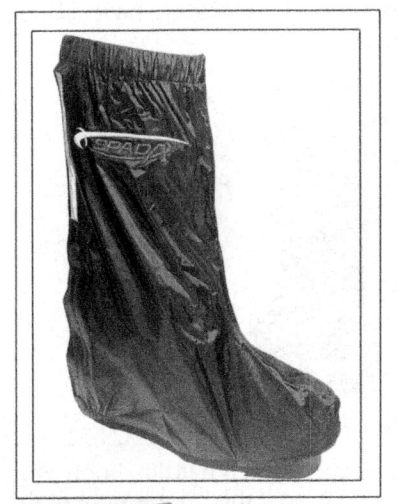

If the going gets tough on the road and the weather gets wetter and wetter and/or cold, then think about some waterproof over boots. They don't win any awards for style, but they do help keep the rain and cold away from the feet.

At about £20 they pack down ok and don't weigh too much. In really wet or cold weather they might make the difference between a great tour and a bad one.

Top Tip

To keep smooth leather boots in super tip top condition, clean the boots and then apply some Nikwax Waterproofing Wax for Leather, then buff off the excess.

For other materials like a nubuck finish use Nikwax Nubuck & Suede Proof from time to time to restore the durable water repellency (DWR).

Jacket/Trousers

As with the other sections, there is no definitive 'best option' for motorcycle clothing, as its down to personal choice, but there are some pointers and advice than can be given to help on the way to buying a jacket and trousers.

Not so long ago the only option was leather, it is a proven tough item, and quite breathable, but it's almost impossible to make a leather jacket waterproof. Bike jackets and trousers made of leather are heavy, and really not suited for touring in hot weather.

With advances in textile technology over recent years, textile clothing really is the way to go for touring.

A good textile jacket should be a nice comfy fit, not too tight and have Velcro adjusters for the neck and wrists and an adjustable waist. Pockets should be plentiful to stash small valuables whilst riding (at least one internal pocket) and have waterproof style zips.

You can't take two sets of bike gear, so most textile clothing has plenty of zipped ventilation (usually on the chest, arms and back to allow a through draft) for the warmer days, and for the cooler times they usually have a detachable thermal windstopper layer which can be zipped into the outer item.

The outers are normally made out of some form of ballistic nylon (cordura) which is easy to clean, very tough and light in comparison to leather. Further critical area armour protection at key points (shoulders, elbows and knees) is usually built in and should be CE approved.

If the clothing is waterproof, the waterproof quality of the garments will differ from manufacturer to manufacturer. Some have a zip in waterproof (gore-tex or similar) liner, others proof the outer with a durable water repellency coating. There are many different waterproof breathable materials on the market now, so a read of the label will be required. The more common ones are Gore-tex, Sheltex, eVent etc.

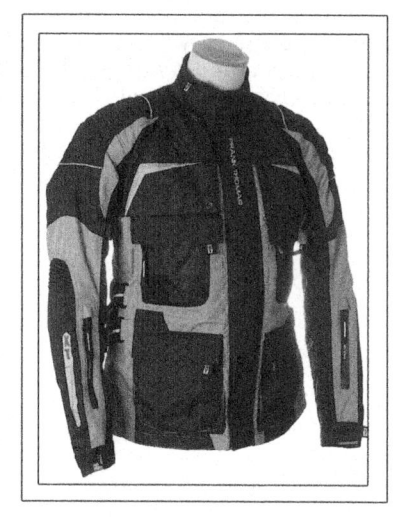

As an example, the Frank Thomas X-Terrain jacket, right, is made from highly abrasion resistant Hypertec material and offers Aquapore Advanced waterproof and breathable membrane lining, CE approved Arma-Flex shock protectors at the shoulders and elbows, detachable Anti-Freeze thermal lining, stretch panelling, pull through D-ring and Velcro fastening sleeve adjusters, double side waist adjusters and two chest and sleeve ventilation openings on the front; together with rear ventilation, either two zipped vents or the removal of a whole panel produces a manageable airflow. There are four outer waterproof pockets, two outer mesh pockets two hand warming pockets and one zipped inner pocket along with a rear pocket.

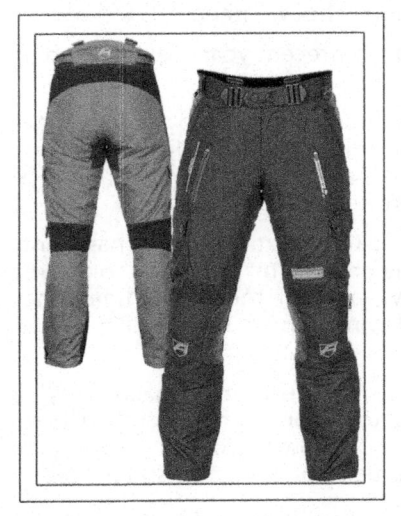

Ideally the trousers should have the ability to zip to the jacket; this will add a little extra warmth on the chilly days. Also look for venting, armour, and knee stretch panelling. If the trousers are the same make/style as the jacket the same characteristics of the material and waterproofing should apply, if not and waterproof is required look for Gore-tex, Sheltex, eVent, ISOTEX etc. (always read the label for full information).

When trying on a jacket and/or trousers, don't just stand in the shop (if it's a dealer) ask if you can sit on a bike to see what the fit is like actually in a riding position.

Jackets/Trousers are available from many manufacturers from the cheap to the very expensive and everything in between, so as always look around and try to get the best value for money without skimping. Examples of textile suits include BMW Rallye III, Hein Gerickle Summit, Frank Thomas X-Terrain, Vanucci Okovango, Held Hakuna, Akito Desert, Klim Lattitude, Rukka, even Touratech Companero Suit.

Some of the examples are not cheap at upwards of £500 for a jacket!

Socks

No don't laugh! If you already have a few years under your belt with motorcycles, then socks are not an issue, but if you are new to touring then this might help.

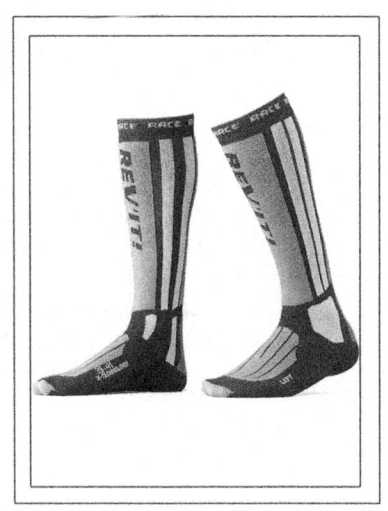

One thing to make sure is that the extremities are kept warm (feet and hands). It's no good just putting on a pair of normal work a day socks and hoping for the best.

Ski socks which are available from most outdoor shops are really quite good, but in hot climates can get a bit hot and sticky.

Merino wool based ones are very good at regulating heat and have anti-bacterial properties. They cost a little more but can really be worth it.

Motorcycle socks usually have some form of simple padding across the top of the foot and chin. Oxford, Revit, Klim, Sidi, AlpineStars along with many more. Available from all good bikes shops and sometimes Aldi and Lidl have offers which are quite good.

For waterproof socks it's got to be SealSkinz. These use a patented technology, giving waterproof and breathable protection for the feet.

Great on cold wet days, the waterproof technology keeps you warm and dry. Even when it's warm, sweat is wicked away from the feet and leaves through the breathable membrane. At £30 for a pair of socks some may say that's expensive, but they really do keep your feet dry, warm and toasty.

A friend of mine swears by antibacterial football socks from Primark, so don't just got out and buy something that has motorbike in the title. Have a look around and see what works for you.

Layering System

What ever type of person you are (see section intro), the layering system is probably the best option when riding for control of body

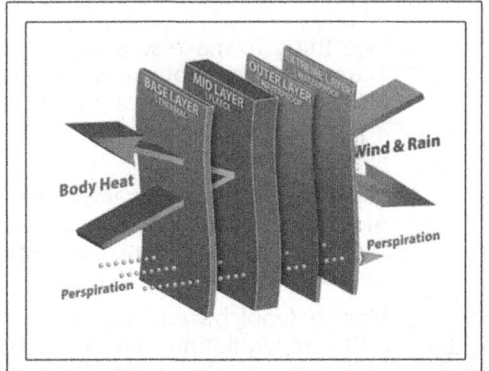

heat. This is based on the same method that is used by walkers, skiers etc. Base, Mid, Outer, Extreme.

Now, with technical breathable and wind stopper fabrics it's quite easy to layer up and not look like the Michelin man.

For all the layers in the system, don't just look at 'biker' options, look at outdoor shops as well, or sometimes even supermarkets have special offers on items like base layers.

Base Layer

This is the one next to the skin. Try to avoid cotton based garments as they can absorb 10 times their own weight in water (or in this case, sweat!) and they take ages to dry. Because of this they can suck away body heat very quickly when damp or wet.

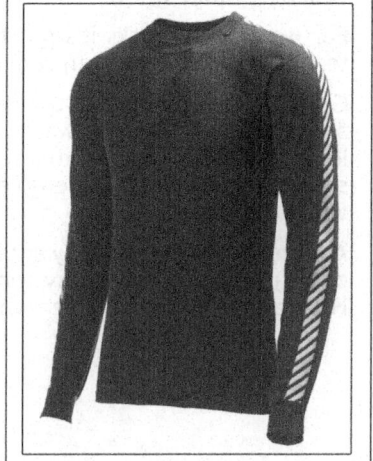

Look to use a good synthetic 'wicking' fabric which will allow perspiration to evaporate, but retain body heat in cooler conditions.

Another alternative is a merino wool based layer. Merino wool is natural soft wool that has great temperature controlling qualities and anti bacterial resistance. Merino wool items can be expensive, but if you shop around bargains can always be found.

Manufacturers include Helly Hansen, Berghaus, EDZ, Icebreaker Merino, plus many others

Mid Layer

This layer is for warmth and insulation. The idea is to trap warm air around the body. Fleece, softshell or wool based garments are good for this layer. Depending on the person a couple of thin technical fleeces may work better than one traditional layer.

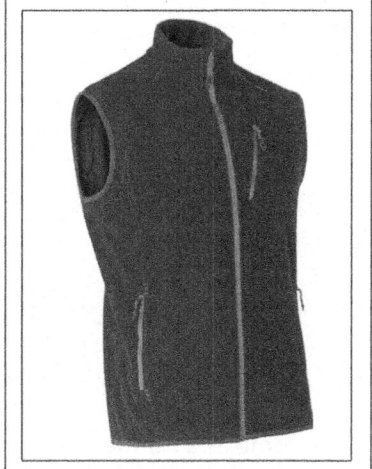

Another option if you don't like things too warm is a windstopper fleece Gilet. This will keep the body core warm while, (as the name suggests) help stopping wind chill.

Again there are many makes designs and colours available for this layer. All ranging in price and quality.

Outer Layer

This is the motorcycle jacket providing protection from the elements, made from a tough material and incorporating some form of armour or protection.

See Jackets & Trousers for more information.

Extreme Layer

Extreme weather protection to go over the motorcycle jacket and legs. Not just for extreme rain, but also to stop wind getting through and extreme cold. This type of waterproof jacket and trousers should be able to pack well and be light, as they are probably not going to be used all the time.

Make sure both items will easily fit over the motorcycle layer, but not be so baggy they blow up like balloons as this will totally defeat the object of this layer. Also make sure if you go for waterproof legs that they go on whilst wearing boots.

Try to double up on uses, so try to get a style of jacket that may also be worn off the bike as a casual waterproof layer over a t-shirt or fleece whilst sightseeing (or walking to the pub in the evening).

Neck Tube

If you are already a rider then you will already know the importance of a neck tube. A little bit like vacuums are called Hoovers (trade name); neck tubes are often referred to as Buffs (trade name).

These very handy items fill the gap between the helmet and the top of the jacket collar to stop wind blowing down the front of the jacket and around your neck. *Don't leave home without one.*

They can also be used as face masks if pulled up, hats, sweat bands, hair bands and a multitude of other odd uses.

They come as a normal tube or if its really chilly fleece lined ones are available (but a little more bulky); and available in a multitude of colours and printed designs.

Major brands include Buff, TrekMates and Comfy, but other brands are available. Prices start from about £10 and are available from all outdoor shops and most motorcycle shops.

Heated

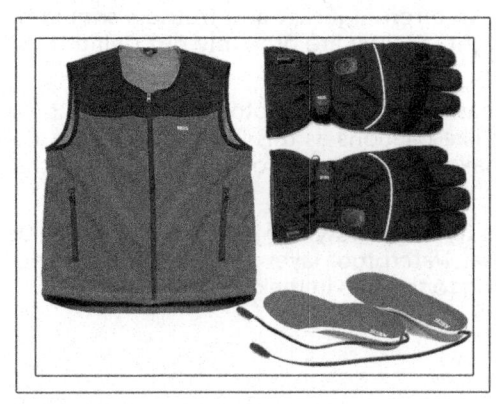

When you get cold, the blood supply starts to leave the extremities and move into the core of the body to protect vital organs. If you can warm the core then the blood will flow back out to the extremities.

You are sat on a 12v generator, so if you really feel the cold, or you are riding in cold weather look at plugging in some toasty heated clothing items.

Far from the rigid, uncomfortable, uncontrollable heat vests of not so long ago, modern motorcycle heated clothing is actually pretty comfortable and at first glance looks like normal clothing.

Heated gilets, gloves, trousers, boot insoles and even socks can all make for a better riding experience in the extreme cold.

Heated kit is not always cheap, Gerbing's T1 heated textile gloves are about £95 and prices in their range for gloves go up from there. Keis produce a pair of heated under gloves for about £50.

As can be seen in the picture, if you go for a full set of heated clothing the wiring system can start to get a little fiddly.

The more popular brands include Keis, Gerbing, the Exo2 range along with several 'own brand' offerings.

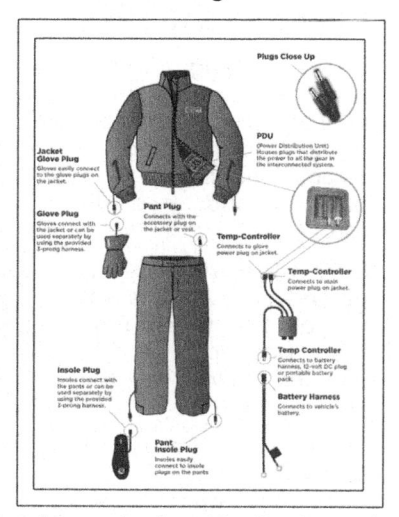

If you are unsure about heated clothing have a look at Maplins heated clothing before taking the plunge on the more expensive brands. Its usually battery operated so no having it switched on all day here, but if its just for occasional use, a heated gilet at £29 and heated insoles at £24 might be worth looking at. The heated gloves sound good value at £25, but remember they are NOT bike gloves and have no protection.

As a side note: In some situations, a pair of heated gloves are far better than heated grips. As the heat is all round the hand, top and bottom as opposed to grips that just warm the palms.

Packing the Bike

One of the biggest mistakes when getting ready for a bike trip is over packing. One school of thought is to get everything laid out on the floor and then put at least half of it back in the cupboard. Another is to get a large shopping bag and fill it; once full that's all that can be taken. Then there is the credit card traveller who only needs to pack a passport and a credit card!

Over a few trips what is packed and what is left will be fine tuned until the packing list is whittled down to the essential items.

Centre of gravity is something that's mentioned quite a lot when talking about motorcycles and packing. No manufacturer publishes that information and of course the CoG will change depending on how heavy the rider is, how they sit, and how luggage is loaded and packed.

If you are into trigonometry then the CoG for a bike can be calculated, but as a basic rule of thumb, keep heavy items in the panniers and as low and forward as possible within.

A motorcycle with a high centre of gravity will be harder to ride at slow speeds, as it may feel top-heavy. A motorcycle with a low centre of gravity will feel more stable at lower speeds, but may not feel as smooth in cornering at speed, as it will take more weight-shift to angle the bike on its side.

When loading up always think about the CoG. The obvious locations for camping gear are in the panniers or over the rear seat. What this will do though, is put a lot of the weight over the rear tyre. If possible try to move some weight towards the front of the bike as well.

Try to avoid packing too high at the back of the bike or filling up top boxes to bursting. As the heavier the back of the bike the lighter the front will be, making the front tyre footprint smaller and may produce light steering and handling.

Obviously for camping trips more storage space is required, so try to place it low and within the bikes centre of gravity.

When packing, as well as weight think about what items can in theory stay on the bike/in panniers. For example a puncture repair kit should hopefully not be needed that often, so it can go towards the bottom.

Clothes and camping kit should only be needed once a day so can be packed up and left. Also, think about stops on the trip. If using a camera, keep it handy in a tank bag, small tail pack or at the top of the panniers. Mobile phones, wallet, maps, etc should also be easily accessible.

As panniers are packed make sure they are well balanced and similar weights to keep weight distribution even over the bike.

Use stuff sacks within panniers and roll bags to help keep them organised. These are available for a few pounds from outdoor shops in a variety of sizes. Buy a waterproof stuff sack for your tent. Then if it's packed wet it won't make anything it touches damp.

Get it right and everything has a place and can be found easily. Get it wrong and you will be rummaging through the contents looking for what you want – and you can guarantee it will be raining!

It may take several 'dry runs' to get it right, but the more touring you do and the more times you pack, it will become second nature and a system that works for you will develop.

Securing the load

When attaching bags to the bike always make sure they are secure, a loose bag could cause you to lose balance or the bag may even come off completely causing danger to yourself or others.

Loose luggage might also cause damage to the motorcycle through movement and rubbing. Be sure luggage is kept away from hot parts of the bike and don't allow loose straps to get near the wheels or other moving parts.

Over time everyone develops their own system of securing the load to the bike using any combination of straps, nets etc. Try to keep it a simple yet secure arrangement.

Think about other retail outlets for straps as well as motorcycle shops, as these sometimes carry a higher price.

Below are a few commonly used solutions.

Bungee Straps

These have fallen out of favour over the last few years, as if they are not handled right there is a strong possibility you will have someone's eye out or get hit by one. But if caution is used they are quite a flexible means of fixing. They also have a tendency to fail and weaken over time.

Cam buckle straps

This type of strap uses a pull-to-tighten system rather than the crank-to-tighten features seen in ratchet straps. This can be important when over-tightening could cause damage to the bike/roll bag. With a good break strength capacity, cams offer considerable strength and easy tightening. Just thread the loose end through and cam and pull tight, perfect for securing roll bags and the like to the bike.

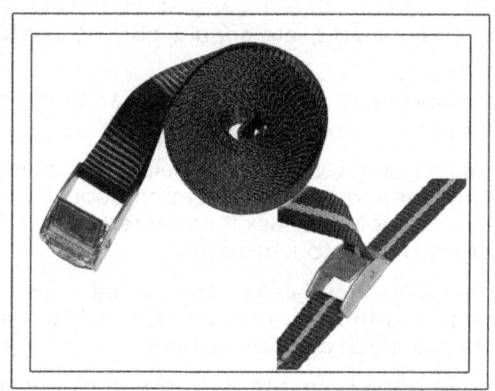

Available from the likes of Touratech at about £15 for 2x1m straps. But as mentioned throughout the book, think laterally - Screwfix set of 2x2.5m straps for £10; also many outdoor shops stock them.

Rok Straps

These straps are becoming the replacement for the traditional bungee straps. They offer better functionality and ease of use. Think of them as a safe alternative to the bungee.

Available with either a closed loop end or hook end they are easy to attach, buckle and adjust. The integral elastic band keeps the strap under tension and secures a load even under tough riding conditions.

At the end of each section of the strap, there's a small loop. Hook the

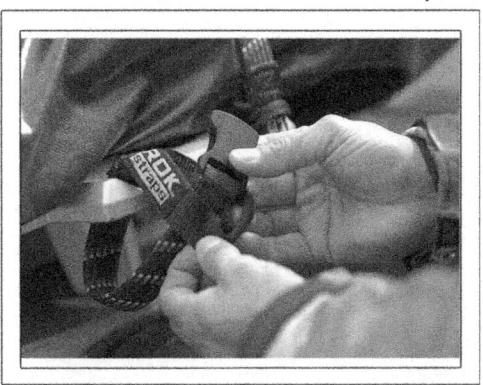

loop around any hard part of the bike, and then thread the strap back through. Repeat with the other part of the strap. Pull the straps over the luggage, snap the buckles together, pull the loose end, and the elastic strap secures your gear.

Andy Straps

Similar idea to Rok Straps but utilising heavy duty Velcro to fasten the two parts of the elasticated strap together. These can be used in much the same way as bungee straps, but safer.

Bungee Nets

Don't solely rely on bungee nets to secure anything to the bike. Use them almost as a final just in case over the already secured luggage. They are also handy to stuff gloves under when filling up or paying tolls.

Arno Straps

These are slightly lighter weight to cam buckle straps. But are non-

slip, have spring loaded metal buckles, are easily cut and sealed (carefully melt the cut end with a lighter) to the required length, easily adjusted and released. Even if you don't use them for securing luggage, try to pack some as a just in case multi-purpose strap.

Available in different lengths from most outdoor shops for a few pounds per set.

PacSafe eXomesh®

There is only so much that can be done to protect kit on a motorcycle. But if/when paranoia kicks in then look into a PacSafe set up. Originally designed for rucksacks and the like when in transit, the Pacsafe system is an adjustable high-tensile stainless steel mesh, designed to cover and protect the bag from tampering and theft.

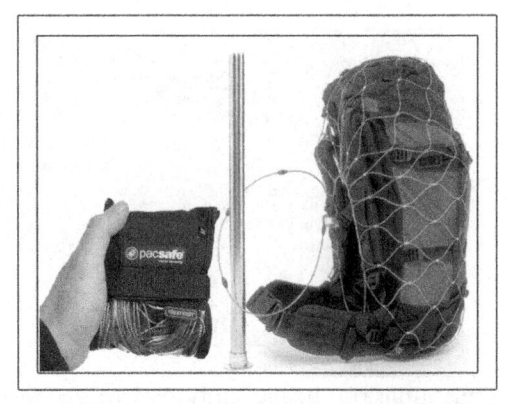

The roll bag is strapped to the bike as normal, and then if the need arises put the PacSafe over the rollbag locking it to the frame of the bike.

When not in use they pack down really quite small into their own pouch, but they add more weight. Available from most outdoor shops in several sizes.

Once ready to set off, always do final checks of all the luggage before you ride; never overload as this may increase the risk of making the bike difficult to handle, or the luggage becoming loose or coming off the bike completely.

Top Tip

If travelling in mainland Europe (or anywhere that drives on the right) try to put tools and emergency items in the right pannier – the side which will be away from the road/traffic if roadside maintenance is required. It's scary how fast and close a truck passes when the bike is parked up at the side of the road!

Pre Trip Bike Maintenance

Even the less mechanically minded should be able to undertake some very basic maintenance and checking before setting off on a bike trip. Below are some simple areas that should be checked or decided on in plenty of time before departure.

Tyres

First things first – if the tyres that are on the bike are staying on the bike, do they have enough tread on them to complete the journey and perhaps another 300/500 miles? Only you the rider will know the answer to that question as you know at what speed you get through tyres. If in doubt – change; and maybe keep the old ones as a spare set.

TWI (Tread Wear Indicator). These are little crosspieces in the profile furrows, which indicate the wear limit. These crosspieces are usually optimised for the US market and indicate the remaining profile depth of approx 1.0 mm. In the UK its 1.6mm, so if the TWI's are showing, get the tyres change. The location of TWI's can be found by locating a small triangular arrow on the tyre wall.

Choice of tyre is initially down to where the chosen route is going to take you, the type of terrain and style of bike.

If you have gone for new tyres, they must be run in using a cautious driving style for at least 100miles. The tyre needs this time in order to fully set onto the rim and to achieve its optimum bonding due to the roughening of the profile.

Types & Tread

For both adventure style and road style bike there are many options to choose from. Most manufacturers do a range of tyres from road, intermediate to full off road knobblies. At the end of the day tyre choice is a compromise between grip and wear rate.

Under normal circumstances when touring round Europe, the standard tyres that are recommended by the bike manufacturer will be up for the job (unless you are looking at doing off road work on an adventure/duel sport bike). But as can be seen from the photo previous, there are a huge range of tread patterns and styles for different applications. If unsure, seek advice from a professional fitter.

Pressure

A quality tyre pressure gauge is an item that should always be part of a motorcyclist's tool kit both at home or touring. When touring try to check the tyre pressures at least once every other day, if not every day. Always do it with the tyre cold, ideally first thing in the morning. Doing this will also highlight a slow puncture before it's too late.

Running a bike with under inflated tyres tend to affect handling and braking as the lack of pressure means the tyre wall isn't firm enough to properly cope with the forces exerted on it. (Try turning sharp corners with a severely under inflated tyre – it's like having a large 50p as a tyre).

Over inflation can also result in deterioration in handling, as well as a reduced contact footprint with the road. This can result in a lack of grip under braking.

For normal road journeys with solo touring luggage the tyre pressure should be increased to that of with a pillion. Check the owners handbook for more information.

As a note: There are times when different tyre pressures work better; usually when off road, in sand or on a dirt road and are travelling slower. Below is a very rough overview showing the tops of the pressure range.

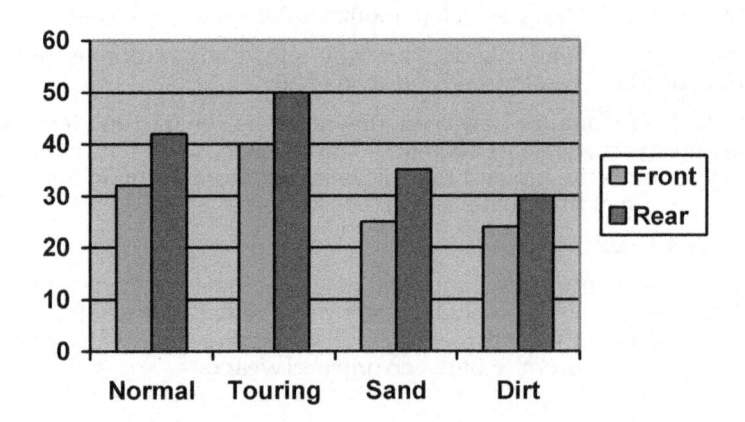

Chain

Incorrect chain tension can result in premature sprocket and gearbox wear, unsmooth gearshifts, snatchy transmission and reduce the life of the bike's chain.

Check your workshop manual for how to adjust your bike's chain to the correct tension. Remember to set the tension with some load on the bike (preferably with someone on it) as the chain will tighten up once a rider's on board.

Refer to the owner's manual for the correct torque settings for each bolt. To do this properly a torque wrench is required.

Remember to also lubricate the chain while you're at it, as this will help prolong its life. Don't forget to take a small can of chain lube along with you on the trip so the chain can be re-waxed whilst on the road. Also, re-check the chain and adjust if required while on the road.

Battery

If the bike is used as normal then the battery should be in a good state.

But for a belt and braces approach; ideally, remove the battery from its holder before carrying out any work. Remember, batteries contain strong acid, which can be harmful if it comes into contact with your skin.

Check the acid level in your battery by placing it on a level surface. If the level's low, then top up with de-ionised water before placing the battery back in the bike. Remember not to overfill, as acid will drain out the overflow pipe when you're on the move. *Many modern batteries are sealed units, so you won't be able to top them up.*

Greasing the bike's battery terminals before placing the battery back in the bike will help avoid corrosion build up. Just remember not to touch both terminals at the same time!

Coolant

Touring on a bike will make the engine work hard especially in warm weather.

Check the owner's manual to locate the bike's expansion tank if it has one; high and low levels should be marked on the outside of the tank. Alternatively, remove the radiator filler cap to check the level. Only do this when the water is cold. If low, then top up with a correct mix of water/anti freeze. Check the level again after a test ride.

Oil

Again, touring is hard on the engine, so make sure the oil is topped up (with the correct grade), or if there is time change it for fresh.

Check the owner's manual to locate the bike's oil dipstick or level window. High and low levels should be marked. If the oil is very black think about a full oil change.

Oiling and Adjusting

Oil and adjust the bike's cables to make for a smoother riding experience. Over time, the oil/grease put into the cable housing in the manufacturing process will dry out, leaving the bike's throttle or clutch action impaired.

Also adjust them to take out any unwanted slack. This will give a better response.

Hydraulic Levels

Check the level of break fluid in both the front and rear reservoirs. If

required top up with the correct fluid (most commonly DOT4). Also, check the bikes hydraulic clutch reservoir (if it has one). These should be checked with the bike on level ground and vertical.

Suspension

As the bike will be carrying extra weight the suspension will need adjusting accordingly. On most adventure style bikes this can be a quick and easy job with a hand adjuster; on a more road bias bike it can involve removing the seat and adjusting with a spanner. Check the owners handbook for more information.

General

The bike will also benefit from a squirt of the right sort of grease/lubricant in the right places; lubricating footrest hinges, levers, locks, stand hinges. And giving the bike a good general once over.

Tool Kit

So, you are not going round the world, but carrying some tools always helps. Admittedly some bikers just pack some clothes and go, but you never know when the occasion may arise when a size 10 hex key is needed. Its much easier being self sufficient than having to start shopping when something simple goes wrong. We are not talking about carrying full socket sets here; just take the ones you know fit the bike.

A good, but simple tool kit can be assembled by using a strong fabric style wash bag. Most of the tools will easily fit into one and can then be kept in the pannier ready for the next trip.

Original Bike Toolkit	Spanners (only sizes that fit bike!)	Chain Wax (small can)
Bike Repair Manual	Screwdrivers (cross & flat head)	WD40 (small can)
Puncture Repair Kit	Allen / Torx keys	Oil (engine)
Length of Wire (for electrical work)	Pliers	Cable Ties (assorted)
Length of Heavy Gauge Wire (for tying & fastening)	Gaffa Tape	Surgical Gloves
Small Selection of Nuts & Bolts	PVC Electrical Tape	Spark Plugs
Electrical Spares (bulbs/fuses/choc block etc)	Knife / Multi Tool	Spare Packing Straps
Tyre Leavers**	Tyre Pressure Gauge	Small Air Compressor*
Right Angle Valve Adaptor	Rag	

* nice to have **if tubed tyres

Above is a basic toolkit for riding through Europe, no need to have spare tyres strapped to the bike, or spare speedo cables. Worst case you can nearly always limp to a garage within Europe. Obviously for riding further a field, then a more comprehensive kit would be required.

Bike Repair Manual

See Paperwork & Documentation section

Puncture Repair Kit

First off, if you don't know, find out whether the tyres are tubed or tubeless. Secondly; don't leave home on a long trip without knowing

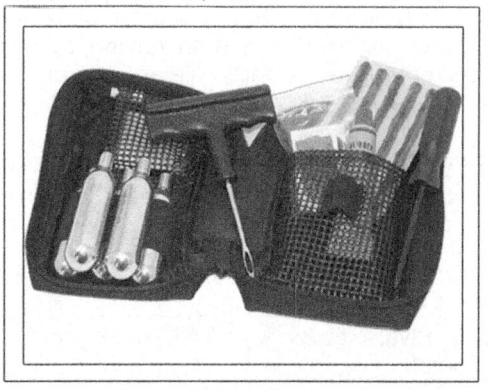

how to fix a puncture. It's probably the most common 'breakdown' that could stop a bike trip.

Usually kits are available in three types; tubed, tubeless or a kit that has the bits to do either (normally a little more expensive).

There are two main types of tubeless repair kits; ones that use glue strips or string plugs (above) and ones that use a twist in plug (below). There are other types, but not as popular as the two mentioned.

Basically, they do the same thing; enable a temporary repair to be made without having to remove the (tubeless) tyre. They can plug a hole up to about 4mm in diameter once the foreign object has been removed. Once repaired the tyre is re inflated using the CO_2 cartridges that come as part of the kit. Using the tyre pressure gauge from the tool kit check the pressure is at a usable level. Once back on the road seek out a garage as soon as possible to replace the CO_2 with normal air.

As a quick word of caution; try not to exceed about 40/45mph after a repair, and get the tyre professionally looked at within 250miles.

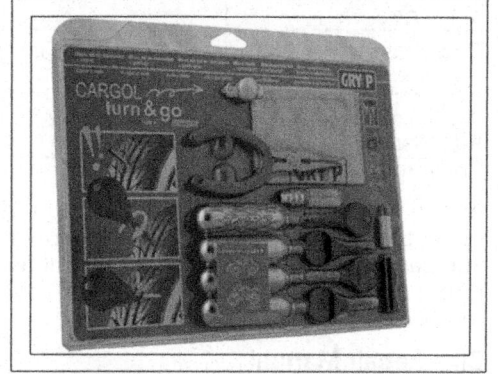

Kits from manufacturers like AirPro - Premium Tyre Repair & Inflation Kit; Stop&Go – Tire Plugger; Gryyp – Cargol turn & go kit should be available from most good motorcycle shops, halfords, some caravan/touring shops and the internet. Prices vary depending on make and offers. But have a starting budget of about £15/£20 in mind.

A puncture kit can easily sit in the bottom of a pannier and be forgotten about until it's required.

As an addition to the toolkit a small air compressor might be a good option to really make you self sufficient. Stop&Go tubeless puncture pilot is a great kit that includes everything including a mini compressor for about £50, and it all fits into a 7"x4"x3" case.

Repairing a tubed tyre is not such an easy process, but it's the same principal as a pedal cycle (just on a much larger and sometimes tougher scale). Below is a brief overview of the process involved.

- Remove the affected tyre.
- Remove any remaining air, then remove the valve and slacken base nut and push the valve into the tyre.
- Apply pressure to push the bead of the tyre away from the rim
- Insert a tyre leaver to lift the tyre over the rim. Repeat the process with a second tyre leaver, and work round the tyre.
- Now remove the inner tube.
- Locate any foreign object in the tyre and remove.
- Refit valve and inflate tube. Listen for air escaping, or pass the tube through some water and look for bubbles.
- Mark the position and release the air.
- Roughen the area up with sandpaper and coat the area with rubber solution glue and wait until touch dry.
- Apply a suitable sized patch, press firmly down
- Dust the area with chalk/talk to cover any remaining glue
- Do a test inflate of the tube to verify the fix.
- Remove air and reinsert the tub into the tyre
- Reverse the removal process being careful not to snag the tube.
- Make sure the valve is at right angles to the wheel, fit valve locking nut and inflate.
- Once bead is remounted onto the rim check the pressure is constant
- Refit wheel onto the bike

So, a nice straight forward routine to practice if you have tubed tyres.

As a preventative option there are tyre sealants which are injected into the tyre (tubed or tubeless). If a puncture occurs the air forces the solution into the hole and solidifies, thus sealing it.

Slime & Ultraseal are two of the more popular brands.

Other tool kit items

A small can of WD40; these can be picked up from most supermarkets and discount shops for about a pound or so. Holding about 100ml they are just the right size to pack for a loner trip.

Chain oil/wax in a nice handy small aerosol should really be taken if the bike is not shaft drive or does not have an automatic oiler fitted. (Scotoiler or Tuturo for example) For their size they can be quite expensive at about £5 for 100ml, but its better than carrying one of the large cans round Europe. And the chain will need lubricating ideally every day when touring

Bike oil, again can be taken as a just in case. The best way is to purchase a small 100ml/200ml plastic bottle of 3 in 1 or multipurpose oil. Drain it out and leave to stand upside down to get all the original oil out of the container. (It needs to be totally clean). Then refill with correct grade bike oil. (Always label anything not in its original container). Now if the bike starts to use a little oil it can easily be topped up by squirting in a top up.

Right Angle Valve Adaptor

Not a very exciting piece of kit, but an easy solution for valves that

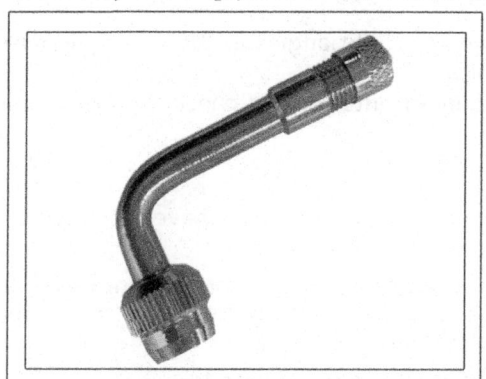

seem almost impossible to get at especially if you have spokes wheels and you need to use a garage air hose. Just screw it onto the valve and it allows normal air hoses to reach. You just never know when you might need to inflate a tyre when touring.

Cost about £4/£5 from all bike part retailers and online companies.

Food & Drink

Everyone is different when it comes to intake of food and liquids. Some people can go for much longer periods than others without eating, but dehydration on a long bike trip can be quite common

especially when riding in warmer than normal conditions.

It is essential that the body is kept hydrated throughout the day. Being properly hydrated will stave off early fatigue which could affect the ability to ride safely. Signs of dehydration include headaches and general fatigue.

Having the ability to carry a daily amount of water and snacks is a must, even through western Europe. By doing this, even at a simple roadside pull in a swig of water (even if you are not thirsty) and a small snack can bring the body back to life. At coffee breaks and lunch stops try to stay away from alcohol. Not only does it speed up the dehydration process it also impairs the ability to ride safely.

See Liquid Transportation section for some ideas; or carry at least a 1ltr sigg style bottle in a tail pack or easily accessible in a pannier. If travelling through much hotter climates a water bladder on the back might be an option.

Bottled water is widely available throughout Europe, and in some

areas its best to try and drink this as the tap water can contain minerals your body is not used to. It's not considered a marketing and sales heaven, it's a necessity, so prices are quite cheap.

Good snacks for the day include items like dried fruit, nuts, cereal bars, chocolate, boiled sweets or jelly babies.

On the road to Andorra

The road to Andorra

Camping in Spain

Crossing the Rhein at Kaub Germany

Camping in Scotland - Shiel Bridge

Two bikes, five sisters - Scotland

Doing the SellaRonda - Dolomites Italy

Passo Valparola - Italy

It's not always sunny and dry on a bike trip! - David Carson getting very wet. Passo Gardena - Dolomites Italy

Ampolla - Spain

B869 - Scotland

Ullapool - Scotland

Time for a brew - Canazei Italy

Aberfoyle - Scotland

CAMPING

Camping is a great way to mix motorcycling with the great outdoors. There are no two ways about it, if you are going touring and have decided to camp then there is the issue of the extra kit involved and the weight. But this does mean that you are self sufficient and can overnight at any campsite, or (if available) wild camp.

If you are new to camping, the first thing you should do is become familiar with the basic camping gear that you will need. Probably the best way is to talk to a seasoned camper, and maybe even go on a trip with them. You can quickly and easily learn from them.

Basically, you need a shelter, which could be a tent or cabin, you need a bed, which will be a sleeping bag paired with a sleeping mat, and food, which also includes a stove and cooking utensils.

When starting out on any new venture, its not always advisable to spend spend spend, just in case it doesn't work out. But on the other hand, don't skimp on items, for example buying a £4.99 tent from the local supermarket – it will leak.

At the end of the day, camping is fun and a laugh. Yes it can be cold, it can be wet but hopefully this will not be the case on your first trip, if it is there is always someone else there in the same boat, so go share a beer with them.

Throughout the section are some sample lists to base a final packing list on.

Tents

Once you have decided to take the next step and try motorbike touring and camping, one of the first things to start looking at is a tent. (It's a necessity really). The tent will be your home while touring so has to be right for you. No good riding to France to find out you don't like it, or you don't fit!

If you have been a car camper in the past, don't just pick up that tent and go; well actually you probably wouldn't go as the tent may be too heavy and not pack down enough.

In times past, a tent was a tent and that was that. Nowadays, tents are available in more and more styles, sizes, features, weights, materials etc. As well as tents, the lightweight camper can also look into tarps (bashas) and hammocks.

So for the new motorbike camper the choices can almost be overwhelming. Time and time again on forums and in magazines are questions like… "What tent?" or "Which is the best tent?" These is no best tent for bike camping as factors like budget and tent features required all need taking into consideration.

Firstly, go to an outdoors shop and look at their tent display with them setup. Don't just buy a tent from a picture on the shop wall and believe the sales staff. Get in them and have a stretch about, look at them packed, feel how heavy they are, talk with the sales staff for advice.

Single/Double Skin Tents

Single skin tents have only one waterproof layer of fabric, comprising at least roof and walls. To minimize condensation on the inside of the tent, some tents use waterproof/breathable fabrics. They are usually lighter than double skin tents, but can suffer badly from condensation.

Double skin tents are like two tents in one. An inner and an outer. The outer tent is a waterproof layer which extends down to the ground all round. The outer tent may be just a little larger than the inner tent, or it may be a lot larger and provide a covered porch area separate from the sleeping area.

The 'inner tent' provides the sleeping areas. An inner tent is not waterproof, but allows water vapour to pass through so that condensation occurs only on the outer. The double layer may also provide some thermal insulation. As the warm air rises it condenses on the outer and then runs down the outer and to the ground leaving the inner tent (where you sleep) dry.

Single skin tents are especially prone to condensation as the warmer air has nowhere to go, so condenses on the tent wall and runs down to where you are sleeping. Double skin tents have an insulating gap between the inner tent and the flysheet, and it is this that reduces the temperature difference at the surface of the flysheet and thereby reduces the amount of condensation that occurs. The inner tent should ideally not touch the outer otherwise the inner will become wet.

Single Skin Tent	Double Skin Tent
Cold Air Outside	Cold Air Outside
fly sheet or outer tent	
Warm Moist Air — condensation	Cool Air
inner tent	Warm Moist Air

Either the outer skin or the inner skin may be the structural component, carrying the poles; the structural skin is always pitched first, though some tents are built with the outer and inner linked so that they are both pitched at the same time.

So as a rough rule of thumb head toward the double skin tents as they should keep you dryer, but single skin are usually lighter.

Ventilation

Ventilation helps reduce the effects of condensation. When people breathe, they expel quite a lot of water vapour. If the outside of the tent is colder than the inside (the usual case), then this vapour will condense on the inside of the tent, on any clothing lying about, on the outside of a sleeping bag, etc. Hence ventilation helps to remove the vapour, and let cooler air in to circulate.

On some tents at the cheaper end on the scale mesh 'windows' may have to be let open at night to help with the ventilation. At the other end of the scale, good ventilation is probably 'built in' with vents that spring out when the tent is erected.

Styles

With modern materials, tent manufacturers have much greater freedom to vary types and styles and shapes of tents.

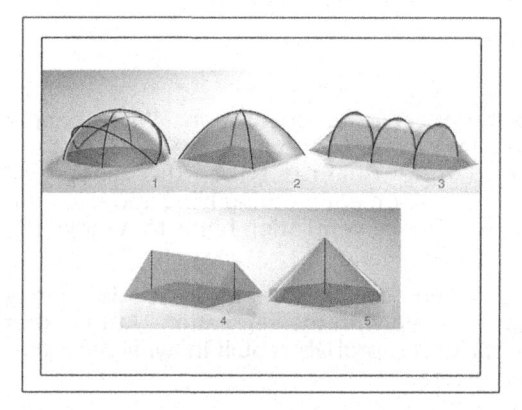

Left are the main types of tent design.

1. geodesic tent
2. dome tent
3. tunnel tent
4. ridge tent
5. pyramid tent

Geodesic tents are basically dome tents with two or more extra poles

which criss-cross the normal two poles to help support the basic shape and minimise the amount of unsupported fabric. This makes them more suitable for use in snowy conditions and in strong winds. To help withstand strong winds they are rarely more than 120 or 150 cm high (4 to 5 ft).

Dome tents have a very simple structure and are available in a wide variety of sizes ranging from lightweight 2-person tents with limited headroom up to 6 or 9-person tents with headroom exceeding 180 cm (6 ft). These may be single skin. Depending on the pole arrangement, some models pitch outer-tent first, while others pitch inner-tent first. The former helps keep the inner tent dry, but the latter is easier to pitch.

The basic dome has a rectangular floor and two poles which cross at the peak; each pole runs in a smooth curve from one bottom corner, up to the peak, and then down to the diagonally opposite bottom corner. A common variation is to add a third pole which supports an extension of the flysheet, to give a porch/storage area.

Tunnel tents may offer more usable internal space than a dome tent with the same ground area, but almost always need guy ropes and pegs to stay upright. These are almost always double wall tents. Sizes range from 1-person tents with very limited headroom to quite large multi person tents.

A basic tunnel tent uses two or more flexible poles, arranged as parallel hoops, with tent fabric attached to form a half-cylinder or tapering tunnel. The most common

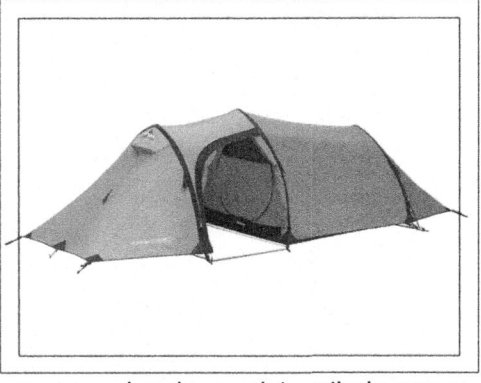

designs have a sleeping area at one end and a porch/vestibule area at the other, though porches/vestibules at each end are not uncommon.

Ridge tents or "wall tent" in their traditional form are not so popular with the solo or 2 person camper. They are mainly used as patrol tents sleeping four to eight persons. Most of them are single-skin designs, with optional fly sheets made of thick cotton. Designers are always twisting the boundaries of tent design, so some ridge tents don't look like ridge tent.

If you draw a tent this is they stereo-typical tent.

Pyramid tent Single pole tents based on the traditional tepee or even the old-fashioned Scout's bell tent get more popular all the time so most manufacturers have now introduced a tepee or something similar in the last year or so.

Tepees may look great on site, but most don't have inner tents so are probably best suited for 'fine weather' camping. However, there are exceptions - the traditional 100 per cent heavy cotton tents used as patrol tents by the Scouts and Guides will withstand pretty much anything the British weather will throw at them.

Fly Sheet/Outer Tent/Hydrostatic Head

The fly sheet or the outer tent is the component that is going to protect you from the elements and keep you dry.

It has to be fully waterproof and have fully taped seams. This is rated as the Hydrostatic Head. The majority of the tents are made from polyester and of those the vast majority rely on a PU (polyurethane) coating to make them waterproof. These coatings come in different strengths; this strength is measured in Hydrostatic Head (hh). The higher the hydrostatic head the more waterproof the material and the longer

How Waterproofing Is Measured

6000mm
5000mm
downward pressure of water column
4000mm
3000mm
minimum level classified as waterproof 1500mm
1000mm
500mm
fabric under test resisting 5000mm water column

the waterproof coating will last.

The term hydrostatic head is used to denote the amount of pressure of water that is required in order to penetrate a given fabric. The Hydrostatic head is tested by placing a column of water $1cm^2$ over the fabric and then adding water to the column. At the point where the water is forced through, it's measured in millimetres giving the hydrostatic head.

Ratings vary from brand to brand but be sure to check this rating meets at least 1500mm before buying a tent. For example, 1500 hh means that the fabric will withstand a 1500mm (about 5ft) column of water for more than one minute before a single drop might appear through the fabric.

The British standard for any fabric to be classed as fully waterproof is 1500mm. Flysheets can go up to and beyond 5000hh, while ground sheets can be even higher.

As a rule, the higher the hh the outer tent is rated, the more water it can repel for longer, thus keeping the inner tent dry.

Ground Sheets/Footprints

A groundsheet is used to provide a waterproof barrier between the ground and a sleeping bag. Normally tents or the inner tent will be supplied with a sewn-in groundsheet. This is basically the bottom of the tent.

A strong recommendation here would be to always purchase a separate groundsheet or footprint. It doesn't matter how well the ground is cleared of sharp objects and stones, its better to damage the footprint that cost a few pounds rather than the built in tent groundsheet, as then the tent itself is compromised. It also adds a second waterproof layer between you and the ground; and prevents wear and tear of the tent against the ground.

A groundsheet usually is a generic term and item, and can be bought from most camping/outdoor shops. Find the size of the tent and buy a ground sheet accordingly. (Make sure the groundsheet is smaller than the fly or outer tent). A footprint is usually an accessory from the tent manufacturer and is designed to fit the tent exactly. Official tent footprints are usually lighter, but more expensive than generic groundsheets.

Again, sometimes thinking laterally might work. Builders' merchants and big DIY shops sell inexpensive polythene sheeting in various widths and thicknesses, and can be bought by the meter. A trailer tarp also makes a great ground sheet for a tent.

Porch/Vestibule

A Porch is a very nice luxury to have. It means once the tent is up you can take off bike gear undercover but outside the living area. It also means you don't have to sleep with sweaty boots next to you all night. And it's a sitting place to eat and watch the inevitable rain!

It adds a bit of weight and packing bulk – but it's worth it

One safety note – never cook inside the porch! By all means have the stove outside and sit inside, but never have a lit stove inside the porch.

Seasons of a Tent

Tent season ratings are a little like the old sleeping bag ratings. It's used as a rough guide as to how suitable a tent will be for the chosen conditions. All tents can roughly be sorted into four groups. Before purchasing a tent decide what the worst possible weather conditions it will be normally out it. (Better to get a tougher tent than one that will leak and collapse)

1 Season – ideal for sheltered summer camping, for use in warm, relatively calm conditions. Generally speaking they are made using lightweight materials with high ventilation to reduce condensation. Ideal for short showers but will not withstand consistent rain.

2 Season - summer, late spring and early autumn, slightly more robust than above, and are designed to handle prolonged rain. They are also normally heavier.

3 Season – This is the season rating that is ideal for the UK and easily the most popular. A tent in this rating should easily handle autumn conditions of prolonged rain and will insulate in cold weather conditions.

4 Season – These are the more technical tents and are more suited to mountaineering. Featuring a minimum of four poles, plenty of guy attachment points, tough construction and sometimes a snow skirt. This is all reflected in the price.

Doors

This can be put simply down as your entrance and exit to your tent, but also is a major influence on condensation and the ventilation of your tent.

If the tent is a double skin style then, then there are least two doors that need to be taken into consideration.

The outer door in the waterproof fly is the main entrance to the tent, so its location has to be right. The inner door ideally needs to have some form of midge netting. This is essential for keeping out the smaller unwanted guests and aiding ventilation.

Poles

Most tents nowadays have colour coded poles; this helps with identification and assembly of the tent as the right pole goes in the right pole sleeve on the tent – makes pitching nice and easy

Normally the more a tent costs, the lighter and stronger the poles will be.

The more you pay for your tent the lighter and stronger your poles will be. Most poles are now linked via elastic shock cord, this makes pitching much quicker. Aluminium poles are lighter and more durable than fibreglass poles, and much lighter than steel.

Steel - steel poles are the strongest that you can find but also the heaviest by a long way. They are best used for larger family style tents; however some lower-grade tents also use them.

Fibreglass – This used to be the pole of choice for many manufacturers. Poles out of fibreglass are still quite popular, but usually only at the lower end of the tent ranges. Fibreglass is lightweight and cheap, but is not nearly as sturdy as aluminium. The concern with fibreglass is that it's prone to breaking if bent too much.

Aluminium - When it comes to tent poles, aluminium and aluminium alloys are currently the most popular variety available. These poles have great strength to weight ratio. Higher quality poles are often made from aircraft-grade aluminium.

Carbon Fibre - used in higher quality and more expensive tents. Its simple advantage is in its lighter weight. As with most things, the better quality the item the higher the price tag. Carbon fibre poles are not the norm in most tents due to the cost.

Pegs

In its most basic form a tent peg is a spike, usually with a hook or hole on the top end; originally made from wood, now metal, plastic, or composite materials are used. They are pushed into the ground for holding a tent down, either attaching direct to the tent's material, or by connecting to guy ropes attached to the tent.

Normally cheaper tents are supplied with steel pegs. These are ok to get you started, but aluminium pegs are lighter. Yes its daft, but any weight saving is always good when bike camping. If you have the money titanium alloy pegs are even lighter!

Top Tip

Always carry a couple of spare pegs just in case

Overall Pack Weight

Even though the tent is not going to be physically carried as its going on a motorcycle, weight is still a major issue. The weight of a tent also can relate to the final pack size too, so, in general, the lighter the tent the smaller the pack size.

The final weight depends on many factors – single skin, type of poles, large porch area, and type of material.

So it's a personal trade off between price, features and size. But always keep the final pack weight in mind.

Example Tents

The following pages have some examples of tents with a breakdown of features, weight, pack size etc. These have been based on a solo biker. The listed prices are the RRP but will probably be available cheaper on a shop by shop basis. The tents range from about £50 to £600 so is a good cross section of available tents

Always keep mind, just because something has the word 'biker' or 'motorbike' in its title does not mean it's always the best option.

Brand: Vango
Model: Omega 250 **Size:** 2 person
Price: RRP £180
Contact: www.vango.co.uk

No fuss alloy poled tunnel tent with extended porch give a large

living/storage space with an equally generous sleeping area for a comparatively low weight.

Perfect for cycle/motor bike touring and trips where you can afford a bit more weight for the large living space. If you are pedal cycle touring, a quick removal of the front wheel will soon see your bike safely stored in the porch area. The Omega has a large porch ideal for storage or sitting in when the weather is bad.

This tent is quite popular with touring bikers.

Total Weight: 4.25 kg	Groundsheet: Polyester 6000
Pack Size: 47 x ø18cm	Poles: PowerLite® 7001-T6 alloy
Flysheet: Protex® HC 5000 polyester	Pitching: As one or Flysheet-first
Inner: Breathable lightpolyester	Tent Style: Tunnel construction

Other Info:

Riser Groundsheet® in porch area : Colour coded alloy poles :TBS® II Tension Band System : Fire Retardant fabrics : Mesh ventilation : Mesh door covers in one flysheet door : Multiple reflective points : 'O' shaped inner doors : Rain stop flysheet door : Inner tent pockets :Supplied with compression Stuff Sac

Pitching time 10 Minutes

Brand: Vango	
Model: Spirit 200+ **Size:** 2 person	
Price: RRP £300 :	
Contact: www.vango.co.uk :	

Designed to accommodate two people the Vango Spirit 200+ tent is reliable lightweight and robust in all types of weather as well as being packed with design features and innovative fabrics and pole technologies to keep it light without worrying about stability and reliability.

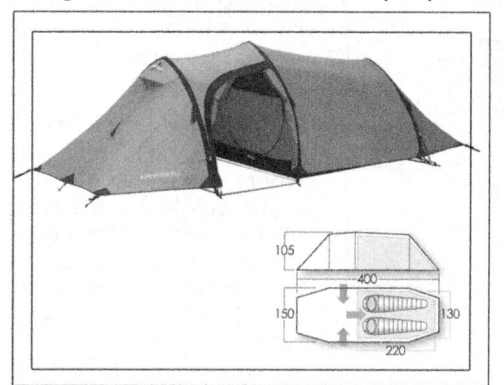

The inner can be pre-attached to the flysheet and the pole sleeves are all colour coded - so pitching this tent is certainly quite straightforward. It can also be pitched outer first.

There is a completely enclosed porch where it is possible to easily store two panniers, a roll bag, bike gear and still have enough room to sit and watch the rain. If you are over 6'3" you might be a little bit cramped in the sleeping area.

Total Weight: 2.9 kg	Groundsheet: HD nylon groundsheet
Pack Size: 44 x 15cm	Poles: 7001-T6 alloy poles
Flysheet: Protex 5000HH SPU ripstop nylon 40D	Pitching: As one or Flysheet-first
Inner: Breathable ripstop	Tent Style: Tunnel construction

Other Info:

TBS Pro-Tension Band System : Flat pole sleeves : Pole sleeve tension adjustment : Line-Lok guyline runners : Colour coded poles : Orange high strength guylines : Gothic Arch pole structures : Rain gutter zip covers : Flysheet door/vent : Entry from both sides (2012 version) : O Shaped inner door : Rain stop flysheet door : Multiple reflective points : Flysheet vent with mesh covering : Part mesh inner door : Compression stuff sac bag : Pitching time 10 Minutes

Brand: Vango
Model: Soul 200 **Size:** 2 person
Price: RRP £50 :
Contact: www.vango.co.uk :

Simple to set up and comfortable to use, the new for 2013 Vango Soul

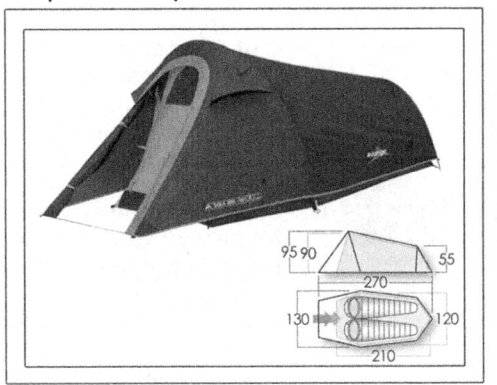

200 is an ideal starter tent for those taking their first steps into the world of camping. With just two poles and an easy to pitch tunnel design, you can pitch the tent in minutes leaving plenty of time for the more important things - like relaxing with a cold drink on a warm summers day.

The down side is the porch. There isn't one to mention really, but some small bits could be stored in it.

It does what it says on the tin – It's a good basic starter tent

Total Weight: 2 kg	Groundsheet: PE & waterproof to 10000mm
Pack Size: 51 x 14 x 14	Poles: PowerFlex® fibreglass
Flysheet: 70D polyester fabric 2000hh	Pitching: Inner-first
Inner: Breathable polyester	Tent Style: Tunnel construction

Other Info:
Part mesh inner door : Lantern loop : Vango Orange guylines : Handled bag for simple packing and carrying
Pitching time 7 Minutes

Brand: Coleman	
Model: Coastline 2 Plus **Size:** 2 person	
Price: RRP £99 :	
Contact: www.coleman.eu:	

Manufacturer's description: Perfect for touring campers, this 2 person

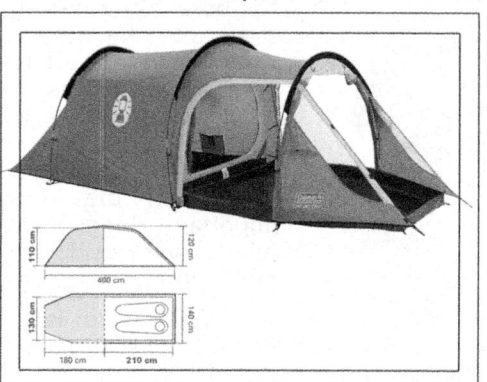

tent benefits from a quick and easy to erect tunnel design that is pitched in no time at all, so that you can sit back and relax within minutes of reaching the campsite. Internally, this design makes optimum use of space, providing ample sleeping and storage space for all of your kit. The addition of the new rising groundsheet increases protection from the elements while providing exceptional ventilation to avoid condensation and keep the air flowing inside the tent. A large PVC window allows plenty of light while storage pockets and a power cord vent add to living convenience at the campsite.

Total Weight: 4.71 kg	Groundsheet: PE 120g/m2
Pack Size: 50 x 16 cm	Poles: Fibreglass
Flysheet: Polyester 185T, PU-coated	Pitching: As one or Flysheet-
Inner: Breathing polyester 185T	Tent Style: Tunnel construction
Other Info:	

Sizeable porch: (LxBxH): 180 x 140 x 120cm : Three entry points : Rectangular carry bag with zipper opening : Y-guy-lines : Colour coded poles and pole sleeves : Internal pockets

Pitching time: 8 minutes

Brand: Coleman
Model: Bedrock 2 **Size:** 2 person
Price: RRP £50 :
Contact: www.coleman.eu

Manufacturer's description: Quick and easy to erect 2 person tent, a

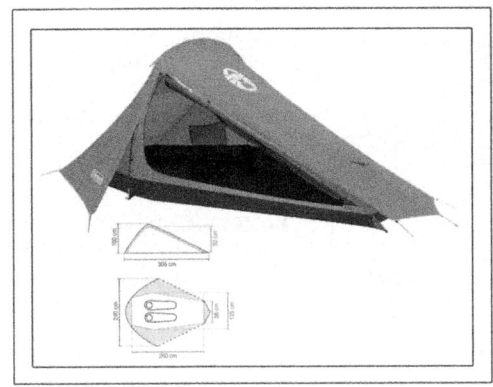

lightweight companion that is perfect for multi-stop trips. The inner first construction means that in warm conditions the inner can be used separately as a ventilated shelter. Additionally, the tent features one door and storage area on each side.

Due to the steep angle of the tent at the foot end, it might not be suitable for the taller biker.

The two storage areas should be able to accommodate quite a bit of bike gear.

If you're looking for a cheap, small pack size, lightweight tent that's perhaps your first tent, this maybe worth a look.

Total Weight: 2.5kg	Groundsheet: PE
Pack Size: 54 x 14 x 14 cm	Poles: Fibreglass
Flysheet: Polyester 2000mm PU coated	Pitching: Inner First-
Inner: Breathable polyester	Tent Style: Tunnel construction
Other Info:	

Fully integrated PE groundsheets : Two doors : Storage space : PVC windows : Fibreglass poles are lightweight and strong in adverse weather conditions.

Pitching time: <6 minutes

Brand: Coleman
Model: Phad 2 **Size:** 2 person
Price: RRP £179 :
Contact: www.coleman.eu

Manufacturer's description: An extremely sturdy structure and

compact, lightweight design are some of the key features that set the Phad™ X² apart from the rest. The 2 person, semi-geodesic structure, durable aluminium poles and tear resistant flysheet ensure that you are protected whatever the conditions. The tent consists of a living area with a generous storage space. Reflective trims on the zipper cuffs make the tent easy to spot at night. Also features an integrated groundsheet that can be zipped on and off.

For a solo biker there is enough room inside for loads of gear and rider. The porch area is good for getting out of the rain to take your boots and wet gear off without soaking the inside.

Total Weight: 3.45 kg	Groundsheet: Nylon 5000 mm, PU coated
Pack Size: 42 x 17 cm Ø	Poles: Aluminium 7001-T6
Flysheet: Polyester ripstop, 4000 mm PU coated, taped seams, UV Pro	Pitching: Inner First-
Inner: Polyester breathable and no-see-um mesh	Tent Style: semi-geodesic
Other Info: Generous storage space : Two doors : Reflective trims on the zipper cuffs : integrated groundsheet that can be zipped on and off. Internal pockets : highly visible bright green guy ropes Pitching time: 5 minutes	

Brand: Easy Camp	
Model: Eclipse 200 **Size:** 2 person	
Price: RRP £50 :	
Contact: www.	

Manufacturer's description: This tent offers an ideal combination of sleeping and living space. It combines the spaciousness of a dome for the sleeping area with the convenience of an extended tunnel-shaped porch for gear storage. The porch has 2 entrance points giving this area great versatility. It pitches flysheet first, with poles on the outside for convenience and includes a porch area groundsheet.

For the money this looks to be an ok tent. The hydrostatic head is quite low, so under some conditions may leak, but for £50 or less another good first time tent.

Total Weight: 4.1kg	Groundsheet: polyethylene
Pack Size: 54x16 cm	Poles: Fibreglass
Flysheet: fully taped, PU coated polyester 2000hh	Pitching: As one or Fly First-
Inner: Breathable polyester	Tent Style: dome

Other Info:
Detachable groundsheet for porch area
Pitching time: 8 minutes

Brand: Hilleberg
Model: Nallo 2GT **Size:** 2 person
Price: RRP £645 :
Contact: www.hilleberg.com

Manufacturer's description: The Nallo 2 GT offers an exceptional space

to weight ratio, and one of the most spacious living spaces of any compact trekking tent on the market. The Nallo Tents excel in any situation where the lightest possible tent is needed, but where true all season strength and reliability might be required.

The GT's extended vestibule boasts an entrance on each side, so that you can always position one out of the prevailing wind. Vertical inner tent entrance makes access easy, especially in the dark. Clothes line and two inner pockets make organising inside simple.

What a tent, but at that price what more do you expect.

Total Weight: 2.6kg	Groundsheet: Nylon 90g/m PU 5000mm HH
Pack Size: 20 x 55 cm	Poles: DAC Featherlite NSL Aluminium
Flysheet: Silicone Kerlon 1200 2000mm HH	Pitching: As one -
Inner: Nylon 42g/m	Tent Style: tunnel
Other Info: Pitching time: 6 minutes	

Brand: Terra Nova
Model: Voyager XL**Size:** 2 person
Price: RRP £509 :
Contact: www.

Manufacturer's description: The 2 Person Terra Nova Voyager XL Tent

 offers a spacious design for your bike gear with a highly ventilated porch with a side opening for convenient access. This lightweight 4 season tent has the strength to withstand windy conditions benefiting from durable DAC Featherlite poles and multiple guylines featuring reflective clamcleats enhancing visibility.

Not the biggest porch, but should still be able to store quite a bit of bike kit.

Total Weight: 2.35kg	Groundsheet: PU Nylon 7000mm
Pack Size: 55 x 15cm	Poles: 8.84mm DAC Featherlite
Flysheet: 6000mm hh	Pitching: As one -
Inner:	Tent Style: Semi-geodesic

Other Info:
Reflective guy lines : Large porch area with 2 entrances
Pitching time: 10 minutes

Brand: Redverz

Model: Series II Expedition Tent **Size:** 3 person + a bike!

Price: RRP €399 :

Contact: www.redverz.co.uk

Manufacturer's description: The new Series II Expedition Tent from

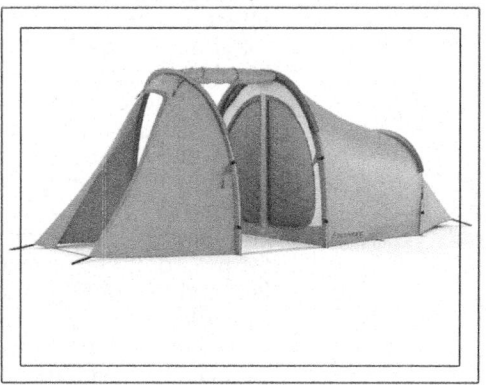

Redverz adds to the appeal of the original design which shelters riders, motorbikes and gear in comfort, out of the elements and under one roof. Expedition-grade ripstop nylon ground cloth and floors offer superior protection, while the double wall design of the sleeping bay helps eliminate condensation. Double J-door entries to the sleeping bay simplify entry and exit the Series II offers more while packing to the same size and weight as the original tent.

The 'garage bay' designed for sheltering motorbikes, has evolved far beyond the original vision. The bay serves as a sheltered utility area or dressing room with enough height to stand up and change gear.

Total Weight: 6.7kg	Groundsheet: PU Nylon 7000mm
Pack Size: 25 x 53cm / 10 x 21 inches	Poles: Aluminum 7005 T6
Flysheet: Coated ripstop nylon 68D 210T 4000mm	Pitching: Fly first -
Inner: 75D 190T/P breathable	Tent Style: tunnel/hoop

Other Info:

Large porch area : 4 doors : 2 Vestibules : multiple inner pockets and hang loops : Once pitched, the Series II is huge: 77 inches tall, 100 inches wide and 201 inches long.

At 14.9 pounds, it weighs nearly three times more than a typical 3-person backpacking tent and, when packed, it is significantly bulkier (21x10x9 inches).

Pitching time: 10 minutes

Brand: Khyam	
Model: Biker **Size:** 3 person	
Price: RRP £209 :	
Contact: www.khyam.co.uk	

Manufacturer's description: The Biker has been designed to be just the

right size for the back of a motorbike and by using the Rapidex pole system (fixed external pole system with hinged locking knuckles) means that it will pitch in minutes. The extended porch also ensures that there is plenty of extra space for anything from panniers to helmets.

Pitching is quick, though whilst the main body of the tent goes up quickly, threading the pole for the extending porch is as fiddly as any other type of tent that uses a pole and sleeve system.

Taking it down is as easy as putting it up - remove the porch pole, fold the legs, and then roll the tent around them.

Total Weight: 5.8kg	Groundsheet: Polyester 185T F/R
Pack Size: 60x20x20cms	Poles: Rapidex® Solid fibreglass
Flysheet: Polyester Weatherweave Pro	Pitching: Fly first -
Inner: Breathable Polyester	Tent Style: dome

Other Info:
Large porch area : 3 doors : flame retardant : integral door tent tidy : Inner tent pockets, Double loop shock corded pegging points :
Pitching time: 5 minutes

Brand: North Ridge	
Model: Torre XL **Size:** 2 person	
Price: RRP £180 discount card holders £75 :	
Contact: www.gooutdoors.co.uk	

Manufacturer's description: The Torre XL is the bigger brother to the

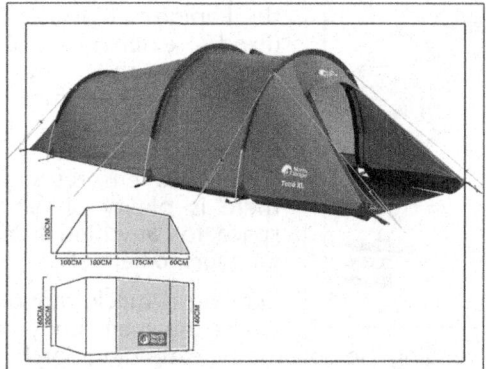

Torre, and in a similar nature, it is a durable and tough backpacking or weekend tent, built for adventure, with enough space for 2, or a luxury home away from home for one.

The Torre XL has been built with protection in mind. Strong alloy poles add in plenty of strength to support the 3.95kg of weight, whilst the ripstop, waterproof polyester provides fantastic all round coverage from the elements.

As well as a spacious inner, the Torre XL offers plenty of room for movement, so you can relax comfortably after a hard day on the bike.

North Ridge is Go Outdoors own brand, which they are expanding all the time. If you are a discount card holder, it must be worth having a look for £75.

Total Weight: 4.4kg	Groundsheet:
Pack Size: 57 x 17 x 16	Poles: Alloy
Flysheet: 3000hh	Pitching: Fly first -
Inner: Breathable Polyester	Tent Style: tunnel
Other Info: Extended porch : 2 doors :: Pitching time: 10/15 minutes	

Brand: VauDe
Model: Taurus 1 **Size:** 2 person
Price: RRP £150
Contact: www.cotswoldoutdoor.com

This 2-person tent is a modern classic. It doesn't get much easier than

this, a simple 2 pole semi-geodesic design that can be erected within minutes. Inside there is plenty of room for two, plus a spacious vestibule for storage. Revised guying at the foot end further improves stability.

Poles (2) and pegs (10) are very light and assembly is very easy even for one person.

Pitching is easy, thanks to the unique external frame design and the addition of adjustable pegging points. The tent is reasonably stable too. Like many Vaude tents, the Taurus gets a superb outer door design that uses four zip pullers to allow it to be opened in pretty much any direction. Porch space is probably just about large enough to store a bit of bike gear.

Total Weight: 2.4kg	Groundsheet:70D polyester 5000mm hh
Pack Size: 53x19cm	Poles: Alloy
Flysheet: 75D polyester; 3000mm hh	Pitching: Fly first -
Inner: Breathable polyester inner	Tent Style: 2 pole ridge

Other Info:

This 2-person tent is a modern classic : a lot of mesh on the inner, allowing good airflow :

Pitching time: 7 minutes

Tarps & Bashas

This is for the true light weight camper, but limited comfort and protection if used by itself.

They can also be used for adding an 'extension' to the tent, either at the door or for somewhere to sit out and stay dry if it rains.

If a larger style is used they can easily be pitched and used as a covered area for a few riders to sit under either for shade or for shelter from rain.

The photo left shows a Coleman tarp pitched for communal shelter. Its secured using guy lines to three trees at the back and guy lines into the ground at the front.

Another option, they can be pitched over the tent as an extra layer of protection from heavy rain.

As an example of weight, a 3m x 3m tarp is about 750g. With plenty of attachment points there's always a way to pitch it. Pack size is quite good (can easily fit on top of a pannier).

Available in a variety of sizes, styles and colours from manufacturers like Vango, DD Hammocks and available from Field & Trek, Go Outdoors, The Bushcraft Store, most outdoor shops who sell tents etc.

Pitching The Tent

One can say with certainty that a well pitched tent is a safe and secure one. Always follow the tents own instructions for pitching.

See the Setting Up Camp section for more information.

Quick Tent Tips

Person Size Rating

All tents have a person size rating eg: "2 Person Tent" or sometimes "2 man tent". Don't take this literally! For pure lightweight camping this is ok. If you want a bit of 'wiggle room' always go for one size larger, so if you are solo, go for a 2 man tent, if you are two up, go for a 3 man tent. Best option is to go to a shop that has a tent display with them all set up and get inside and physically try for size.

Before Going Away

Have a practice session pitching a new tent. There are good reasons for doing this:

It will allow you to familiarize yourself with the pitching process of your tent.

In the unlikely event of a defect, you will have the opportunity to resolve this before going away.

Condensation

Condensation happens in most tents & is often confused with leaking. To minimise condensation: Ensure all available vents are fully open, keep all storm flaps rolled up unless needed.

Shake off or wipe away any moisture inside the flysheet; wiping will not impair the waterproofing of the flysheet.

Pole Care & Repair

When folding poles, start from the centre to prevent excess strain on the shockcord.

If shockcord fails it is still possible to pitch your tent with care. New shockcord is available from most camping/outdoor stores.

Replacement pole sections for most tents are also available from most camping/outdoor stores.

Top Tip - Getting The Tent Back In the Bag

When you first get the tent home, don't rush to get it out of the stuff sack. Carefully take it out making a note of how it comes out and is folded (take photos at different stages to refer back to).

Then after pitching lay the stuff bag near to where you are packing the tent so you have an idea of the final size it has to be.

Fold in reverse order from how it came out, and it will go back in the stuff bag easily.

After a few times it will be second nature.

Sleeping

Once a tent has been purchased, gear for a comfortable nights sleep needs to be looked at. A sleeping bag and sleeping mat are the minimum components required.

Keep looking at pack sizes and weight of bags and mats, as at the end of the day they need to be packed onto the bike.

Sleeping Bags

As with the tent section, there are now many different makes, models, types and features to look into before a purchase is made.

You can even buy them at a local supermarket – which is sometimes no bad thing (some people swear by these sleeping bags)

If you are new to motorbike camping and seeing if it's your 'bag' then maybe look towards the cheaper end and test it out in the summer months. Cheaper bags will be as warm as an expensive bag in the summer months, but due to their manufacture, will not compress into such a small space.

Six basic feature to consider are: comfort rating : weight : pack size : filling length and fit.

Bag Seasons

Just to throw another rating into the mix to slightly confuse/simplify things, there is also the season rating to look at.

1 Season Sleeping Bags – Best for summer - Usually Around +4/5 Degrees

2 Season Sleeping Bags - Later spring to early autumn when it's not sweltering, but when you are unlikely to be on the receiving end of cold snaps or snow. Around 0 degrees

3 Season Sleeping Bags - More technical than a 2 season bag, these are best for mild to cold nights, without frost, but with a very low temperature 0 to -5 degrees

4 Season Sleeping Bags - The most technical bag. These are made for very cold winter nights in the outdoors. These are typically more bulky and weigh more, but they do keep you exceptionally warm. Usually to -10 degrees.

Seasonal ratings are the 'traditional' way of grouping sleeping bags. Sleeping bags have ratings simply because what is a comfortable bag in for the summer won't be warm enough to use in winter. Seasonal ratings are the 'traditional' way of rating sleeping bags, that is before a method of testing called EN 13537 was introduced.

The EN135357 standard was introduced as there is a big problem with seasonal ratings, in that there is no one main way of identifying a season. A 'season' in Norway will be different to a season in the UK, perhaps by 10 degrees! So what bag should you take?

The main advice is that no-one should blindly buy a certain season of sleeping bag without looking at the specifics of what it can handle. Above is a 'general guide' you can look at for an idea of how sleeping bags are rated. As you can see from above, 1 season bags are great for hot conditions and 3 and 4 season bags great for colder weather.

EN 13537 Ratings

The problem with seasonal ratings is that whilst a 4 season bag is designed for extremely low temperatures, it will probably be quite hot and uncomfortable to sleep in during the summer months, so it's perhaps not a four season bag at all but a 1 season (winter) bag. It is very hard to define a season alone.

In 2002, EN 13537 legislation came in which ensured that all manufacturers use high-tech sensors on heated mannequins in bags to determine how cold the bags can get. This is to standardise how sleeping bags are sold, and get away from the very subjective 'Seasonal ratings'.

So now on most sleeping bag stuff sacks is printed a table with:

Upper Limit/The Lower Limit - This upper limit is a temperature a man can sleep without sweating profusely. This is tested in normal 'summer' sleeping conditions, so the mannequin doesn't have a hood on, and has open zippers. The Lower Limit Temperature is the temperature a man could sleep at for 8 hours without waking up.

This temperature limit is at what temperature the bag will still keep you warm/cool before it starts becoming a matter of survival/extreme discomfort. At this limit, you are probably not as comfortable as you would like to be, but you should be able to sleep.

The Comfort level - This is the limit that a woman could sleep comfortably at and is the temperature you can be comfortable in. Obviously, the widest range here is what you should be looking for, so you can use your bag in a variety of situations.

An Extreme Temperature - This test is for emergencies only! The test shows the minimum temperature a standard woman can remain for six hours without dying in the cold. This is the maximum (lowest) coldest temperature that you could use this bag in without freezing. This won't be a number you will feel comfortable at all, but you will survive.

The problem with any rating system is that everyone is different – some people really feel the cold at night, while others can be happy sleeping in a much thinner bag.

Lab tested ratings are great, but as any couple knows, one partner can wake up roasting in the night, whilst the other freezes.

Examples of the ratings panel:

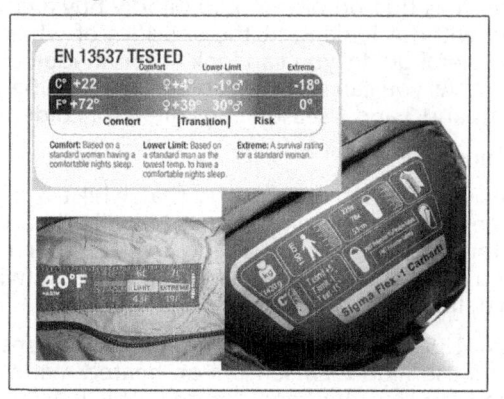

Backpackers/Climbers who camp in cold weather usually purchase

winter bags rated to below zero. These bags typically are higher priced than summer bags and require more space to pack.

Motorcycle campers should not need winter or severe cold bags as they are probably not camping when the weather turns to below freezing (Unless you are going to the Elefantentreffen). Instead consider buying a good three season bag which will be good for the spring and autumn and ok for the summer – sometimes three season bags can be too warm in the summer. These bags pack relatively small and can keep you warm on cool autumn nights.

Bikers who plan to just camp in the summer months could get away with a good two season style bag, and usually packs smaller than a three season, so saving space on the bike.

Weight

As with everything to do with motorcycle camping, weight is another consideration to think about. Lightweight bags can really be compressed down and weigh very little, for example about 700g for a Vango ultra light 350.

Fill

The fill is the thermal insulating material used to fill the bag. There are basically two types of fill to think about, down or synthetic fibres.

Down is the fine layer of fluffy feathers underneath the normal feathers on water fowl, usually geese or ducks. These bags are usually lightweight compress well and have a longer life span than synthetic fibres. But they also usually cost more, loose their ability to keep you warm if they get wet, and require a long time to dry. There needs to be enough space for the down to 'loft up' as it traps air, but not too much, as this allows the down to migrate and leave areas without insulation.

The American market uses a different rating system to the UK/EU. The general rule for conversion is 600 US fill power is, 500 EU fill. (Generally take off 100 of fill power for an EU/UK conversion.)

Down is Mother Nature's best insulator. It provides incredible warmth for minimal weight and is highly compressible and resilient; but it comes at a price.

Synthetic Insulation as its name suggests is a man made, synthetic insulation made using polyfibres, the lab made equivalent of natural down. Synthetics are used to attempt to replicate the warming and heating effects of down, without the bulk, and with the chance to achieve higher levels of breathability, all at a lower cost.

Well- designed bags will overlap, or offset, insulation layers so that cold spots are not created; look for terms such as 'shingle' or 'double-offset layer' in the more advanced bags which describe such construction.

With rapidly advancing technology, new synthetic fill materials are being created all the time. Some of the most popular synthetic insulations are: Polarguard®, Primaloft®, Thinsulate®, Thermolite®.

The main advantages of a synthetic filled bag are: they usually cost less, they stay warm even when wet and they dry much quicker than down bags.

Is there a winner in the down vs. synthetic debate?

The fact of the matter is that down is better except when synthetic is better. The distinguishing line gets more blurred every year. Just a few years ago, down was unmatched; but today's lighter, warmer, and more compressible synthetics are slowly closing the gap. In order to find your best match, keep these key things in mind:

Down works well for just about everyone - unless you frequently find yourself in wet weather. – That will be the UK then!

Synthetic insulation is a good choice for anyone new to camping because of the lower cost and quick drying properties.

Down still wins in terms of weight, compressibility, and durability, but synthetic is the hands-down winner in the cost department.

Continuous technological advancements in synthetic materials are giving down a run for its money. You may not be able to tell the difference.

Down or Synthetic Insulation- At A Glance

Down Bags Pros	Down Bags Cons
Extremely warm for its weight	Performs badly when exposed to dampness/wetness
Extremely compressible	More expensive than synthetic insulation
Retains its shape and loft and, with proper care, can last a lifetime.	Care required when cleaning and storing for optimum performance
	Needs to be kept dry
	Lacks breathability

Synthetic Bags Pros	Synthetic Bags Cons
Good value for money	Poor weight to warmth ratio when compared to down insulation
Less care required in cleaning and storage	Bulkier than natural, high quality down
Provides plenty of circulated heat with more freedom of movement.	Loses heat quicker than a traditional down fabric.
Performs in the wet	

Fit

In general there are two main types of design for sleeping bags: Rectangle/Envelope and Mummy.

Rectangular bags are basically a quilt folded in half with a zip up the bottom and side. They are quite roomy, but not very heat efficient.

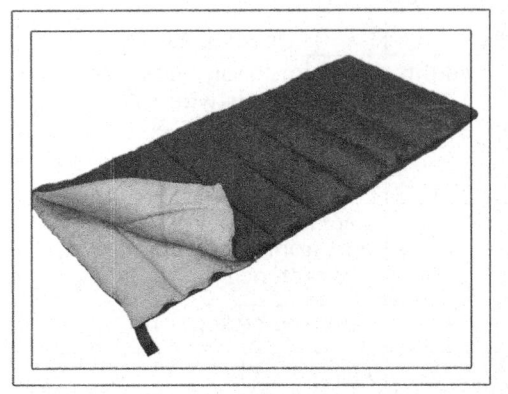

Rectangle bags are cheap and cheerful, and can serve well for brief, short, good weather trips away, but because of their weight and pack size, lack of hood are not ideal for long trips.

They can be zipped together though to make a double bag. If you want to do this you need to look for Left or Right handed bags. If you get a right side zip and a left side zip, they can then be attached together.

In general rectangle bags are being produced less and less year on year.

Mummy style sleeping bags get their name because they are shaped like an Egyptian mummy-wide at the top, tapering to slimmer feet, so the feet should warm up nice and fast. Just from looking at them you know they are going to be warm and the heat should stay in. They can be restrictive, especially if you are used to a

rectangle shaped sleeping bag, however the design will keep you warm in almost any condition. Most of the time, they also incorporate a hood for snuggling into to keep even warmer. These bags tend to have a much shorter side zip than the rectangle bags. Because mummy sleeping bags are made with less bulk, they also weigh less.

These are now easily the most popular style of bag.

Length

As a very rough guide, look to buy a long bag if you are over 6ft 2inch tall. There is specific information on height on most bags. If not, don't just get what you think is right – ask the staff for assistance, better still get in one and try it out.

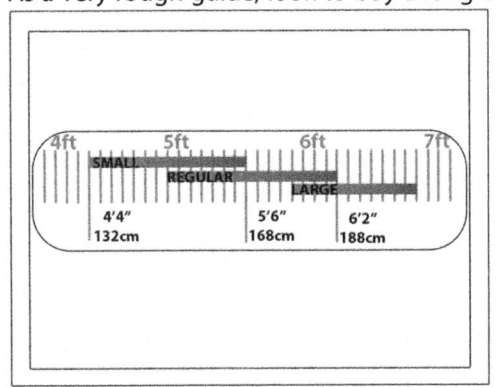

Sleeping Bag Quick Tips

Decide what the lowest temperature is that you are likely to encounter. Choose a bag that will perform to this temperature (and ideally a little below for extra peace of mind).

Synthetic bags tend to be cheaper and easier to clean than down bags. They also provide reasonable insulation when wet and dry out more quickly than down bags.

Down bags provide the best warmth to weight ratio, compress smaller and will last longer than synthetic bags.

A mummy shaped bag will provide the most efficient insulation compared to a rectangular bag which will give more space to move around in (but also to heat up).

Be sure the bag is the right size, based on the fit information.

A sleeping bag is no good if you don't have insulation from the ground; use a suitable mat to get the most from your bag.

Buy the best bag you can afford.

Fluff out your bag as early as possible before use, especially if it's a down filled bag. Try to open up the bag immediately after setting up the tent to fully restore its loft by bedtime to get the greatest warmth.

Sleeping Bag Care

By taking good care of a sleeping bag, it may not need to be replaced for several years. Follow these tips to help make the bag last:

The best way to maintain your sleeping bag is to use a liner. This will help keep it clean – See *Sleeping Bag Liner* section.

After any trip, take the bag out and clean off any marks with a sponge.

Dry out the bag immediately after every use.

Never pack away a wet sleeping bag for longer than it takes to ride home from your destination. Hang it out to dry or tumble dry it at low heat as soon as possible.

Always follow the care instructions for your bag if it needs washing. If you misplace them, wash the bag by hand with a very mild detergent and tumble dry on low heat (with a clean tennis ball to fluff the bag).

or

Wash in an oversized front-loading washer on a gentle cycle. (30 degrees or below). Tumble dry on low heat (with a clean tennis ball to fluff the bag). It does not need spinning too hard. DO NOT use an agitator top-loading machine.

If the bag is made of Primaloft or similar, then don't use any detergent of softener; it might degrade any kind of DWR (durable water repellent) treatment that's been applied to the bag.

As an alternative to normal detergent look at Nikwax Tech Wash or Down Wash which are non-detergent soaps, and clean without harming water-repellence, and help to restore the bag's loft.

After washing, keep the bag open - ideally on a washing line to dry off naturally.

Down filled bags can be problematical to wash and it's all too easy to ruin a £200+ bag. Take it to a specialist cleaner. (Franklins in Sheffield has been recommended for down bags)

Store the bag in a cool, dry place and never leave it jammed inside a stuff sack, or it will eventually lose loft and will permanently become less effective. If possible keep it stored flat and use a large storage bag.

Sleeping Bag Liner

Sleeping bag liners perform a few useful functions. Firstly, they keep the sleeping bag clean and stop the need to wash it too often which

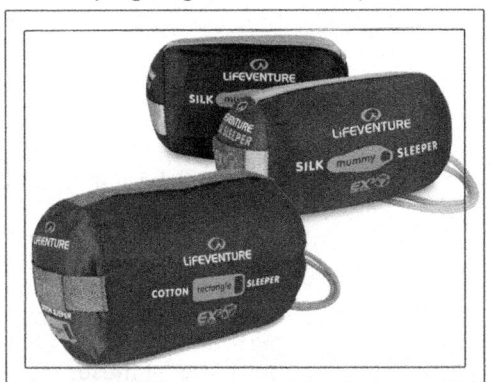

could reduce its performance. Secondly they can also add a few degrees of warmth into the rating of the sleeping bag by adding an extra layer of material and air. Thirdly they can be used instead of a sleeping bag in warmer climates making them perfect for use in hot countries.

Liners come in a variety of materials, but cotton or silk are the more popular. Cotton is much cheaper than silk, but silk is much lighter and packs down to nothing. (Lifeventure silk liner packs to 10x7cm and weighs about 120g) Some liners also have an insect repellent and antibacterial agent built in. The price range is quite large (Gelert cotton liner £9.99, Sea to Summit silk liner £49), so buy what you thinks best/budget will allow.

For short trips they can be kept inside the sleeping bag, thus reducing packing, or on longer trips take them out and store them in their own little stuff sack.

Sleeping Mat

If you have ever spent a night sleeping directly on the ground you will probably have had a restless night and been cold. Sleeping mats are essential if you want a good night's sleep.

Lightweight and easy to pack, sleeping mats are designed to preserve body heat, as the ground sucks heat away from you, and to provide a barrier of comfort over hard or uneven ground. The comfort provided by a sleeping mat by insulating you from the ground and providing a smooth surface to sleep can't be over stated enough.

Sleeping mats are either self inflatable, blow up yourself, or closed cell foam, which requires no work.

Designs are all very similar, and most accommodate roll up straps to help prevent it bouncing back as you roll it away, as well as a stuff sac to keep it all tidy.

The Classic Closed Cell Mat.

A closed cell is a classic camping mat (originally known as a karrimat) that looks like a yoga mat, firm yet flexible. These are cheap, easy to carry and even easier to pack away. Closed cell refers to the construction of the mat, which acts as a cellular barrier against moisture. They provide a simple form of insulation from the ground that works well, but since newer styles of sleeping mat have been developed these have fallen out of favour. For about £5 one can be picked up from most outdoor shops.

Self Inflating Mats

As its generic name suggests, this type is capable of self-inflation due to the open-cell foam that fills the internal cavity. For many years this design was protected by patents held by Cascade Designs (Therm-a-Rest to you and me), and were a premium item. But since these patents expired there has been an explosion of this type of sleeping mat and now they are commonplace.

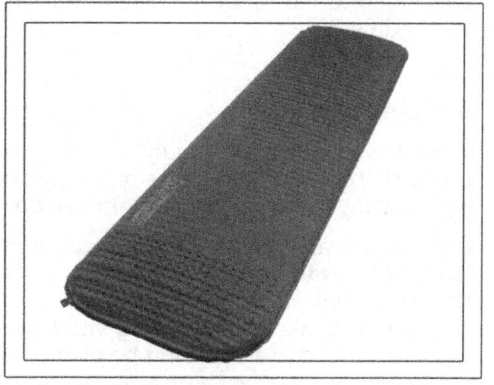

To inflate, there is a valve at one corner, when the mat is laid out flat and the valve is unscrewed, air is sucked in and the open cell foam expands. Now even though its 'self inflating' they nearly always need finishing off with a few blows to speed up the final part of inflation. Once full, just close the valve.

To deflate, just undo the valve and roll up the mat. As the mat is rolled the air that's inside is squeezed out through the valve. Once at the end, close the valve.

The most popular brand for this type of sleeping mat is Therm-a-Rest who now make over twenty different types and styles, the cheapest being about £50. Many other companies now also make self inflating mats and can be bought from as little as £10.

These mattresses are lightweight and pack to a small size.

Air Beds

Yes you will have a bouncy comfy nights sleep with an air bed, but as

 their name suggests, they are full of air, so there is no insulation material and it will take on the ambient temperature while you sleep.

Also a pump (12v or manual) or a pair of very big lungs will be required to inflate an airbed. There is a lot of extra weight to think about if this is the sleeping mat of choice.

Is there really a place for airbeds when 'lightweight' camping on a motorbike? Mmmm, a good question, but I personally don't think so!

Available from all outdoor shops and some supermarkets etc.

Pillow

Pillows! Yes it all sounds a little luxurious but a pillow of sorts really can help with a good nights sleep. We are not talking nice fluffy types like on the bed at home here, we are talking about small inflatable ones, or an instant on the spot camp made pillow. But they do make a difference.

Small inflatable pillows can be bought from any out doors shops for a few pounds. It packs to nothing and can be rolled up in the sleeping bag stuff sack while travelling.

A camp made pillow can easily be made by filling a spare stuff bag with a fleece or a couple of worn t-shirts. It's basic, but so often not thought of and can be just what is needed for a better nights sleep.

Other Items To Pack

Not really miscellaneous items, but items that don't really fall into a section.

Stuff bags

Not necessarily an item to pack, but an item to help packing. You can never have too many stuff sacks to organise clothes, panniers roll bags etc. They do make packing much easier. Available form all outdoor shops; depending on the make and if they are waterproof can be bought for a few pounds.

Bin Liners

They don't take up much space or weight and they can be used for several jobs. Wrap wet/muddy camp boots up before being packed, thus stops anything else getting wet. Wrapping up the tent stuff bag if the tent is packed damp. Rubbish bags while at camp. Shopping bags can do the same, so while at camp keep them to one side.

First Aid kit/First Aid

First aid kits are designed to be used as a way of treating minor accidents. First Aid is not to be confused with serious healthcare, and is only to be used for minor treatments. It's about stopping a flow of blood and stabilising an injury or condition until the person can receive proper medical attention if required. You don't need to carry a portable clinic with you!

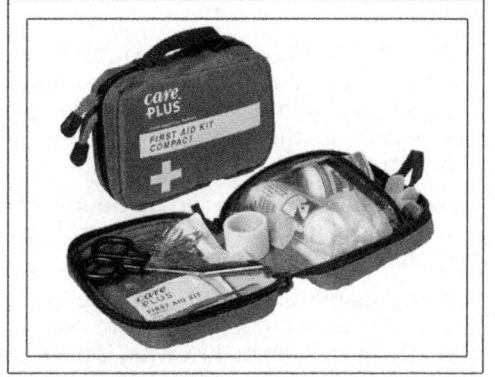

In this book Third World Travel is not covered, but as a future guide, if travelling in the Third World Countries and Africa especially, a sterile set is essential so that use of potentially contaminated equipment can be avoided.

First aid kits can vary in price and what they offer. With a little forward planning a good first aid kit can be assembled. Just because it's a motorcycle trip doesn't mean a 'special' motorcyclist's first aid kit has to be bought; but it can be if you want.

You can either make your own up from scratch using a small Tupperwear style box or nylon bag (little black travel bags can be bought at pound shops that work well), or purchase one from an outdoor shop (that way the bag will be more visible being red). As a start, look for one around the £15 pound mark (pack size should be nice and compact). Then there should be about 11/12 items already included and you can add to it for a more personal kit. Usually ready made kits also have a little 'How To' guide which if you are new to first aid can be handy (if very basic).

Items to make sure are in the first aid kit or that can be easily added to one:

Care:	Medicines:
Antiseptic wipes/Antiseptic cream	Pain relief (Paracetamol/Ibuprofen etc)
Sterile or vinyl gloves	Antacids
Plasters	Anti diarrhoea medication
Sterile plasters	Rehydrating salts/tablets
Mircopore tape	Burn gel/cream
Gauze bandages	Insect bite relief
Gauze pads	Prescription medicine
Safety pins	Blister pads
Small low-adherent dressing	Foil blankets*
Woven bandage	Aftersun*
Small crepe bandage	Lemsip Max (a couple of sachets)*
Scissors & tweezers	Antihistamines*

* not essential – and other items can be included

First Aid Notes:

Not wanting to put a 'downer' on proceedings, but riding any distances away from home over several days inherently increases the risk of accident. (Though riding safely anywhere shouldn't impact any more than normal).

If in any doubt about any injury or illness seek medical advice as soon as possible. Only move a seriously injured person when really necessary. Moving can potentially make the injury worse.

Before setting out on a bike tour try to have a 'gen up' on how to recognise symptoms and apply treatments.

Basic First Aid • Dehydration • Bleeding • Heat Exhaustion • Altitude Sickness • Burns • Fractures • Shock • Bites & Stings

For further information on first aid and how to administer it enrol on a St. John Ambulance training course. They are about £30 for a three hour course, and well worth it.

General

A couple of other items that should be carried when touring, but not necessarily in the first aid kit (as they may be needed throughout the day) are, lip balm, sunscreen and insect repellent.

Lip balm and sunscreen; as being outdoors whether riding or at camp exposes the skin to the elements and UV. Even on dull days on the bike your face and lips will catch the sun.

Insect repellent; you just never know when those little annoying flying insects are going to show up to make life unpleasant (in Scotland that's most of the time!) Options here are chemical based insect repellents or a proven alternative is Avon Skin So Soft! It keeps the little insects away and makes you smell oh so nice at the same time.

If going down the Avon Skin So Soft route don't take the big bottle as it's big and weighty. Go to a pound shop and buy a little travel pack of bottles and decant some into one. Always label up anything not in its original container.

A couple of other natural (if not immediate) options are an odourless garlic capsule in the morning or Vegemite/Marmite on toast for breakfast.

ICE – In Case of Emergency

No one wants to think about the worst happening on a motorcycle trip – but it can!

ICE Information

One of the things that most people forget about when travelling alone or not with a family member is the need for information In Case of Emergency. There are several ways this can be done. One is to write the information on a piece of card and carry it with you. Another is to add a name in your phone just as ICE and have the number set as an international code; so for UK +44 <miss off the first 0 of the area code><number> eg 00441141231231 (but make sure you don't have a keylock on the phone!)

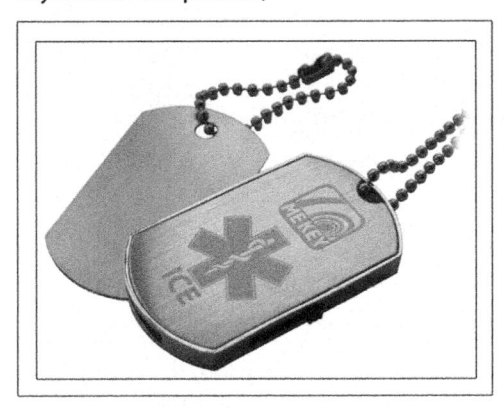

Another option is an ICE tag. These tags plug into a USB port on a PC and can contain personal details, medical information, emergency contact details and much more. They also translate into five languages.

The internationally recognised paramedic star and ICE is engraved or printed on them, so are highly visible.

Not necessarily to be used at a scene of an accident, but if you cant communicate then this will allow emergency services to find out who you are, what medications you are taking and who to contact. Also, they are very easy to update, unlike an engraved tag.

Available from www.mekey-icetag.co.uk for £20

See Paperwork & Documents section for more information.

Whistle

Always carry a whistle in a motorcycle jacket pocket. If you are riding by yourself and somehow come off the road and in a ditch (along with the bike) no one will see you or hear you shouting. You can blow a whistle for much longer than you can shout. Blasts on a perry whistle can be heard further away than shouting, and it takes less energy (which should be conserved in a survival scenario), the piercing tone carries well over distance.

They cost a couple of pounds from any good outdoors shop. Go for the perry whistle as they are plastic and pea less. So they won't pull your lips off in the cold or not work when the pea falls out!

112

This is the European wide emergency phone number, available throughout the EU (Austria, Belgium, Bulgaria, Cyprus, Czech Republic, Germany, Denmark, Estonia, Greece, Spain, Finland, France, Hungary, Ireland, Italy, Lithuania, Luxembourg, Latvia, Malta, Netherlands, Poland, Portugal, Romania, Sweden, Slovenia, Slovakia, United Kingdom), free of charge.

It is possible to call 112 from fixed and mobile phones to contact any emergency service (ambulance, fire& rescue or police).

Operators in many countries can answer the calls not only in their national language, but also in English or French. If the caller does not know where they are, the operator can identify where the person making the call is physically located which will be passed on to the emergency authorities.

112 doesn't replace the existing national emergency numbers. In most countries, it operates alongside them, but simplifies emergency contact where countries have several numbers. (Eg Spain: 062 - civil guard, 091 - police, 061 - health emergencies, 080 - fire, 092 - local police).

However, some countries have opted for 112 as their main national emergency number. 112 is also used in some countries outside the EU, such as Switzerland and South Africa.

It is also available worldwide on GSM mobile networks where it gets automatically transferred to the national emergency number.

Clothing

When you have been riding all day in a bike suit, one of the best tings to do once the camp has been initially set up is to get into some 'civies'.

When looking at clothing to take in the initial planning stage, start to look at materials/fabrics, weight and pack size. Also start to think about the layering system and what set of clothes will keep you dry and warm or cool and comfortable depending on the predicted weather at camp (not necessarily at home when packing). Ideally you want to have the maximum flexibility with the minimum fuss.

When choosing clothing for camping trips on the bike (or any camping trip) ideally look for items that compress, are fast drying, wicking, insulate, breathable and lightweight.

Straight away that really should ring some bells and that pair of jeans really shouldn't be packed.

Clothing items can be bought over time as you develop knowledge of fabrics and their properties. See the motorcycle clothing section for more information.

Items that compress well and are relatively light in weight are good as it allows a selection of clothes to be carried without bulk and weight. But don't over pack clothes – how many time do you return from a holiday with unworn clothes. These unworn clothes on a motorcycle trip take up room and add weight.

Fast drying items are a must. At some point in camp you will get wet, be it from rain, splashed water, a paddle in the sea or lake or an item of clothing that just needs a wash. Technical clothing aimed at walkers will dry much quicker than denim or cotton.

A good example are the Craghopper Kiwi trousers shown previous. They are lightweight, have loads of pockets including a couple of zipped security ones, made of SmartDry Nano Water repellent and quick dry textile, UPF40+ fabric, and can convert into sorts – so two items in one!

For an insulation layer a technical fleece is one of the best options. They pack small and are lightweight. Leave your favourite big fluffy comfy woolly jumper at home.

In hot countries loose fitting cotton is a good option to keep you cool.

Footware

Soft lightweight approach style boots or shoes. Your feet will love you after being in motorcycle boots all day.

Available from all outdoor shops, supermarkets like Aldi and Lidl sometimes have special offers. Makes include Merrell, The North Face, Jack Wolfskin, HiGear, Karrimor, and many many others. Usually have a Gore-tex or similar upper with a tough grippy style sole. Prices vary considerably dependant on make.

Teva style walking sandles. Your feet will love you after being in approach boots if it's hot! Only take these if your destination is going to be really hot. Like approach boots these are available from all outdoor shops. Prices vary considerably dependant on make.

When packing these always put them in a bin bag first – that way any mud, dust or damp will not end up anywhere else.

Hat

Another daft thing to write about, but if the destination of the trip is going to be hot and sunny, then don't forget to pack a hat of some sorts. One with a wide brim to help shade the face and neck is a good option. Also if going up to Scotland when the midges are out then one with an inbuilt midge net might be handy.

If the destination is cooler, then a hat will help keep you warm in the evening as a large proportion of the body's heat is lost through the head.

Packing Clothing

Everyone eventually develops their own routine for packing clothing. But try to get clothing into a smaller space as possible. Fold items down small and then roll tightly. Some systems here are to roll up a days worth of clothing into a shopping bag (and then roll the bag around the clothes). Then each day just take out a bag, at the end of the day return the clothes to bag, but turn the bag inside out for identification as being worn.

Another is to use nylon stuff bags to keep clothing organised once they have been folded and rolled. One for clean and one for dirty

If the trip is for more than a say six or seven days then look at washing clothing in a shampoo solution when at a campsite for more than one night. That way pack size and weight will be smaller and the clothes will smell nice.

T-Shirts	Walking Sandals (if destination is hot)
Long Sleeved Fleece	Hat
Trousers (ideally not jeans)	Underwear
Shorts	Socks (not bike)
Approach Boots	Waterproof Jacket

Everyone always over packs clothes, so don't take more clothes than are needed. For example; you don't need seven pairs of normal socks on a seven day bike trip! (Each pair will only be worn for a few hours a day, so maybe take three or four pairs).

Top Tip

If there are no facilities for washing clothes in a sink then a good way to wash clothes is to have a medium sized waterproof stuff bag, half fill it with water, add a little bit of shampoo or shower gel. Then add the item of clothing that needs a wash. Fold over the top of the stuff bag and give it a good shake, squash down and rub about. Leave for a few minuets and repeat, then remove the clothing, rinse and dry.

Wash kit

Everyone has been away from home before on a holiday, so has a rough idea of what's included in a wash kit. But here are some pointers and ideas to maybe get you looking at things again.

Firstly start a new wash kit for bike trips; nothing that is put in it will have a short 'use by' date. Doing this will allow you to assemble it once, keep it with the bike gear and then the next time you go touring it just needs a quick check and it's ready to go. But do try to keep toiletries to a minimum; there is no need to take a hair dryer!

Don't spend money on special small tubes of toothpaste; wait until a normal one is 3/4 empty and then put it to one side for the wash kit.

Some pound shops have travel kits which contain a travel toothbrush, a small micro fibre cloth and a couple of small squeeze bottles. This is a good starting point.

Toilet Paper	Deodorant	Shampoo**
Baby Wipes	Hairbrush	Micro Fibre Towel x2
Small Bar of Soap	Razor/Shaver	Feminine Hygiene
Toothbrush*	Shaving Cream	Contact Lens Solution
Toothpaste	Shower Gel**	Wash Cloth
Universal Sink Plug		

* from the travel kit mentioned above
** decant from larger bottles into smaller ones from travel kit

The above list is obviously quite a generic list so just tailor it to your own requirements.

Once everything is assembled try to pack it into a small stuff bag or small purpose made wash bag. (The smaller the better).

Depending on the facilities when camping (or lack of) showers/water etc, you can always go a couple of days by using some large baby wipes. It's quite impressive how clean these things can keep you! Always carry a pack.

Towels

Don't pack your favourite terry towel beech towel. Microfibre towels are the way to go. These pack quite small for their unpacked size, are light, quick drying and can 'hold' more water than an ordinary towel. The majority of modern microfibre towels are now impregnated with an antibacterial agent. This helps stop mould and smells that can occur by leaving the towel packed damp over extended periods.

Think about carrying a couple – one large/X large (for the times you have access to a shower or a swim!) and one much smaller for drying after a normal wash. (some come with a karabiner allowing them to be attached to the outside of the tent for hanging up to dry)

They are a bit strange the first time you use one as they are not a normal towel. People either love them or hate them; but for travelling light a normal towel just takes up too much space.

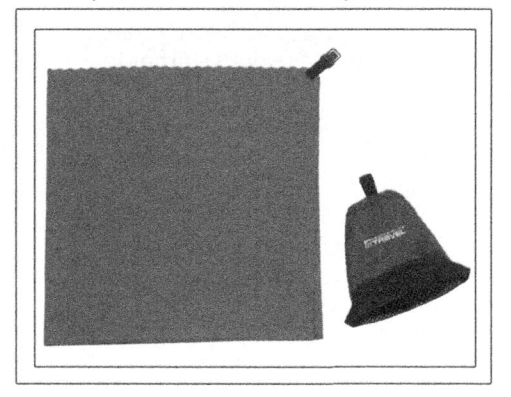

Not wanting to teach you how to dry yourself, but these towels work better if you dab and don't rub as you would with a normal towel. If it gets totally wet while in use, just wring it out and start again!

Available from Mountain Warehouse, Go Outdoors, most outdoor shops, Amazon, TKMax and Aldi sometimes have good offers. With prices from £3 for a small every day towel to £30/£40 plus for an XL towel. Prices are dependant on make; an XL towel can be purchased for around £10 or less.

Always wash the towel before its first use.

Universal Sink Plug

If you always like a full bowl of water when having a wash, then this is a must have item. Many campsites on the continent don't have plugs

in the sinks; the idea being people don't walk off with the taps running and plugs in causing floods. They can be picked up for a couple of pounds from most outdoor and camping shops. Or you could just have a wash under running water.

Top Tip

Take a plastic shopping bag to the shower with you. It's handy for holding the wash kit and clean clothes on the way in; holding watches, glasses, jewellery etc and clothes while showering and on the return trip it can have the dirty clothes in.

Campsite tools

When setting up camp and while camping there are a few tools that might make life a little easier.

Multi Tool

These are fantastic items to have when camping. As its name hints at they have a multitude of uses around the camp without having to carry several individual items. Knife (sometimes a couple), pliers, screwdriver (flat & cross head), scissors, can opener, bottle opener and corkscrew. Even better if the design allows for the tools to be locked out for safety.

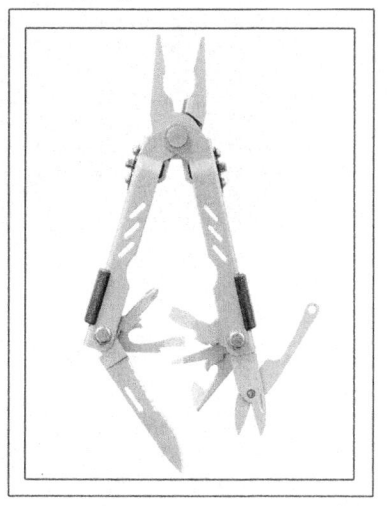

The day you go on a trip without it is the day you realise how much you use it!

Available from some outdoor shops, Springfields of Burton, army stores as well as online. Examples include Gerber – Compact Sport 400 (£50), Leatherman – Wave (£80), Draper Expert (£25)

Paracord

Not really a tool, but one of the worlds best inventions. Can be used for all sorts of things, from emergency tent guy lines, to hanging a tarp, to a washing line. Buy a good length of it and keep it handy.

Tent Kit

Yes they are bulky and yes they are heavy, and it's moving away from lightweight a little, but if room and weight allows then it's sometimes

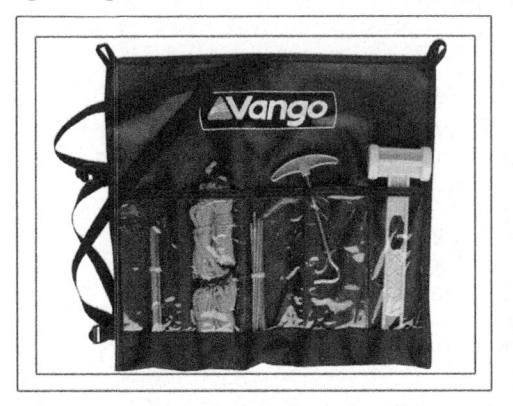

handy to have one of these. It contains a plastic peg mallet, spare pegs (hook and V), peg remover, spare guy lines and runners. The mallet is a little light weight, but it does help sometimes. If you got a tent repair kit with your tent, then put that in one of the pockets, then all the tent accessories are kept together.

Setting Up Camp

So the end of the riding day has finally come and you have arrived at the campsite of choice. After checking in at reception the first thing to do is have a steady ride or walk around to see what pitches are available.

Choosing A Spot

Below are some basic pointers for choosing a location to pitch the tent.

- Always aim to get to camp well before the light starts to fade. That way there should be plenty of time to look around and pitch in daylight.

- Never pitch the tent next to a stream or lake, if the water level rises so do you!

- Try to see if the pitch has good drainage – Pitching a tent in a slight dip or low spot means it could flood during rain.

- Try to find a level pitch (or with a very slight angle for rain drainage). If you do pitch on a gradient, pitch the tent in line with the fall (if possible) and always sleep with your head at the highest end.

- See where a fresh water supply/facilities are to the chosen pitch, if too far and there are spaces, then look around again.

- Find shelter – Hedges, low walls, even other tents can form great windbreaks on an exposed site.

- Trees are a bit of a catch 22 issue. It can be appealing to pitch in the shade of a tree, but the grass is often poor because it's protected from the rain, pine trees can drip sap and birds have a habit of roosting and inevitably marking the tent. Rain will also drip from trees long after a storm has passed. It can also be dangerous to pitch under a tree if there's a thunderstorm.

  But saying that it is handy having a tree or two close by to cast shade if the sun is hot, to break up wind and rain or to tie a tarp to.

- Privacy – How close is the chosen pitch to other people. Obviously if you want a little solitude then don't choose a pitch right next to other campers.

- Check to see if the bike can be parked up close by. If so test the ground to see if the bikes side stand will hold up or sink. If it looks to be sinking then use a mud bud to spread the weight.

Setting Camp

If the weather is favourable, briefly consider the layout of the camp before pitching the tents. Where to cook? Wash up? Eat? Light a fire? (If allowed).

Once you've chosen a pitch, check it's free from anything that could damage the groundsheet of the tent, including old tent pegs, branches, rocks or roots. Find a longish stick and give the area your tent will rest on a quick rake over to clear it of any detritus.

Now comes the most important part. Getting the groundsheet set right. It sounds simple, but check the direction of the wind; the tent should have its back facing into the wind, not across it.

Have a think about the door of the tent; this needs to ideally be away from the wind. (But if the pitch is on a slope and you sleep with your

head near the door, it should be higher than your feet. Do not sleep with your head downhill as you may suffer from headache due to increased blood flow. Now once those tasks are done peg out the groundsheet so it's nice and taught and flat. This normally takes less than a minute to do.

Get the tent out of its stuff bag and lay it on the groundsheet. At this point all tents have different methods of pitching, so follow the instructions for pitching the tent precisely, step by step, and in order.

As a guide; position it so it's roughly in the right place (door where it should be). Make up the poles and take care inserting them. Most tents now have a handy colour code to help you work out which pole goes where. If they don't slide in easily check to see if they are caught on the fabric. Always push the poles through to keep the joints tightly together. Never pull a pole through as the joints will pull apart.

Once the poles are in (depending on the style of tent) lift and start to peg down. If pitching in strong winds then there is always a little bit of fun at this stage, so always try to fix the windward side first; this should

stop the tent catching the wind and blowing over.

Start pegging out the tent. Pegs should be pushed into the ground diagonally at an angle of 45 degrees (normally), with the point towards the tent and right up to the hook. But the peg should always be 90 degrees to the guy line

Tent Peg Angles

(see example picture previous) So sometimes the angle may need to be shallower. This means that if the tent is blown about the force is trying to pull the peg through the ground, not out of the ground. Don't put the peg in vertically as the guy lines will ride up and the peg will pull out.

Depending on the ground it can sometimes be handy to have a mallet (it could save ripping the sole of your bike boots!) Or hit them with a rock and swear loudly at them!

Guy lines need to apply a downward pulling force to the tent. They normally follow the line of the seams, but on tunnel tents they need to pull the poles down and away from each other. So always read specific instructions for the tent.

Guy lines should be at ground level at the peg with the peg pushed in right up to the hook

Position the runners so there's room for adjustment and check them regularly to make sure they're not loosening or getting too tight.

Once the tent is fully up, adjust the pegs and guys so that they are positioned as far out as possible (this also maximises tripping potential); a taut tent means the outer will not be touching the inner, so a dry inner tent.

If you expect a lot of rainfall dig a drainage moat around the tent for excess water to collect in and then flow away (some camp sites don't like people doing this).

Top Tip

Tent stuff sacks are light weight so can blow away. Weigh them down with unused pegs or put them in a pocket.

If strong winds are forecast, place a rock over the peg (but not touching the guy line, as

the sawing motion may cut through the guy.) Or, double peg your main anchor points (guys, corners, seams etc) Place two pegs through

the elastic or guy but make them cross each other at a good angle, keeping the correct angle to the guy.

Alternatively connect an 18 inch length of paracord to the anchor point and run it past the peg maintaining the same line, so if one pulls out, it's backed up by the second.

A tent is a living thing, so if the tent is to be pitched for a few days, keep checking it and adjusting the pegs and guy lines.

To avoid tripping over guy ropes, tie a plastic bag half way up them.

Sleeping Kit

As soon as the tent is pitched and secure get the sleeping kit sorted. Unroll the sleeping mat, and if it's self inflating, open valve and lay it flat out on the tent floor so it can start to inflate.

Once the mat is inflated and the valve closed, unpack the sleeping bag, place it on the mat and give it a good shake to allow it to regain its loft. If possible open it up a little to allow some air into it.

Moving In

So tent is pitched and secure, sleeping kit is airing, and you are still in your bike gear. So now its time to take everything required off the bike and move in. If the tent has a good sized porch it may be possible to put panniers and roll bag in there keeping the living quarters tidy for sleeping. Time to get changed into 'normal' clothes.

Maintaining Camp

This is a bit of a broad title, but it's really an all encompassing heading for things that need doing at camp, and items that will assist in making a camping trip more fun and or easier. Cooking, lighting, seating, hygiene and general organisation are all in this section.

Lighting

Now unless you are camping up in the land of the midnight sun, there are no two ways about it, some form of illumination will be required; from after dark reading/journal writing, walking back to camp from a pub, late evening socialising, to a late trip to the loo etc.

There are many different options including handheld torches, Mag lights, oil lamps, head torches, candles, LED cluster lights. Any light that has a naked flame has to be removed from the list straight away due to fire hazards. (As nice as they may be to look at).

Normal handheld torches are good for light, but can be weighty, large and need a hand to hold them where you want the light. Small Mag lights are not too bad as they are light and small and produce a decent beam of light.

Head torch – now this is the way to go for personal light. Compact, shines light where you look and are hands free. Things have come a long way since the ever faithful Petzl Zoom head torch, which was quite large, weighty and ran off Duracell MN1203 4.5v batteries.

Now modern head torches are compact, light weight and LED based so the batteries last for much longer.

Before making a choice of headtorch areas that need to be looked at are price; batteries, bulbs and burn time; features.

Bulbs used tend to be Tungsten, Halogen, Xenon and Krypton and LED. Tungsten bulbs are not that bright and don't actually last a long time. Halogen bulbs give the brightest output but also eat battery life like it's going out of fashion. Xenon and Krypton bulbs are commonly found in headtorches and give good battery life without compromising the brightness. The longest burning times comes from LED bulbs that last over 20x longer than the others put together!

Headtorches are available from all good outdoor shops with prices reflecting quality and make. £10 for a HiGear Mini Headlight; £13 for a Wynnster 12 LED headtorch with a burn time of 30 hours; LED Lenser H5 at £40 has a light range of about 170ft; Petzl Myo RXP at £70 with all the bells and whistles.

LED cluster lights are quite good value and are quite multifunctional 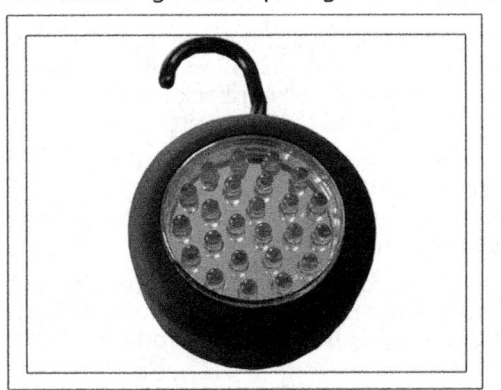 with integrated hook and magnet. They can be picked up for about £5 from most outdoor shops. One of the popular makes is Sunncamp. If the tent has an apex hook then these little lights are great to hook up. And it's easily found in the dark. They are cheap and cheerful, but are quite handy.

If there is more than one biker, then some form of social light is always a nicety and a bit of a luxury. A small LED lantern is always nice to illuminate the area. Space and weight is always an issue with luxury items.

Top Tip

If the tent has pockets along the inner, always put the torch in the same pocket last thing at night. Then if required later in the night there is no fumbling around trying to find it.

Seating

Seating really can be an issue with riders when camping. Some take nothing at all, some take foldable chairs, others small stools; on top of this some spend three or four pounds while others spend quite a few pounds.

If you think about taking nothing and are going to sit on the floor or crouch, then you will regret it. (You could always sit on a pannier). Having somewhere to sit once the camp site is set up is luxury, but it really is needed.

Don't just look at the seat when it's unfolded; look at the pack size and the weight, as these are important when packing for touring.

There is a massive range of options here from a simple three leg fold out stool for £4 or £5 from most outdoor shops (pack size 30x30x43 and weights 780g);

Quechua Low Chair from Decathlon at £9.99 (pack size 17x17x58 and weights 1.9Kg); the Helinox Chair One direct from Oz at £65 + shipping, import duty and VAT (pack size 35x10x12 and weighs 897g) or Amazon at £80; to the Kermit Chair at over £90 + shipping, import duty and VAT (which could make the final cost over £140 plus!) (10x15x60 and weights 2.4Kg).

There are quite a few makes and models in the £5 to £15 bracket that fit the scope of light weight and small pack size.

Cooking

Some bikers who tour and camp never cook! At the end of the day they setup camp, get washed and changed and then off to a café/pub/restaurant for food. That's great if they are available and the pub is always good for a beer to two.

But if there is no easy way of getting to food when camping, then you need to have the facilities to cook your own. It doesn't have to be complicated, but at the same time it doesn't have to be boil in the bag every night. (And unless you are short of water and/or cooking fuel, don't use the same water to make a coffee!)

Always try to make sure you have a couple of day's food on the bike. That way all bases will be covered; pub, café or cooking at the campsite. If the camp is going to be a base for a few days a walk to a local shop to buy provisions is always a good way to spend some time. While there, look for different menu options so food intake is varied.

Kit

There is so much kit out there these days to choose from that a lot is down to personal choice. There is no need to buy the most expensive of everything (just because the sales man says so) – just grow into what's best for you.

One thing is for sure – everyone will tell you that theirs is the best!

Stoves & Pan Sets

When looking for a stove for use when motorcycle touring look at ones designed for hiking campers as having a nice dual ring with grill is just not an option. Stoves need to be lightweight and compact, and make the most of the space they do take up in your luggage.

The cheapest and very cheerful option would be a small solid-fuel stove (hexi blocks). These are lightweight and small, but are slower to cook on, leave your pots black, it takes a lot of fuel tablets to generate any decent heat and are totally uncontrollable. On a plus side they can be picked up for about £5 from most outdoor shops.

Alcohol/Meths or Trangia System - All-included systems from Trangia and other brands include a small meths burning pot and a system to collect the heat and feed it up through pans. Meths stoves take a bit longer than gas or petrol stoves to heat up food and water, but they are cheap to run. The flame from the burner is often invisible so care needs to be taken. When burning meths, pots will have a tendency to retain a black residue on the outside (to reduce this add a bit of water to the meths). Because of their design meths stoves cook food faster when it's windy.

All the pots/kettle/burner all fit inside one another and pack into one item. A gas adaptor for Trangia's can be bought separately; it's expensive but very good, and allows for two fuel types to be used.

Prices vary depending on which version/size the 27-2UL is a one to two person size, and comes with two 1ltr pans, a non stick frying pan, pan handle, a kettle, meths burner, simmer ring and upper and lower windshields.

A gas stove has the advantage of being easy to use, heats food and water very quickly and doesn't make your pots black. They are

lightweight and tend to pack away quite neatly.

A gas stove with a hosepipe attachment is probably better than the ones that simply screw on top of a gas bottle. Having the burner close to the ground usually results in a more stable setup and there is less chance of your long-awaited dinner ending up spilled over the grass. However for the lightest pack weight, screw on top stoves generally are better. Try to get a stove that uses self seal screw on gas canisters, as these can be swapped and changed easily. They do loose power as the canister pressure runs down.

Gas canisters are widely available throughout the UK & Europe. Outdoors stores and campsite shops almost always have a selection of different sizes to suit the length of trip you are going to take.

The Coleman F1 lightweight is a good example of a screw top type burner, and weighing only 77g once packed it's totally un-noticeable. RRP £25, but can be purchased for less.

Multi Fuel Stoves – These are efficient and cheap to run, they boil water in no time and many of them can run on a variety of different fuels such as unleaded petrol, Coleman fuel, white fuel, kerosene or aviation fuel and others. So while ever you have a bike fuel tank with petrol in, you can cook.

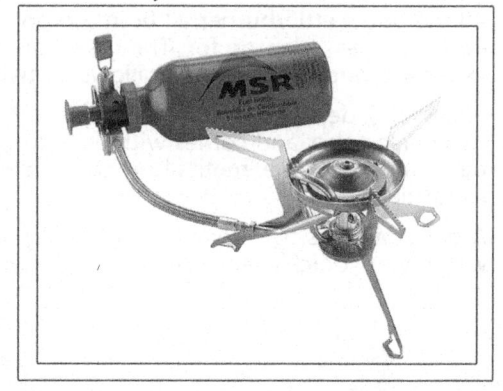

The downside to these stoves is that depending on which fuel used, they can require a bit of maintenance to keep the burners clear and running properly. They are also heavier than other stoves mentioned here at 309g. It can also be a bit daunting the first time you use a petrol camping stove as the whole pumping, priming then fully lighting process seems fairly complex (oh and the noise and smell!) Once it's been done a couple of times it becomes easier.

The MSR Whisperlite at RRP£100 available from all good outdoor shops is a great example of a multi fuel burner.

For a petrol stove a proper fuel bottle is required. See Transporting Liquids section.

As mentioned previously, buy what is right for you. For ease of use its gas. For compact all-in-one units buy meths. For performance and flexibility buy petrol/multi fuel. And if you feel a bit manly then go for it and build a fire! (Check with the campsite first).

If the stove of choice is not a Trangia all in one system then some form of pan set will be required.

A pan set (as its name suggests) is a set of pans that will be used with the stove for cooking. Normally the pots and pans nestle inside each other like a Russian doll to save on space. With any outdoors kit there is a balance between having something long-lasting and durable, and having a low pack weight. Aluminium is typically used as it is a lightweight material, but it is easily dented. On the other hand stainless steel or titanium cookware sets are a tougher alternative to aluminium, but are heavier, in the case of stainless steel, or more expensive, in the case of titanium. And is a titanium cook set really necessary when bike camping?

They are available from all camping shops, army surplus shops and websites like Amazon.

Depending on budget, or if it's a first time cooking and camping there are many different makes and types of pan set – there is no reason why you have to start out with the most expensive set. Sometimes it's good to spend a little money first to see if it's for you before splashing out on the latest titanium pan set.

Ideally a pan set should have a couple of pans and maybe a small frying pan. A kettle is a nicety (but you can boil water in a pan). In its most basic form a pan set consists of a mess tin; simple no frills cooking.

For a simple basic pan set the HiGear festival set is good enough to get you going. It contains two mess tins, one folding solid fuel stove, some solid fuel and a simple knife, fork and spoon all for £10

Some people swear by keeping it all very cheap and simple, and use a basic aluminium pan set from the likes of Trekmates (see picture). They are tough, light, no frills and do what it says on the tin. If anything gets lost or broken it's cost effective to just buy another set at less than £10.

In the £10 to £30 bracket there are so many makes, styles coatings to choose from; there will be a pan set in this bracket to suit almost everyone. Makes include Coleman, Outwell, GSI, MSR, HiGear, Gelert, Quechua, Vango, and others.

The Quechua 1-person non-stick cookset looks like good value at £13 when compared to a similar offering from Touratech at £91! The Quechua set is about twice as heavy at 720g, but even this is not that heavy.

The MSR Quick 2 System is a versatile multi-part cookware system. With a choice of multiple plates and mugs, it will easily serve a couple of bikers, and its non-stick, so very easy to clean and maintain. It includes: 1.5L Duralite

DX Pot, 2.5L Hard Anodised Pot, with strainer lid, Talon Pot Handle, 2x Polypropylene Deep Dish Plates, 2x 35.4 gram insulated mugs. Weight: approx. 800g and pack size: approx. 13x20 cm. Available from camping and outdoor shops from about £67 or Touratech for £102.

Whatever set is being thought about, look at the way the handles work. Are they fold out thin plastic coated wire handles, fold out rigid ones, or is a separate claw handle used. There are pros and cons for all types, so have a play in the shop to see which you could work with while cooking at a camp.

When camping by yourself a little bit of weight can be saved by making simple one pot meals and eat from the pan. Saves carrying a plate and saves on washing up.

This is now going to sound daft, but don't forget a mug - It has been done! Mugs come in all shapes and types but a titanium mug for £52 is pushing the envelope a bit. Plastic or metal, but never the best china, as long as it holds coffee then job done.

Knives, forks and spoons are simple items that some campers think good money needs to be spent on (not sure why). A simple fit together steel cutlery set can be bought from most camping shops for about £3 a more refined light weight set for £20 or a super light weight titanium set for £45.

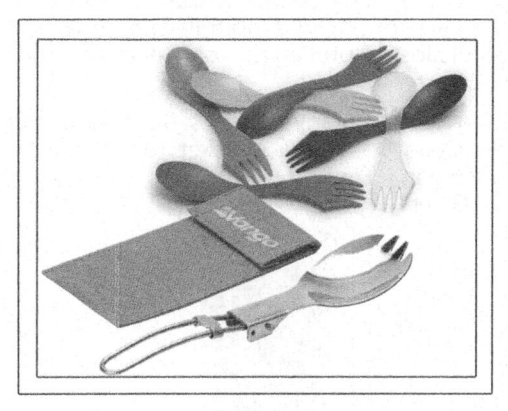

To keep things simple, the ever handy sporks are a fantastic little item. Spoon, fork and a small cutting edge all in one handy item. Plastic ones are available from all outdoor and camping shops for a couple of pounds. Taking it to the next level is the Vango foldable metal spork. Made of stainless steel, folds in half and weighs 60g.

BBQ

If the camp is to be a base camp for a few days then a BBQ is a great way to get that real outdoor smokey taste without having to build a fire.

Simple one use disposable BBQ's are available from nearly all supermarkets for a few pounds for some impromptu BBQ fun; just remember some campsites don't like you burning their grass, so sit it on some bricks.

Another option is a small portable barbecue. The Grilliput barbecue is a cracking bit of kit. It's fully collapsible and when packed down its 11.5"x 1" and weighs 590g. The fire bowl packs down to 7"x7"x3" and weighs 370g. It can be used with wood or charcoal/lump wood.

Not a cheap item with the griddle at about £30 and the firebowl at £15.

This is a 100% luxury item for when you want to do something totally different at a base camp or on a wild camp. It won't replace a good camping stove, but if the weather is right then nothing can beat it.

Food Prep

Before any cooking can take place some basics need to be gathered together. With a few basic utensils quite a wide range of food can be cooked on a camp stove or BBQ.

Knives x2 (1 basic cooks knife in a sheath 1 multi tool knife)	Baco Cook in Bags
A small non stick spatula	Kitchen Roll
Spork	Sanitising Hand Gel*
Olive oil (in a small plastic squirt bottle)*	Water Carrier
Spice mix/mixed herbs (in a small plastic bottle)	Washing Up Liquid*
Self seal sandwich bags	Washing up Scrubbie
Medium Freezer Bags	Chopping Board
Lighter or Matches	Can Opener

* decant into small plastic bottles

Cooking Knife

Don't take the best kitchen knife from home, go and buy one from a supermarket for a couple or three pounds and then keep it with the bike trip gear. Make a simple sheath out of some cardboard and gaffa tape.

Non Stick Spatula

Not really a necessity, but it does come in handy for all types of stuff, 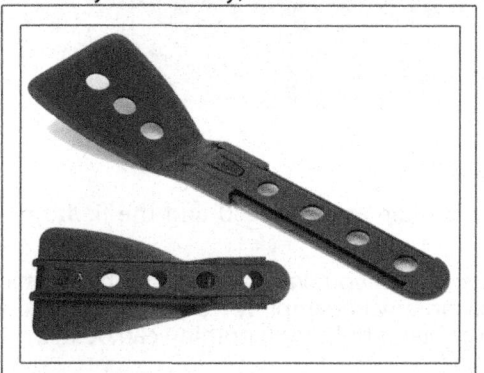 and if the frying pan in the cookset is non-stick it will help to prolong its life as it shouldn't scratch like metal would. They fold down, weigh almost nothing and can easily be packed with the panset being only about 8cm when folded down.

Chopping Board

Ones designed for lightweight camping can be bought, but are very thin. Buy a cheap plastic chopping board from a supermarket, cut it down to size and it will slip into a pannier with no fuss and minimal weight.

Top Tip

Cut out a circle just a little smaller than the frying pan from a cheap plastic kitchen chopping board. Then it can fit inside the frying pan when the cook set is all packed up. Another way to save a little space.

Water Carrier

When camping in the same spot for a few days these are great items and much better than bottles as when they are empty they reduce in size. Try to look for a soft plastic roll up type as these pack up better than the hard plastic type.

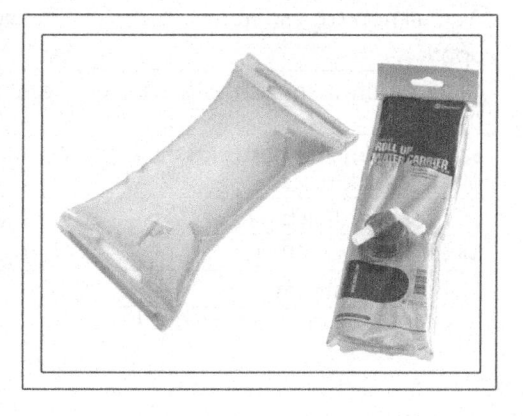

They hold about 10ltrs, which is quite a bit of water. Having a supply of water close by is always handy when cooking.

 **Top Tip**

Before the first use, wash it out with warm water and baking soda! You may have to do this a couple of times, but it works. Two teaspoons of baking soda, fill it up with water, give it a good shake, rinse, repeat and perfect drinking water. Otherwise the water will taste real bad.

Before moving on after breaking camp, empty and wrap in a bin bag just to be double sure no water dribbles out.

Can Opener

If you are right handed then there should be no problems here as there will be one on the multi tool. If you are left handed then you either need to pack a can opener that works for left handed operation, or simply look at the cans you buy first to see if they have a ring pull. Doing this also saves carrying another item.

Kitchen Roll

You can never have too much kitchen roll! If the panniers have space at the top after packing, put a couple of rolls in there. They will help to stop things moving in the panniers when riding, and once at camp they will get used.

Sandwich bags (self seal)

These bags can get used for all sorts when camping; wrapping food for a later date, wrapping bread to help stop it going stale etc. Always have a few handy just in case.

Olive Oil

Decant some into a small plastic squeeze bottle. Before packing wrap in a self seal sandwich bag (just in case). Can be used for cooking, a salad dressing or just to dip bread in.

Ketchup/Mustard/Brown Sauce/Salt/Pepper

Don't pack bottles of these, they take up space and add weight. Whenever you go into a café either just before the trip or during the trip, pick up a couple of sachets extra of what you might fancy, or need for the evenings cooking.

Coffee/Tea/Sugar/Milk

It goes without saying that these need to be packed. Decant coffee from a large jar into a small plastic one (don't carry glass jars). Sugar can either be carried in a zip loc bag or another plastic container. Milk; either learn to go without or have powdered until you are at a camp for a few days.

Hygiene

Sometimes when riding and camping, people can easily forget about food hygiene if soap and water is hard to come by. Because of this

some campers may not wash their hands as thoroughly and as often as they would at home. Also basic food management (cross contamination) sometimes suffers. This could result in bad stomach aches or worse.

It may sometimes be difficult to do, but always follow good food hygiene practices. Wash hands well after any visit to the loo. Always pack a small bottle of antibacterial hand sanitising gel. Small 50ml plastic bottles can be picked up from all good supermarkets (Aldi 70p), out door or camping shops.

Wash hands again before starting to cook. Make sure the chopping board is clean. Wash hands straight after handing any raw meat. Wash any food prep items that have been used with raw meat straight after to avoid cross contamination.

Once cooking and eating has finished clean up the area, wash all pots and pans and pack away. Don't leave them lying around for later, and definitely don't leave them overnight.

Put any leftovers in a sandwich bag and seal up before putting in a bin.

Recipe ideas

When the weather is nice sunny and warm, why would you want to boil a packet of 'food' and then use the same plastic flavoured water to make a coffee. Try and move away from this whenever possible.

Saying that, there are some good quality pre-packed food lines available. The 'look what we found' range is good and because it's packaged in a pouch it packs better than a can. Available from most supermarkets. So buy a pouch when it's on offer to have in your pannier as a standby meal.

Mug Shots in pouches are another handy standby. Hot pasta and sauce in a mug in five minutes.

Breakfast All Wrapped Up

Serves 2	Pots 2
Cooking level *	Washing up level *

This is a cracking chilled way to start a great day on the bike – sat outside the tent with a breakfast wrap in your hand.

Pack of Tortilla Wraps Chutney 4 Eggs 4 Rashers of Bacon 4 Sausages 4 Slices of Black Pudding Mushrooms 2 Big Toms

1. Hard boil the eggs, cool, peel and roughly chop
2. Chop bacon, sausages, black pudding and mushrooms and fry until cooked
3. Spread chutney onto tortillas
4. Fill with egg and fry-up mix
5. Wrap it all up and enjoy with a nice hot coffee

M's Spicy Sausage Stew

Serves 2 to 3	Pots 2
Cooking level **	Washing up level ***

If you fancy a twist on a chilli out of a can then this is the one for you

1 TBSP oil
3 Chicken Breasts
1 Can Chopped Tomatoes in Chilli Sauce
1 Can of Chilli Beans
½ Onion
½ Courgette
Rice – Uncle Bens Express Rice
OR Normal Rice

1. Pour a little of the oil into a pan and brown the chicken on both sides.

2. Drain away any excess fat. Pour in can of toms and beans. Stir, cover and cook over a gentle heat for about 20 mins until chicken is cooked. Meanwhile, dice the onion and courgette.

3. Heat remaining oil in a pan, add the onion and courgette and cook till soft.

4. Add the rice and cook for a minute.

5. Add 30ml of water, bring to the boil, and then simmer for 3 mins. Serve the rice with the chicken and sauce.

Note:

If using normal rice at #4 add 200g long grain rice. Cook for 1 min, pour 550ml of water, stir and cook at a simmer for 15 to 20 min.

Pitta Bread and Houmous

Serves 1	Pots 0
Cooking level *	Washing up level *

Can't be bothered to cook, but fancy a nibble

Packet of Pita Breads
Big Tub of Houmous
2 Carrots
Rocket leaves

1. Finely slice the carrots

2. Open bread down one long edge and spoon in some homous. Add carrots and leaves

3. Dip in and relax

For more cooking ideas see the sister book to this, 'One Motorbike, One Tent and I'm Hungry'.

It contains a great selection of recipe ideas, designed for camping and using only a Trangia and occasionally a BBQ for a cooker. All the recipes have sensible cooking times, unlike some campsite recipes that say..."and simmer for 2 hours".

Available from Lulu, Amazon and www.2bikes1mission.co.uk/books

One Motorbike, One Tent & I'm Hungry

a camping cookbook & journal for motorcyclists (yes some of us do need one!)

Richard Mawson

End of the Day

When its time to call it a day, there are still a few things that should be done before finally getting into the sleeping bag.

Have one final look around to make sure all gear and unused food/beer/wine etc has been packed away. If there has been a camp fire or BBQ make sure it's properly extinguished. If there is any rubbish then have a quick collect up and put it in a bin bag (its easier and more hygienic to keep tidying up as you go than to have litter laying around). Oh and go to the loo!

Try not to enter the tent with outdoor boots on; at the end of the day open the tent and leave them in the porch or put one either side of the door under the flysheet. Every effort should be made to keep the inner tent clean and dry.

Try to get into a routine and do the same every night. If the tent has pockets running along the inner, always put a torch there so it's easy to find. Make sure valuables are inside the inner with you. If you use a bumbag for valuables then move this into the sleeping area with you. If there are any electricals that need charging, then sort them out.

Not until all the little tasks that need doing are done should you get into the sleeping bag. That way once you are in, you are in.

Striking Camp

Routines are everything when camping, and striking camp is no different. After a few times everyone develops their own routine for packing away and moving on.

In an ideal world it will be a dry sunny day when packing away, but it's not always the case, so plan a routine that keeps gear as dry and clean as possible for as long as possible.

First job is to pack away all the sleeping gear – so sleeping bags rolled into stuff bags, sleeping mats rolled and packed.

One of the best ways to strike camp when on a bike is to do it with bike clothes on. That way all clothing can be packed inside the tent keeping it clean and dry.

When the tent is empty its ready to be taken down. If it's wet try to shake or wipe off as much moisture as possible. Reverse the pitching routine to get the tent back into its stuff bag. If the tent is packed wet then put the stuff bag into a bin bag before packing. Finally the footprint needs to be shaken and re-packed.

At this point everything should be round the bike ready for packing onto it. Panniers, roll bag and any other 'on bike' luggage. Before starting to pack the bike have a quick look around to make sure nothing small has been left laying around.

Now another routine of packing the bike comes into play. Take your time and get everything loaded onto the bike they way you have developed. Make sure everything is secure and/or locked. See Packing The Bike section for more information.

Before setting off take one last look around to make sure nothing has been left (tent pegs lying in the grass are the usual) and there is no litter.

From start to finish (at a leisurely pace) it should take no longer than about 40 to 45 minutes to strike camp and be sat on the bike ready to ride.

Top Tip

Lay the tent stuff bag near to where you are packing the tent so you have an idea of the final size it has to be.

Fold in reverse order from how it came out, and it will go back in the stuff bag easily.

There is always at least one stubborn tent peg that refuses to come out. If you have a peg extractor, then use it; otherwise get another peg and run it through the loop of the stuck peg and pull the horizontal peg.

Camp Sites

Most of the time pre-booking campsites is not required, just turn up, register and pick a spot. There is something nice about just turning up somewhere – it all adds to the adventure.

If you have no pre-booked accommodation or pre-researched location of a campsite, always start thinking about where to spend the night by about 3.30 in the afternoon at the latest.

Camping is a lot more popular in Europe than in the UK, so there is quite a good selection of sites. Sites range from the quite simple (almost basic) through to the full on sites with restaurants, bars, swimming pools etc. The price you pay is usually reflected in the facilities and the time of year.

During the months of July and August though, they do get very busy as these are the months everyone takes their summer holidays, also the weekends can get a little hectic towards the end of May and June. So start looking for possible overnight stops a little earlier than normal, just in case the first option is full there will be time to find another.

Also be aware that some campsites don't actually open until May on the continent, especially in northern Italy.

ELECTRICALS

As people now carry with them so many electrical items, there needs to be a way to power them or recharge them whilst touring. There is not always a handy dandy mains socket available for plugging things in to recharge (but if the night is spent in a B&B then first job is to plug everything in to re-charge). First thing to look at though is the current draw of all the items. Then to look at how many different adaptors will be required. Maybe look at a multi charger with adaptors. The plus side is only one set of cables; the down side is only being able to charge one item at a time.

Quick list of possible items: Phone; Camera; SatNav; GPS; Tablet; NetBook; BlueTooth headset; MP3 player; Bike to Bike Comms.

Bike charging

If the bike has a factory fitted 12v take off point (either traditional or the BMW Powerlet/DIN style) then plug in the right adaptor and you are away. If not, then look at fitting one, as there is a bike there with power available (see Bike Mods). Even if it's only used from time to time its handy to have.

As more items are charged via USB look at fitting a powered USB socket to the bike. They are smaller and neater than the traditional 'cigarette' style and the lead will just plug straight in with no bulky adaptor sticking out.

Try not to leave the device attached when the bike is not running.

Solar chargers

The theory behind these is great – a battery to store the electrical energy produced by the inbuilt solar panels. Then in the evening

charge any electronic devices from the battery. Next day start again.

In practise, this is fine if you are travelling under clear blue sunny sky as the battery will charge in about 8/10 hours from flat. Ride under dull conditions and it will charge but take longer.

They usually come with a charging lead and a collection of interchangeable tips to fit a multitude of devices.

Check also the current output from the battery. As items like phones have turned into smartphones their power requirements have changed. Most devices could be charged happily from a 500mA output, but now most devices require at least 1A (1000mA) to charge. So before taking the plunge check the battery can kick out what the device is going to draw. Otherwise the battery may overheat and buzz disapprovingly, or the device just will not charge.

More recent solar charges have been designed with iPads and smartphones in mind and can deliver the required current. The PowerMonkey eXtreme above, houses a 9000mAh capacity Lithium Polymer battery can deliver up to 2A. It does take 15 hours of daylight to fully charge from flat! But in practice this is not so bad, as it can be charged over several days, as one full charge can re-charge an Apple iPhone4 about 6 times. It can also be charged direct from the mains. Costs about £120.

Brands available include Freeloader and PowerMonkey and are available from larger outdoor shops, Maplins and Amazon with prices starting at about £30/40 upwards.

Power Banks

Imagine the battery section from a solar charger with (in general) a larger capacity battery and then you have a power bank. In simple terms a high capacity battery power supply. Similar to the solar chargers, they come with a collection of tips that fit several devices via one lead.

The batteries range from 5000mAh up to about 12000mAh and can kick out 5V at 2A (some of the smaller batteries only give 5v at 1A). Charging cycles depends on the device being charged but as an example, an iPhone 4 can be charged 6 times from one charge of the power bank.

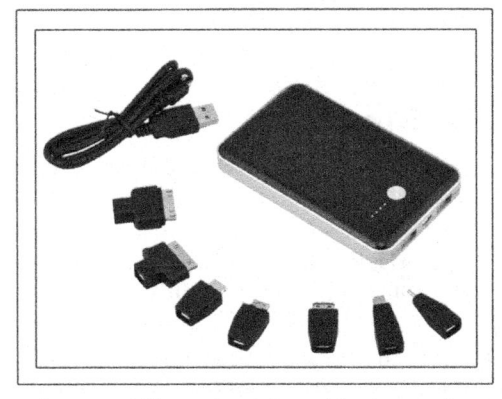

At about the size of an iPhone and weighing between 150g and 400g depending on make and capacity of battery a power bank is a simple solution to power on the road.

One of the down sides is that they do require an overnight mains charge once they are flat. But they can be trickle charged with an external solar panel if required, but this does take quite some time.

Available from several manufacturers including TeckNet, Anker, PowerGen, and available from Amazon, Maplins etc. Prices from around £16 for the smaller capacity batteries. The 12000mAh battery is about £35.

Mains Adaptors

A simple straightforward mains converter will do the trick here. Most of Europe uses the same round two pin style. But just as a curve ball Italy somehow manages to have three different types. So they fit in some but not in others!

These can be picked up from all supermarkets, outdoor shops, boots the chemist etc and on line for a few pounds.

BEFORE LEAVING HOME

As you have come to this section in the book, then planning a trip is probably already on the horizon. The book has already talked about luggage options, packing and camping.

The first proper bike trip that lasts more than a coupe of days can take some planning, even if it's in your own country. (Unless you are a credit card adventure rider!)

If it's a European adventure, then there are a few more things that need to be done before leaving home. See Paperwork & Documents, and Riding in Europe sections.

After the first trip is successfully complete, you will want more, and any trip afterwards should be easier as you will now have knowledge of planning, camp craft and what little tweaks need to happen in your kit to make it even better the next time.

Planning and Prep

Every rider will approach the planning phase of the trip differently. As it's already been mentioned - Preparation and planning is the key to most things in life, but it's a fine balance between over planning and no planning. If you want to do something well, there has to be some element of preparation involved.

Overall Planning

The best way to plan anything is to write it all down. Start a trip planning 'book' either computerised (a spreadsheet is great for it) or old fashioned pencil and paper. The main thing is to keep it up to date.

You either love them or hate them, but also start a collection of checklists and enter in all packing lists and location on the bike, items that need to still be purchased, jobs that need doing to the bike, total running cost of the trip. Some items you may already have, if so tick them off the list and start collecting things together ready for packing.

Possible Checklist Headings

Tool Kit	First Aid Kit
Clothing (casual)	Security
Clothing (bike)	Paperwork & Documents
Wash Kit	Food Prep / Cooking
Camping & Sleeping	Navigation
Miscellaneous	Electrical

Then break the headings down into individual items ready to be checked off. See specific sections for breakdown, or Checklist Example Section (it can look quite a lot, but most of it is small items which pack into stuff bags).

Once a route is in the planning enter possible daily routes with towns and road numbers into the trip planning book as well.

Riding Buddies or Solo

Most riders will instinctively know if they want to ride solo, with a riding buddy, two up on the bike with their partner, or going with an organised tour group.

Riding Solo

Going on any bike trip solo really can offer maximum flexibility. Follow your own thoughts for a route, stop for a coffee when you want, camp where and when you want, make a detour and have a walk round somewhere when you see a sign.

Riding solo really can expose you to the culture of the country you are riding through. You and you alone will have to communicate with people which can really be part of the overall fun of the trip. People usually see a lone biker as less of a threat so will readily come over and chat, or try to help out if you get lost or have any issues.

Riding solo on the whole can give you the full in your face raw experience of motorcycle touring and camping; no little bubble of your home country to keep you safe.

The obvious downside to riding solo is that you are more vulnerable if things don't quite go to plan. (Mechanical, health, safety, navigation etc). Drop the bike, and there is no one there to help pick it up and give you an encouraging pat on the back if all is ok. No familiar face to share in the highs or lows of the trip.

Being alone for long stretches of time is really not for some riders, but for others it's what turns a trip into an adventure.

Riding Buddy

Travelling along and seeing your riding buddy in the mirror or in front of you is as good a feeling as anything. Instantly you feel secure, all

issues, and problems are halved. It gives a much greater level of security that only comes with a group of two or more. Having someone there to share in the highs or lows of the trip really helps with personal morale.

If you are new to motorcycle touring then this is a great way to learn and gain experience, especially if your chosen riding buddy already has some knowledge.

If there are two (or more) and you get on, (personality, riding style and goals from the trip) then there is nothing better than being able to share them.

As with most things there are some downsides. The interaction with locals tends to drop away as you tend to talk more with your riding buddy. This in turn stops locals feeling as secure with you, so tend not to come and interact or to your aid. Route planning has to be a joint decision; there are always different roads and places riders want to see and do; so a bit of give and take is required. At worst there may develop a bad personality clash that only develops after a few days. These need to be sorted as soon as possible to keep the trip a success.

Communication when on the road with others can present problems. For the hi-tech option start looking at bike to bike comms units using either wireless or Bluetooth systems.

If riding with others then plan a system of very simple hand signals so fellow riders know when someone needs petrol or a coffee break etc.

Route Planning

Planning the route is all part of the whole adventure. Time to get the maps out and start seeing a route take shape.

As well as traditional maps Google maps is very good when it comes to route planning. The zoom feature is great as it can show all the twists and turns of the route selected. It does have a couple of downsides; take its timings with a large pinch of salt as it assumes top legal speed on all roads; it can't factor in breaks or overnight stops so the route just becomes one large block of time.

An alternative is MS Autoroute. With this you can pre-program speeds, coffee breaks, overnight stops and fuel costs. The maps aren't as up to date as Google, but it gives a better indication of speed, time and distance.

Everyone's riding styles and fatigue thresholds are different, but in general try not to plan many days which involve 350+ miles, especially if it's the first trip on the continent. Be realistic in your daily mileages and do not overstretch yourself.

If covering long distances, try to break the day up with some motorway and then some time on scenic roads.

Don't expect to be doing huge daily mileage if travelling through mountains. The roads are slow and twisty and there will be plenty of stops for photos. Time can always be made up with a section of motorway riding if available.

Take time to 'gen up' on your chosen route and see what places of interest there are along it that may be worth either stopping at or taking a detour for.

For maps and SatNav; See Navigation section.

Documentation

For trips within the UK you don't have to carry copies of all the bike documentation, insurance etc. But always have your driving license and breakdown card with you on any trip.

For European trips see Paperwork & Documents section.

Gear

See bike clothing; camping.

One or Two Months Before

Routines

Start getting used to always putting items in the same place. For example bike keys always go in the top left pocket of trousers; money, top right trouser pocket; phone inside jacket pocket. It's a simple idea, but you will never loose your bike keys again.

Test pitch tent

This is especially relevant if the tent is a new one. It will give you practice in how to pitch it and if there are issues time to sort them. For an existing tent it's more of a quick check to make sure all is as it should be.

Shakedown trip

If time allows a shakedown trip is always a good idea before a long bike trip. This is a pre-trip trip with the fully loaded and fuelled bike where all the bike gear, packing system, camping kit, and bike can be tested. It gives an opportunity to check out any modifications you have made to the bike; is the packing system right; is the seat comfy; are items in the panniers in the best place. What should have been packed and what could be left behind for the main trip are also areas to look at.

There are so many things that a shakedown trip can highlight if you have never packed for touring and camping before.

Try to make it at least an overnighter and if the main trip is with a companion, try to do the shakedown together.

Check docs

All documents should have already been checked by now, but a final check should be done just in case something has been missed. Start to collect them all together ready for the trip, scan them and upload them onto a MEkey ICE tag as a backup.

Kit

Make sure you know how to use all the technical kit being taken. There is nothing worst than learning how to use something at the side of a road.

Two Weeks Before

Bike Service

Either take it in for a full service or do it yourself.

Final test pack.

This should be the tweaked version of any packing issues that were highlighted from the shakedown trip.

Day Before

Fill Up

Pack

CHECKLIST EXAMPLE

This is an example checklist NOT a definitive list. Use it as a base to get you started and then tailor it up or down to your specific requirements.

Tool Kit	MOT (if required)
Original Bike Toolkit	Bike Service Manual
Bike Repair Manual	Bike User Manual
Chain Wax (small can)	Breakdown Cover
Puncture Repair Kit	EHIC Card
Length of Wire (for electrical work)	Ferry/Tunnel Tickets or Booking Ref
Length of Heavy Gauge Wire	Extra Personal Travel Insurance
Small Selection of Nuts & Bolts	Money
Electrical Spares (bulbs/fuses/choc bloc)	**First Aid**
Tyre Leavers	Antiseptic wipes/Antiseptic cream
Right Angle Valve Adaptor	Sterile or vinyl gloves
Spanners (only sizes that fit bike!)	Plasters
Screwdrivers (cross & flat head)	Sterile plasters
Allen / Torx keys	Micropore tape
Pliers	Gauze bandages
Gaffa Tape	Gauze pads
PVC Electrical Tape	Safety pins
Knife / Multi Tool	Small low-adherent dressing
Tyre Pressure Gauge	Woven bandage
Rag	Small crepe bandage
Chain Wax (small can)	Scissors & tweezers
WD40 (small can)	Safety pins
Oil (engine)	Small low-adherent dressing
Cable Ties (assorted)	Woven bandage
Surgical Gloves	Small crepe bandage
Spark Plugs	Scissors & tweezers
Spare Packing Straps	Pain relief (Paracetamol/Ibuprofen etc)
Small Air Compressor	Antacids
Paperwork & Documents	Anti diarrhoea medication
Passport	Rehydrating salts/tablets
Driving Licence	Burn gel/cream
V5c	Insect bite relief
Bike Insurance	Prescription medicine

First Aid Cont	Shampoo
Blister pads	Micro Fibre Towel x2
Foil blankets	Feminine Hygiene
Aftersun	Contact Lens Solution
Lemsip Max (a couple of sachets)	Wash Cloth
Antihistamines	**Camping/Sleeping**
Clothing (Casual)	Tent / Poles / Pegs
T-Shirts	Groudsheet
Long Sleeved Fleece	Roll Mat
Trousers (ideally not jeans)	Sleeping Bag / Liner / Inflatable Pillow
Shorts	Camp Tools
Approach Boots	Stool
Walking Sandals (if destination is hot)	Head Torch
Hat	LED Backup torch
Underwear	Multi Knife
Socks (not bike)	**Cooking**
Waterproof Jacket	Stove / Fuel
Clothing (Bike)	Pan Set
Bike Jacket	Knives x2
Bike Trousers	A small non stick spatula
Boots	Olive oil (in a small plastic squirt bottle)
Gloves	Spice mix/mixed herbs
Helmet	Self seal sandwich bags
Base Layer / Underwear	Medium Freezer Bags
Mid Layer	Baco Cook in Bags
Bike Sox	Kitchen Roll
Ear Plugs	Sanitising Hand Gel
Buff	Water Carrier (roll up type)
MEkey ICE Tag	Washing Up Liquid
Wash Kit	Washing up Scrubbie
Toilet Paper	Chopping Board
Baby Wipes	Spork
Small Bar of Soap	Knife / Fork / Spoon
Toothbrush*	Mug / Plate
Toothpaste	Coffee / Tea / Sugar / Powdered Milk
Universal Sink Plug	Matches / Lighter
Deodorant	**Navigation**
Hairbrush	Maps
Razor/Shaver	SatNav / GPS
Shaving Cream	Route Plan
Shower Gel	Anaglog SatNav / Cards / Pen

Electrical	Avon Skin So Soft
Solar Charger or Power Bank	Lip Balm
Continental Mains Adaptor	Insect Repellent
USB Multi Charger & adaptors OR	Sun Glasses
Individual Chargers	On Bike Snacks (Cereal Bars / Jelly Babies)
12V Adaptor for the bike	Sigg Bottle for on bike drinking water
Phone	Money
Camera	Visor Cleaner (small bottle)
Communications	Side Stand Puck
MP3 Player	
Security	
Bike Cable Lock	
Lightweight Cable Lock	
Bike Cover (plain)	
Disc Lock	
Miscellaneous	
Bike Keys	
Spare Bike Keys inc Spare Alarm Fob	
Memory Cards For Camera	
Pen / Note Book	

SECURITY

It's a sad thing to have to say, but whenever you stop (sightseeing, shopping, meals or for long periods) don't leave anything on the bike or easily accessible. Even if the SatNav/GPS is in a locked bracket, take it out. The less there is to tempt the safer the bike will be.

Depending on where you end up parking for the night think about taking along a basic plain dark bike cover. Its amazing how these can make the bike almost invisible. If nothing else it should stop the occasional fiddler pressing switches and the like as they go past. For a little added security or if paranoia kicks in when camping or in a really cheap motel, take the panniers off the bike then use a cable lock to fasten them together or to a fixed item in the room.

Bike Cable Lock*	Bike Cover (plain & dark)
Lightweight Cable Lock**	Disc Lock

*A bike cable lock does not have to be a heavy weight type, just something good enough to satisfy paranoia. They can coil up and sit in the bottom of a pannier quite easily.

** These are very handy as a back up or for locking panniers together. Ones used for tying laptops down are quite good, or a small extendable one from the likes of PacSafe or LifeSystems

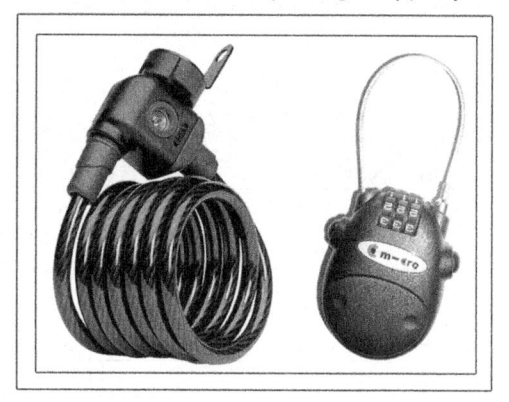

A basic lightweight bike cover can be picked up for about £10. They usually come with a stuff bag, so can be packed down nice and small. Always look for a plain darker colour to help with the blending in. Don't take a bright orange one with KTM written all over it!

PAPERWORK & DOCUMENTS

If you were/are planning on setting off on a round the world trip there would be quite a lot of paper work to assemble, including visas, carnets, insurance, maybe an international driving licence, inoculation certificates and others.

For a European trip it's a little less daunting, but it still needs checking and organising in plenty of time. Don't leave sorting out documents and paperwork while the day before. As soon as the bike trip is planned start organising the paperwork and checking expiry dates.

Always take the original documents with you. Try to keep them on you all the time (maybe in a waist bag) and put them in a sealed plastic bag. Also make colour scans of them and keep them in a sealed plastic wallet on the bike as a handy backup. Its easier (but still a pain) to replace if anything is lost if you have a full copy of the original.

A final backup and for your reference, all the below documents should be scanned, then uploaded & encrypted onto a MEkey ICE tag. Then if the worst happens you will still have copies of all the information (along with personal and medical information; and emergency contact details).

See ICE In Case of Emergency section.

Below is a quick table showing required documentation for Europe

Passport	Breakdown Cover
Driving Licence	EHIC Card
V5c	Ferry/Tunnel Tickets or Booking Ref Number & Times
Bike Insurance	Extra Personal Travel Insurance
MOT (if required)	Money
Bike Service Manual*	Bike User Manual*

* pdf format

Passport

At this point many people are be saying "Who would leave without their passport", but it is an item that A) may need to be found; B) check its not expired (and has a further six months after return); C) needs to be applied for and D) does need packing.

Most of the time passports are only shown when leaving the UK and re-entering. The rest of the time in western Europe you can just ride from country to country. But always have it handy as there are the occasional border checks, so don't pack it at the bottom of a pannier, always try to keep it on your person and safe.

Vehicle Documents

All these bits of paper show you are allowed to travel with the bike. Check to make sure none of them expire before you return. If they do they need to be renewed as soon as possible.

Driving Licence

If it's the newer style with a photo ID card and a separate paper section, both parts need to go. And make sure it's not run out. The photo licences now expire after ten years.

V5c

The vehicle ownership document (even though it says it's not proof of ownership!) Make sure that all the details on this are correct. If in doubt check it tallies up with the bike VIN details etc. If something happens and these are incorrect it could lead to lots of problems.

MOT

If required, make sure it's valid and will still be valid when you get back.

Tax Disk

Like the MOT certificate, have a quick check to make sure it does not run out while you are away – It sounds daft, but it can happen.

Insurance

Make sure it's valid and will still be valid on return. Most insurance companies include up to 30 days European cover. But always check with them first to make sure the countries travelling through are included, and to inform them of the trip.

EHIC Card

If you don't have one, then get one. If you become ill while in the EU, this allows you state healthcare at a reduced cost or free. It will cover you for treatment that is needed to allow you to continue your stay until your planned return.

The EHIC is free to apply for and can be done online at www.nhs.uk (don't use any of the online third party sites as they will charge a fee).

Breakdown Cover

You may be very mechanically minded and think you know everything about your bike. But breakdown cover with repatriation is a must. You may save a few pounds not having it, but you will regret it if things go wrong and they can't be fixed.

If you already have breakdown cover for the bike, check to make sure it includes Europe and repatriation. Some 'free' breakdown cover included with bike insurance does not cover Europe.

Ferry/Tunnel Tickets

Gone are the days when an impressive document folder arrived in the post with nice thick tickets. These days most are what are known as etickets which are basically a printout from an email with the conformation booking reference number.

If crossing the channel on the train, make sure you have the credit card on you that you booked the crossing with online. That way all you need to do is arrive at the Euro Tunnel barrier, insert the card and you are in. If the machine refuses to read the card then make sure you have the booking reference number very handy as you will need to type it in!

Money

See riding in Europe

Motorcycle Service Manual/Owners Handbook

You don't have to take the whole thick paper manual. Either get a copy in .pdf format, or scan relevant pages and then upload it all to a MEkey ICE tag. Then if it's needed you have a copy and it's taken up no room at all.

Travel Insurance

Always make sure whenever you travel a good insurance policy is purchased. Check to make sure motorcycle travel is covered as some policies exclude it, and it covers the countries you are riding through.

NAVIGATION

According to the Oxford Dictionary; Navigate - Assist driver by indicating correct route or the science of finding a way from one place to another.

So basically navigation is the art of not getting lost. And if this is to work you need to know where you are going, but more importantly where you are. It can be as complicated or as simple as you make it.

As this guide is mainly aimed at staying in Europe and probably being used by riders who are not going off road into the wild depths, taking compass bearings and following the track of the sun to work out your position are not really going to be covered.

Maps

What did we all do before SatNavs and GPS units? We all used maps, and there is nothing better than a map to navigate from! By all means

use other devices as a backup or to get out of built up areas, but always carry a map (as they don't break down, or stop working or need recharging). They are sometimes inaccurate or go out of date, so when buying maps always try to get the most recent revision.

Before setting off familiarise yourself with

the map, as maps for different countries do look different depending on who has produced it.

Map Scale

The scale of a map is the ratio of a distance on the map to the corresponding distance on the ground. So for example a map with a scale of 1:2.5million equates to 1cm = 25km and a map of 1:800 000 is 1cm = 8km. Different scales offer different planning options. A map with a scale of 1:2.5million will cover the whole of Europe, so good to get a full idea of the planned route, but lacks enough detail to ride from. Ideally for that a 1:800 000, 1:600 000 or better

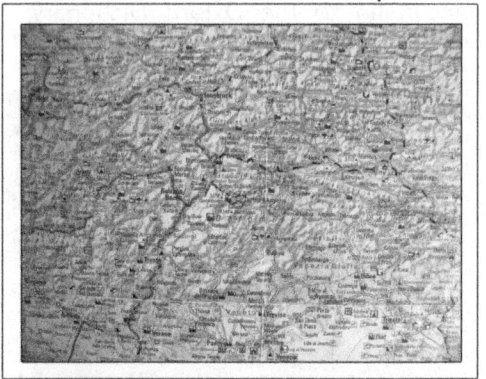

As an example right are three maps with the same central position. The first one is a 1:2.5million scale (good for seeing the whole of a European tour on one map). The second is a 1:800 000 scale, so not too bad for riding from; and the third is a 1:25 000 scale. Probably too large a scale, but gives a great amount of detail and shows all the little roads, and twists and turns of the mountain passo roads. Maps of this scale can usually only be bought locally or ordered through a specialist map shop at a cost.

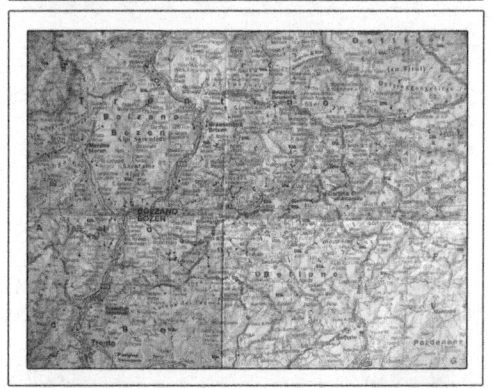

General

Just as for the UK there are several different companies that produce maps for Europe. Many people recommend the Michelin red and orange range of maps. Marco Polo also do some good regional maps for example The Alps (which covers parts of France, Germany, Austria, Switzerland, Italy) at 1:800 000 or Andalusia at 1:300 000. Collins fold out road maps of France and Spain are also quite good.

If you don't already have the right maps, try to purchase them as soon as trip planning starts to familiarise yourself with route options and style of map.

There is nothing better when planning a trip than looking at real maps to plan out a route. Also, nothing is more relaxing at the end of the day to get a map out and start looking at the next day's route and planning which places to go and see.

Keep the map handy at all times. If a tank bag is being used then put it in the clear sleeve so it can be looked at easily.

Top Tip

If you don't want to buy foldout maps, then buy a good scale road atlas of the country or countries travelling through. Then scan in the pages that the route is on and print them out (duplex if possible). That way you are not carrying a whole countries road atlas for maybe two pages of map. It's lighter and takes up much less room.

Use Google maps and zoom into an area of interest and print out the map at a large scale.

Sat Nav/GPS

Satellite Navigation also known as Sat Nav, uses GPS, (Global Positioning System) and some complex software with maps to allow the user to know exactly where they are, in which direction the they are travelling, at what speed, and for how long. Using complex maps and this geographical pin-pointing, Sat Nav is now a globally recognised tool used by millions of people across the world.

GPS, (Global Positioning System), works on a triangulation method. Triangulation is the method of determining a location of a map by using three or more points through which lines of known directions are drawn. The intersection of these lines is the desired location. Ideally, four or more satellites are required to offer an exact position.

Three satellites will work but the fourth will help in accuracy and error checking.

The receiver (your on bike 'sat nav unit') also contains a set of road maps. Using GPS and the maps together, it can plan a route between your current position and any selected destination. It can also plot your progress along the route, by constantly updating your position through signals from the GPS satellites.

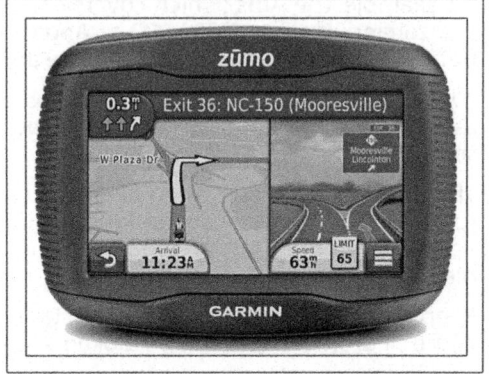

The two major players in the bike specific satnav market are TomTom and Garmin. They both do the same thing but ask any Garmin owner and they will say Garmin is the best and like wise for TomTom. Startup times and GPS fix times will be quoted, even down to the style of bike icon.

Both Garmin and TomTom bike satnavs are designed around a watertight casing, glove friendly software, can give turn by turn voice direction and come with suitable motorcycle mount and hardware.

SatNavs do have handy some handy features like Points Of Interest or POIs. These are pre-programmed in features including filling stations, car parks, camp sites, hotels plus many more. Then if you need a filling station just tell the satnav to direct you to the nearest. These can also be customised to contain your own POIs. For example if you are riding through France it might be helpful to upload the Hotel BB chains POI so then the satnav can direct you to the nearest Hotel BB.

The Garmin range currently has the Zumo 220, 350LM and 660LM. With RRPs starting at £370 going up to £499. The now retired Zumo 550 is still as popular as ever with bikers.

The TomTom range is at present the Urban Rider with either UK only or full European maps installed. A new version is on the horizon which will have European maps and on bike charging mount.

Each new version always comes with more and more features like lane assist, 3d mapping, 3d building view, spoken road names, speed limits etc. But used in their simplest form they are an electronic map with directions.

Bike specific devices can be difficult to see in retail shops, but both ranges are available at Halfords, Argos, Currys (would recommend checking availability first) and other specialist shops, and online from the likes of Amazon or direct. Offers are always taking place, so try to shop around for the best deal.

SatNavs have not yet replaced traditional maps, so take one but read the instruction manual and learn how to use it properly. Test it out on a short shakedown trip first, but also take a map.

One thing to mention though, don't become a slave to the satnav! If you feel things are not right, don't keep blindly following the computerised voice. Stop and look at road signs or a map.

Brackets

All motorcycle satnavs come with some form of fitting them onto the bike. It's usually a basic but secure system that utilises a ram mount,

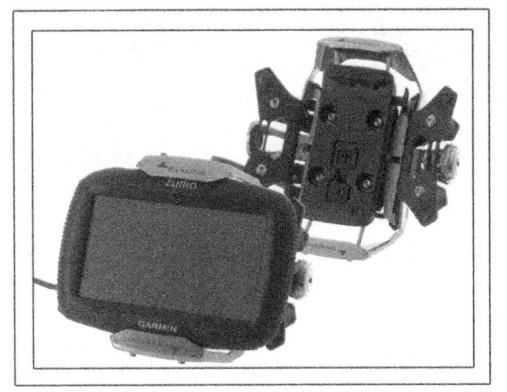

and bracket. There are some quite impressive third party satnav brackets available and some more basic ones which are just slightly more subtle than the standard fitment.

Prices for a fully lockable and anti-vibration bracket are in the region of £130 from Touratech. For a plastic, but functional holder look at buybits.com. They are quite basic, but from a positional point of view they are quite good. (Just remember to take the satnav off when you leave the bike).

Position

Always make sure the satnav is mounted so it does not obscure the dials, or interfere with the normal operation of the bike. One of the best places to mount a satnav is above the dials. It puts the savnav just below the line of sight, so when looking at it, you don't take your eyes completely off the road, as you would with a handlebar mount.

Migsel mount is one of the more popular makes. The photo shows one fitted on a Suzuki VStrom and is available direct from Migsel for €96

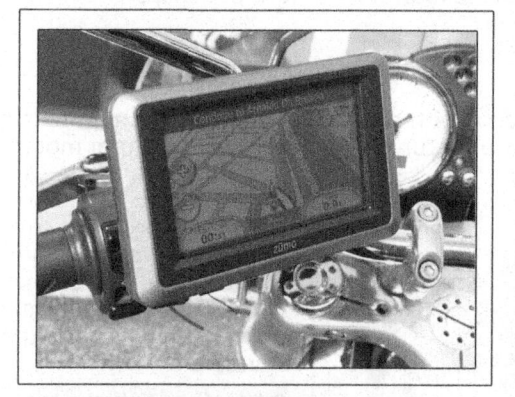

As standard, the bracket that comes out of the box with the satnav tends to be a handlebar ram mount style. While this is good enough to get things going it can be a little awkward. Also make sure none of the bike controls are obscured. The picture left is a bad example of fitment on the handlebars.

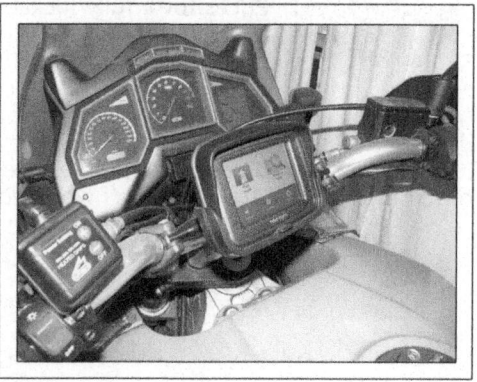

Left is another alternative, which is to fit a cross bar or accessory bar to go across the handlebars. This does bring the device quite close, but there is less physical movement than fitting it up near the bar grips. It's not in the ideal location, but minimal head movement is required to look at it.

Other fittings like stem yoke mounts, short ram mounts, long ram mounts, flex arms are also available to allow for a better fitting of the satnav.

For pre trip route planning, Tyre is a great piece of software (and free) that allows you to plot your route on the PC using Google maps, and then transfer it to the satnav as a route. Makes getting routes into the satnav so much easier and means you should ride on the route you want not what the satnav decides when the next destination is entered.

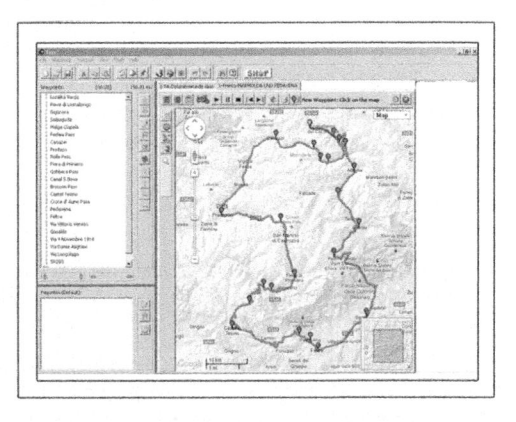

Another alternative is MS Autoroute. With this you can pre-program speeds, coffee breaks, overnight stops and fuel costs. The maps aren't as up to date as Google, but it gives a better indication of speed, time and distance.

Non Bike Specific Sat Nav

There are a couple of things to note here. Bike specific satnavs are amazingly expensive compared to car satnavs; non bike specific

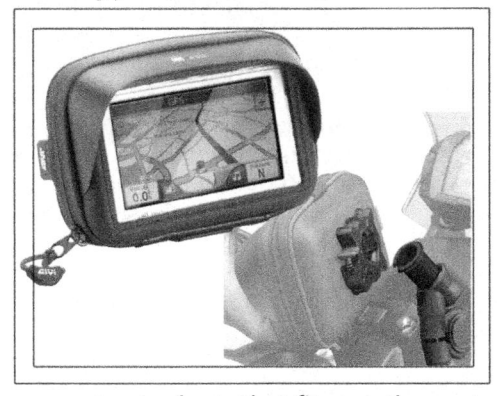

satnavs are not waterproof; car satnavs don't come with mounting kits for bikes. So if you already have a car sat nav or don't want to spend on a bike specific one, by buying a waterproof case it can still be fitted onto the bike.

Mount options include waterproof bags with built in ram mount connectors or bags that fit over the centre of the handlebars. These are now available from several manufacturers and with a range of prices from about £20 or the one above from Givi (S954) with an RRP of £43 which is suitable for screens up to 5" and comes complete with a quick release system.

As an example; a TomTom Start 20 Europe costs £120, couple that with a Givi S945 at £43 and you have a satnav that will fit the bike for £163 as opposed to over £300! It might not win any style points or be the most rugged setup, but it's an option.

There are also similar cases available that fit smart phones like Apples iPhone, HTC, Samsung Galaxy etc.

Bluetooth Earpiece

There is no issue if all you want the sat nav for is a backup to glance at occasionally, but what if you want to hear spoken directions. This is where a Bluetooth earpiece or headset comes in.

Bluetooth allows devices to communicate wirelessly by creating a small network between the devices by pairing them together. This then allows the rider to hear the spoken directions from the sat nav.

Cardo produce a range of Bluetooth headsets within the Scarla range which all support connectivity to sat navs. Most also have other features. Starting from about £139 for the Scarla Rider

Costing £99 The Interphone F2 City can be paired with two Bluetooth devices simultaneously, such as a mobile phone and sat nav. Other makes include Sena, Midland, Parrot, STK and others.

If all you need is sound then the Jabra Clipper is a quite a nice option. With a unit that just sits in a pocket (4.8 x 1.7 x 2.5cm), in ear earpieces so they don't catch when putting on a helmet and it will pair to two devices it's an ideal unit at £30

So, why is it called Bluetooth? you are all asking. Harald Bluetooth was king of Denmark in the late 900s. He managed to unite Denmark and part of Norway into a single kingdom then introduced Christianity into Denmark. He left a large monument, the Jelling rune stone, in memory of his parents. He was killed in 986 during a battle with his son, Svend Forkbeard. So now you know - even if it says nothing about the way the technology works.

Top Tip

What ever happens; road signs are helpful, don't become a slave to the satnav. If a sign says campsite to the left, then follow it; it might be the best campsite you stay at on the whole trip!

Analogue Sat Nav

This is the self phrased term for written route notes!

There are several different types of analogue satnav out there at the moment. Some are notes written on a piece of paper stuck to the screen, others are in a tank bag which can be bigger and more informative, maybe with small drawings of tricky junctions.

Another alternative is a simple and straight forward arrangement that makes some riders laugh when they see it – but it works.

Get hold of an iPlayer or iPhone strap that runners use to strap them to their arm so they can listen to music while running; the ones with a clear plastic window and Velcro closure (these can be bought for a couple of pounds from a well known auction website). Then cut some thin card pieces (the whiter the better) to fit inside and fill the window space.

Now write a simple overview of the route, ideally using a black pen on the card and slip it into the iPhone (now analogue satnav) holder and strap it to your left lower arm. As seen in the photo.

No need to write every left or right turn, just the major junctions and destinations to look out for. It's very simple, but it really does make on the move navigation easier. The route notes right cover about 200 miles through Germany.

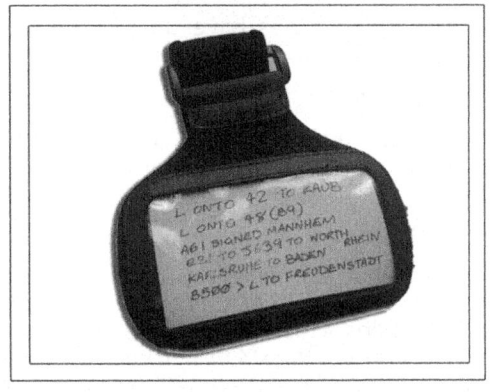

Top Tip

If writing routes down on paper, then hand write them, don't print them from a computer (you can read your own handwriting much better). Try to use a black pen on white card or paper.

RIDING IN EUROPE

This section is 'Riding in Europe' as this book does not really cover RTW trips and similar. So you have taken the plunge and made the decision to go onto the continent.

Europe has some stunning roads, mountains, castles, scenery, the list is endless, and these are just some reasons why every rider should at least 'do' Europe once. You will be back!

First thoughts about riding in Europe can look to be quite daunting; but if a little bit of common sense is used when preparing then things will tick along quite well.

At the end of this section is 'Europe at a Glance' chart showing what's recommended, compulsory or banned. This is designed to be for initial reference and was correct at time of printing. As always do final checks on any countries you are travelling to before you leave.

Kit

Different countries have different laws and rules on what to carry when riding through them.

GB Sticker

This goes without saying that you need one. If your number plate has the blue Euro GB logo on the left then this is good enough, or just go to a car accessories shop and buy one for a couple of pounds.

Spare Bulbs

Many riders ask the question "Do I need a spare bulb kit for <insert country name>" There is an easy and logical answer - Get a full set of spare bulbs & fuses for the bike and just take them with you from now on (touring in the UK or Europe). That way you will always have them and be covered. They don't take up that much room.

Hi-Vis Jackets/Waistcoats

At the moment no countries in Europe require riders to wear hi-vis over jackets or waistcoats under normal circumstances. However, most countries require the wearing of hi-vis if broken down at the side of the road (motorcycles and cars). A hi-vis waistcoat folds up really small and weighs nothing and can cost from as little as a couple of pounds. So again, just pack it every time and then you will always have it with you. In bad weather it may be advisable to wear one, but at the moment it's still a personal choice.

France had been looking to make hi-vis compulsory in 2013. So riders of bikes over 125cc would have to wear a reflective item of clothing. The reflective area would have been on the upper body and cover at least 150 square centimetres. Failure to comply would lead to a fine.

In December 2012, French plans for compulsory high-visibility motorcycle clothing were withdrawn after campaigning by French riders and it also emerged they were in breach of an EU directive. But this could change in the future.

Headlight Beam Deflectors

Now then, here is an interesting one. All riders whose native side of the road is the left are expected to fit beam deflectors by law when riding on the right.

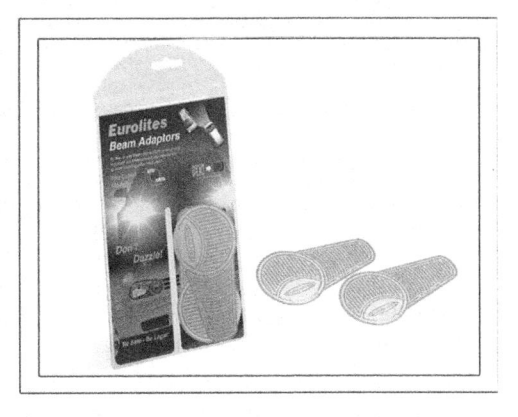

However, unlike a car where the left side flick is quite prominent, a motorcycles light beam does not flick up so much at the left (this is what would need blocking out with beam deflectors) if it does at all. Most bike headlights tend to be straight or with very little flick; also unlike a car you will be riding more to the centre of the lane.

If they are fitted its best to face the bike against a flat wall and see where the beam goes high to the left; this is the part that need blanking out.

Beam deflectors or adaptors can be bought from most caravan touring shops or the AA/RAC; or a strip of PVC tape could be used to mask off the left side flick (be aware that the adhesive on PVC tape will melt).

Most UK riders tend not to fit them due to having straighter beams. Also most are not riding at night which may make it more obvious. For further information look under 'Authors Kit & Personal Views'.

Breath Test Kit

From 1st July 2012 it's been a legal requirement in France for all

vehicles travelling on French roads (regardless of country of origin) to carry at least one breathalyser in the vehicle that conforms to approved French standards (NF).

They are available for about £5 for a pack of two from Halfords, Amazon and the like before you travel or at the port or on the ferry over to France.

Update:

At time of printing, (Feb 2013) French interior minister, Manuel Valls, has suspended the legislation to enable the Conseil National de la Sécurité Routière (CNSR) to look at just how effective the law really is; and if the supply chain of breathalysers really is working.

Manuel Valls is waiting on the report from the CNSR as to whether drivers will again require an alcohol breathalyser in their vehicles, or if the law will be abandoned. One option is to just get a pack – sorted.

Hazard Warning Triangle

This is a requirement for cars, but *not* for bikes – So no origami required to get one to fit on the bike. However, if you want to go the extra mile, you can get helmet bags which have a reflective red triangle printed on them.

First Aid Kit

Again, this is another question that gets asked over and over. The simple answer is yes; always carry one when touring. Its common sense when travelling to have some form of first aid with you. Even if it's just to put a plaster on a cut to keep it clean.

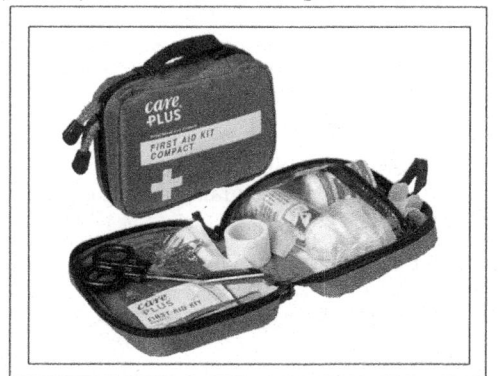

Once the kit is assembled, just leave it with the kit for touring and then it's with you whether touring in the UK or Europe.

See Other Items to Pack in the Camping section for more information on first aid kits and to include.

Money

This is in the Riding in Europe section as under normal circumstances, if touring in the UK money is not really thought of as a packing item. Not really 'kit' but you still need to pack some money. There are several options here, some safe, some less so. Don't get too paranoid about money when travelling in Europe, just take normal precautions and everything should be fine.

Cash

Anyone who has been abroad knows it's nice to have a bit of 'walking out' money. This is money for everyday expenses. If you like to carry a

lot of currency, try to keep it in two places; a small amount that is your 'walking out' money in an easily accessible place. And the backup money stored securely else ware on you.

Don't forget to change money into Euros before leaving if travelling through majority of Europe.

European countries using the euro: Andorra, Austria, Belgium, Cyprus, Estonia, Finland, France, Germany, Greece, Ireland, Italy, Luxembourg, Malta, the Netherlands, Monaco, Portugal, San Marino, Slovakia, Slovenia and Spain

European countries not using the euro: Bulgaria (lev), the Czech Republic (koruna), Denmark (krone), Hungary (forint), Latvia (lats), Lithuania (litas), Norway (krona) Poland (zloty), Romania (leu), Sweden (krona), oh and the UK

Liechtenstein & Switzerland's currency is the Swiss Franc, but after a little cajoling they usually accept Euros (sometimes at a bad exchange rate).

A handy tip for carrying small amounts of money while riding is to wrap it up in a small self seal sandwich bag before putting it in your pocket. This keeps it dry, organised and easy to find.

Debit Card

If you are going to use a debit card for either ATM transactions or to pay for goods in Europe it's advisable to inform your bank before leaving. Otherwise they might just stop the card believing it's being used fraudulently. Most banks charge for using a debit card abroad, so find out how much before setting off.

From a security point of view, the down side to using a debit card is that if it's lost, stolen or skimmed, the perpetrator has access to the funds in your normal bank account. Because of this, think about using a credit card as an alternative, or set up a separate trip account.

As always make sure it's safely stored and take usual precautions as you would in the UK.

Credit Card

As with a debit card, tell the credit card company you are going abroad before leaving as some automatically block the card from being used outside the UK unless informed. But it's another handy secure way to pay for goods and you will be covered for any loss if the worst happens.

Find out what the exchange rate and commission the card company will charge as this can mount up when working out the final cost of the trip.

Some credit card companies advertise no charges for overseas transactions, even some travel/bike publications recommend cards, but look at the small print first. The most commonly advertised 'no charge for overseas use' card by the travel/bike press is the Nationwide credit card; this is NOT the case and they are re-using old information.

As with debit cards always make sure it's safely stored and take the same precautions as you would in the UK.

Traveller Cheques

These used to be one of the safest ways to carry currency before 'chip

& pin' cards became popular. If travelling in 'western' Europe then the benefits don't outweigh the hassle. Having to find a bank that's open, having to pay the bank a commission. They are just not worth the time and effort for most of Europe in the Euro zone. Outside the Euro zone they are still a good option.

Travel Card from Post Office

These cards are the way forward - Basically they are a prepaid MasterCard which can be preloaded with spending money (Euros or US dollars). It provides a safe and easy way to manage foreign

currency and can be used for paying for purchases or to withdraw a couple or three day's worth of local currency from any ATM that displays the MasterCard symbol.

Simply pop into the Post Office and ask if you can have one, load it up with money and you are away (Once you have reset the PIN to one you can remember).

As a word of caution, if buying petrol make sure you have the cash to cover the transaction just in case – some smaller 'independent' filling stations machines for some reason don't accept it.

Mobile Phones

All UK mobile phones should work ok in Europe for voice calls (if you still have a brick as a phone then think about upgrading).

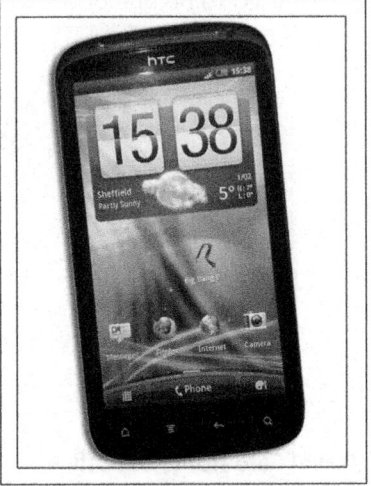

Use your mobile abroad, and you are using 'mobile roaming'. This is when the phone connects to an overseas network and calls are routed via that network provider instead of a home network, at an increased cost.

If you have not taken the phone abroad before, then tell your provider you're going. Most providers have special packages to use when abroad, but unless you ring up and ask, you don't get them automatically. These packages can cut the cost of calls. Some add-ons are free; others require a fee. Calling back to the UK from Europe can be 30p/minute; to receive a call while roaming in Europe costs about 8p/minute.

However it's free to receive texts anywhere worldwide, so ask friends to text you, and not call. It costs around 8p to reply to a text within the EU and 50p to reply outside the EU, but don't play txt ping pong though – it will add up!

Data Roaming or mobile internet can cost proper money, so switch it off before leaving the UK. If you are on Vodafone their standard rate for data roaming is 69p/Mb unless you have a pre-organised package.

Turn off 3G/data roaming on the phone, otherwise installed apps may still be using a connection. If internet access is needed, then use free wi-fi hotspots.

Don't use a smart phone as a satnav in Europe; as the maps are downloaded via data roaming, so again there is a cost involved.

Riding

The doors open on the ferry or train and that's it; you are on the continent. One of the most obvious parts to riding on the continent for a UK rider is riding on the 'wrong' side of the road. Riding on the right is not as difficult as some people think; it's easier than driving a UK car on the right.

First the easy bit – Get into the habit of always reminding yourself to 'ride on the right' every time you do anything on the bike. It's simple; when you set off in the morning, when you start any manoeuvre, when setting off after a break, just say to yourself 'ride on the right'. After a lunchtime break is a classic time when auto pilot can kick in, so again just get on the bike and say to yourself 'ride on the right'.

Riding on the main roads is not always the problem, it's the smaller minor roads where auto pilot can take over, so be aware at all times.

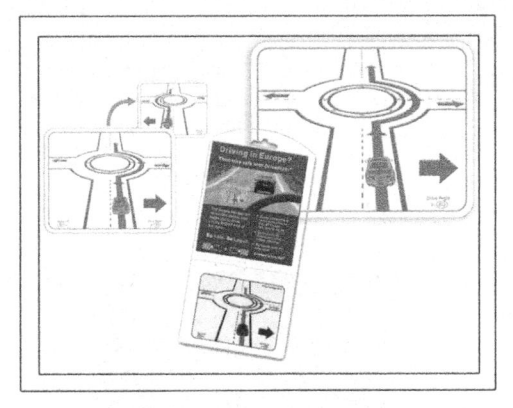

If you think you may have issues with riding on the right; another way to reinforce this is to use a visual aid. You can buy a simple sticker (DriveRight) which goes on the inside of the screen which shows a natural 'sat-nav' view of the road ahead and shows instantly which side of the road you should be driving on. Once back in the UK just flip it round and stick it back on as a quick reminder for the first few miles. Available from caravan/motor home stores, the AA and Halfords etc for about £4.

There is also what could be termed the 'Pooratech' version which is a printed arrow with Right & Left above and below. Stick this to the screen both when on the continent and then flip over as a reminder when back in the UK.

Costs nothing but a bit of time, and gives a visual reminder if unsure. Another option that some riders do is just to put a small day-glow sticker on the right-hand mirror.

Roundabouts

Roundabouts may be the equivalent of the U-Turn in the bike test!

Everyone talks about them and for the first timer they worry so much about them that they can talk themselves out of going!

They feel a little strange at first, but you soon get used to them and rarely cause major problems. If you take time to look at a UK roundabout; you will notice you are pushed slightly to face left (the direction of the roundabout). It's the same on the continent; you are slightly pushed to face right as you enter the roundabout.

As in the UK there is also a warning sign beforehand – except the arrows go the other way (these are very handy when approaching). Once at the roundabout priority is to any traffic coming from the left (usually); so, slowdown or pause, look left to check traffic, set off saying to yourself 'ride on the right' ready for your exit. Remembering to do lifesaver glances.

There are some roundabouts in France where this is not the case, however, although these are few and far between, where priority is given to any traffic joining the roundabout, therefore coming from the right! So if you are on the roundabout, you give way to traffic entering. This type of roundabout is slowly being phased out.

Priorité à droite

There is a very odd rule of the road in France, which is that there are certain places where traffic coming from what is apparently a minor road has priority over the traffic already on what appears to be the major road. This is exclusively when the minor road joins the main road from the right, and although it can be difficult to see, it is usually when there are certain markings on the road ushering the traffic from the right into the main road, or, less helpfully, when there are no lines, dotted or otherwise, across the end of the minor road. IF you are on the main road entering a village look for the signs.

sign entering a village showing you do not have right of way

sign after a village showing you have priority

It is an antiquated law, but although largely eradicated in main towns, it still occurs when you least expect it, especially in small towns, villages and country roads. France is however slowly moving away from the Priorité à Droite rule and on the open road and town bypasses you will often now see a yellow diamond sign signifying that you have the priority. However as you enter a town or village you may see a yellow diamond with a black line through it - signalling the re-commencement of Priorité à Droite so take extra care again!

A general rule of thumb is always be cautious when there is a road joining from the right in France!

Riding in any foreign country it is essential that you have at least a basic understanding of the rules of the road.

Take extra care, as you would in any new riding conditions. The most likely times to go on auto pilot are after you've stopped for a meal or long break, or overnight; or if you're over-tired, so schedule in enough down time for sleeping and relaxing.

Speeds/Speeding

Check local speed limits. Some countries have variable limits that are lower in bad weather, and don't get carried away with the high numbers – they are in kilometres per hour NOT MPH! If you have a digital speedo that can change to read KPH then make sure you know how to flick between MPH and KPH. On some analogue dials the KPH numbers are quite small and can be unreadable if printed in dark red or similar, so just take it steady as on the spot fines are common throughout Europe and can be hefty.

Speed cameras are these days common place all over Europe. Gone are the days of riding fast through France, Germany and Italy. If you cross the channel to France; shown left; is the type of speed camera signs you will see.

These are similar to UK automatic cameras at the side of the road.

Don't rely on the signs too much though as the French Government has advised to start removing the signs and leave the cameras!

Right is a French camera – nearly always rear facing, so don't think bikes can get away with it.

While on the subject of speed Italian and Spanish cameras on major roads look similar to the French. Left is an Italian speed camera on a rural road and below, the sign to look out for.

Styles of Local Driving

Driving styles vary in different countries, so don't assume you can predict what other road users will do. In most European countries most drivers have also ridden scooters or motorbikes, and will be more aware of you than road users in the UK. If they move aside for you to pass, don't forget to give them a thank you nod.

Drink Driving

Most other European countries have stricter drink-driving rules than the UK. But the easy solution is don't! Save the drinking for the evening at the campsite.

Petrol Stations

This may sound daft, but know what type of fuel the bike takes. Most commonly it's unleaded at 95RON

At the pump you will have a similar set of fuel pump options that you get in the UK, but with different names. Example table below:

	France	Italy	Germany	Spain
Unleaded 95RON	Sans Plomb	Senza Piombo or Benzina	Benzin* Super**	Gasolina sin plomo
Super Unleaded 98RON	Super	Super	SuperPlus	Super
Unleaded with 10% ethanol added	E10	E10	E10	
Diesel	Gazole	Gasolio	Diesel	Gas-oil
LPG	GPL	LPG	LPG	gases licuados del petróleo

* 91RON **95RON

Pumps

Unleaded – Green or Red

It is usually available in two grades, 95 octane (Green) and 98 octane (sometimes a red pump).

Unleaded E10 - Blue

Don't fill up with E10; which is 10% Ethanol added to Unleaded and most bikes or cars at best won't run well on it; at worst could damage the engine!

Diesel – Black

Don't be shocked if a little old man comes up to the bike and wants to take over the routine of filling up. Keep an eye on him and the pump and make sure petrol does not spill out all over the tank as sometimes they don't care as much about your bike as you do!

A good phrase to learn if attendant service is: fill it please or "il pieno, per favore" in Italian as an example.

It's common for petrol stations to be closed on Sundays, or to switch to an automatic mode. When in automatic mode the machines tend to only accept local credit cards. If you're carrying cash, try to see if a local will use their card for your cash.

Service areas on the motorways normally stay open on Sundays.

It's also common in Italy and Spain for petrol stations away from the main routes to close between 12.30 and 3.30 in the afternoon.

Belgium

One total oddity throughout Europe is filling up in Belgium. If you are not using one of the automated credit card pumps there is quite a funny routine that has to take place.

- You pull into the self serve petrol station. You need fuel but don't know how much (in money).
- You have to get off the bike, go into the shop and hand over (lets say) €20 and tell them the pump number, they then give you a receipt.
- Go back to the bike to fill up.
- Go back to the shop with your receipt to collect any change.
- Now go back to the bike, ready to ride; and it's that simple!

Motorways

Or French Autoroutes; Italian Autostrade; Spanish Autopistas and Autobahns in Austria & Germany

Most motorcycle riders when planning a trip to the continent will initially say they are going to keep off motorways as much as possible. This is a great idea in theory, but as in the UK motorways are a means to an end – to get somewhere quickly and easily. So if the trip involves getting to Italy and back and you only have 10 days, then some motorway travel is needed to make up time.

As the 'Europe At A Glance' chart (at the end of this section) shows, most countries motorways are toll roads. Only Belgium and Germany are toll free.

France now has quite a few roads that have motorway characteristics that are toll free roads.

Toll Plaza Routine

If you have never ridden on a toll road then the routine can be a little daunting the first time. So this next part is a brief run through of how a toll booth works in Italy. Other countries are similar.

As you enter the motorway (or Autostrada as in Italy) the toll booths await. Head towards the booths marked BIGLIETTO (ticket) STAY

AWAY from the ones marked TELEPASS. Telepass are drive-though lanes for subscribers with a transponder in their vehicle. Enter the lane and at the barrier a ticket should automatically come out of the machine. These machines rely on vehicle weight to work and some don't register a motorbike – If this is the case just hit the red button and a ticket will pop out. Once you get a ticket from the automated BIGLIETTO booth, aim for the right-hand side of the road and find a safe place to briefly park up (there are usually parking spaces). This is a good chance for a brief stop and to safely pocket the toll ticket. Always put it in the same pocket – that way you shouldn't loose it!

Payment is due at the exit nearest to your destination. Before the toll booth aim for the right hand side of the road to safely park up and remove gloves and get the toll ticket and money handy.

There are two payment options: credit cards or cash. If using a credit card head for the blue booths marked CARTE. Insert the ticket, wait for the amount to show and then insert a credit card.

If its cash, then go to the white booths with the coin and cash symbol. If there is an attendant, give them the ticket, the amount owed will be displayed on a small screen. Pay and then as before this is a chance for a brief stop.

At automated cash booths insert the ticket; a screen displays the amount, then place the notes or coins into the machine. Care is needed here for the change; some malfunctioning machines spit change out all over the floor!

Rather than risk an international incident with backed up drivers I have in the past just left a couple Euros on the floor! I'd like to meet the person who calibrated the machine's mechanism.

Vignettes

Vignettes are used in Austria, Bulgaria, Czech Republic, Hungary, Montenegro, Romania, Slovakia, Slovenia and Switzerland. They are a small, coloured toll sticker that is stuck to the screen of the bike to show the motorway tax has been paid.

A vignette can be purchased at most petrol stations and at border entry points. Failure to comply will result in on the spot fines. In Austria a 10-day Vignettes cost about €7 (at time of printing) for a motorcycle. The fine for not displaying one is €240 to €3000! If travelling through Austria some motorways also have an extra toll to be paid. One of these is the A13 - Brenner Motorway if heading down into northern Italy.

Blue Vignettes stickers can be seen on the screens of the bikes above at a service area on the Austrian Italian border.

As opposed to other European countries, vignettes are not issued for different time periods in Switzerland other than a whole year! So if riding through Switzerland via motorway it can be expensive at about €35, especially if you are only in the country for a couple of days. (You may be able to pick up a 'second hand' one off a well known auction site – but this is technically illegal!)

The Swiss vignette price does not include the following tunnels: Grand St. Bernhard Tunnel and Munt la Schera. A further toll must be paid here. If stopped without a valid vignette a cash fine of at least 200 Swiss Franks could be charged.

Tolls

Motorway tolls vary considerably from country to country, but the most expensive have to be the Spanish Autopistas. Usually there is an N road running along side of the AP which is free and can be more fun, if considerably slower.

Riding

At all times while on the motorway ride in the right hand lane. Only move to the left to overtake.

Some slip roads on and off motorways in Europe, but especially Italy, are very short. Sometimes only 30 to 50 metres long, so when entering, keep the speed increasing, look over left shoulder, but at the same time be ready to stop if no one lets you on. When exiting, there are times when some quite heavy breaking may be required, so start anticipating the exit early.

Off the Motorway

Once off the motorways the roads are generally of good quality with fewer pot holes. One element to keep an eye out for though is overbanding. This is where cracks in the road have been filled and joined with liquid bitumen. When wet this can be like ice.

Filtering is allowed and expected, except in Germany where it is strictly forbidden.

Stop signs really do mean stop! To qualify as having stopped a foot must go down. The local police do like to catch bikers 'giving way' when they should have stopped.

Speed limits	Motorway	Open Road	Urban
Austria	130 km/h	100 km/h	50 km/h
Belgium	120 km/h	90 km/h	50 km/h *
Germany	none unless shown	100 km/h	50 km/h
France	130 km/h (110 km/h when wet)	90 km/h (80 km/h when wet)	50 km/h
Italy	130 km/h (110 km/h when wet)	90 km/h (80 km/h when wet)	50 km/h
Switzerland	120 km/h	80 km/h	50 km/h

* (30 near schools, hospitals, churches etc)

General

In general people treat motorcyclists on the continent as normal human beings, unlike in the UK where sometimes you feel like you are from Mars!

Try to learn at least hello, thank you and goodbye in the local language. Even if you get it slightly wrong they will usually understand and help you to correct it.

Another oddity of European drivers are Zebra crossings – They very rarely stop at them, to the point they ignore them, so slow down and ride with caution. If you do stop some drivers may even overtake you over the crossing!

Most motorcyclists wave to each other. The outstretched left arm with 2 fingers is customary and is said to originate from the battle of Agincourt. The English victors cut off the fingers of the French archers, so those that kept their freedom show they still have their fingers. (Well that's how the saying goes anyway).

If you are overtaken or you overtake, a customary 'waved' right foot is used.

Liechtenstein & Switzerland can be very expensive. Be prepared to pay about €9 for a coffee and a soft drink!

Tunnels & Passes

Tunnels

If you like tunnels then these are some fun long ones! Most tunnels have speed cameras in them and there is usually no overtaking.

Fréjus Road Tunnel – About 13km. Motorbikes one way €27

Mont Blanc Tunnel - Motorbikes one-way: €25.80

St. Gotthard Tunnel – 17km. No extra toll (already have vignette)

Tunnel du Puymorens – 4.8km €4.70

Arlberg tunnel – 13.9km €9

Great St Bernard Tunnel – 5.85km. Motorbikes one way €14.70

San Bernardino Tunnel – 6.6km

Felbertauern Tunnel - 5.3km. Motorbikes one way €10

Passes and Mountain Roads

Well there are just so many good mountain pass roads they can't all be listed here, but some of the more famous or scenic are listed below.

Remember to take things easy on the tight mountain pass roads. Uphill, you can use the rear brake during turns, that will stabilise the bike, and it allows you to keep the throttle open during the turn. But downhill, the rear brake is not so good, so go easy with it; the rear wheel carries almost no weight, which means it will stop turning very easily when you apply the rear brake. So easy front break and try to use some engine braking to slow down, break steady and in plenty of time for the corner going down hill, remembering to release the front break before starting to turn.

Stelvio Pass, Italy

At 2,757m it's the highest paved mountain pass in the Eastern Alps, and the second highest in the Alps. With 48 hairpin turns on the northern side, and 12 on the southern side. Once on the pass itself, each of the turns are numbered with stones so you can count your way up!

Dolomites, Italy

The Dolomite Mountains, with their characteristic flat-crested, vertically monolithic appearance, is unique to the Alps, and are one of the great biking regions of the Alpine range. There are many mountain passes within the same area, interconnected with interesting riding routes. There are some nice towns to stay in, such as Corvara, Arabba, Canazei or Selva, putting runs like Jaufenpass and Timmelsjoch well within reach for good day trips. Another option is to do the Sella Ronda circuit which takes in Passo Sella, Passo Gardena, Passo Falzrego and Passo Pordio

Großglockner Hochalpenstraße, Austria

This leads you upwards with numbered hairpin curves, to the Kaiser Franz Josefs Höhe visitors' Centre, with a panoramic view of the Pasterze Glacier and the Großglockner itself. The road has toll booths at Ferleiten in the direction of Salzburg (toll for motorcycles €23). Bikers arriving from the south from Carinthia come through the picturesque mountain village of Heiligenblut. The Grossglockner itself, at 3,798m, is Austria's highest mountain.

Furka Pass, Swtizerland

Furka Pass (2,436m) is a high mountain pass in the Swiss Alps connecting Gletsch, Valais with Realp, Uri. The Furka-Oberalp-Bahn line through the Furka Tunnel bypasses the pass. The base tunnel opened in 1982 and replaced a tunnel at 2,100m. The road can be a little bit narrow in parts, but it offers fantastic views onto the surrounding glaciers.

San Bernardino Pass, Switzerland

Another nice riding route is over the San Bernardino Pass (2,065m), a high mountain pass in the Swiss Alps connecting the Hinterrhein and Mesolcina (Misox) valleys between Thusis and Bellinzona. Located in the far eastern side of the Western Alps it should not be confused with the Great St. Bernard Pass and the Little St. Bernard Pass. The top of the pass represents both the Italian-German language frontier and the watershed. The lake at the top is great when the sun is shining, lots of photo ops and a good spot for a coffee break.

Border Crossings

Within Europe you can pretty much ride from country to country without even knowing sometimes. The only indicator is the language (sometimes) and the road signs, oh and the flags.

Many roads just have the European Stars with the name of the country at the side of the road. A little bit like riding from England into Scotland. However there are still some 'proper' border posts where you may be asked to pull over. If this is the case make sure your passport is handy and not at the bottom of a pannier.

If stopped just be polite and show the official your passport and that's usually that. Sometimes you may get asked some questions about the trip and the bike, but that's usually out of interest rather than officialness.

112

This is the European wide emergency phone number, available throughout the EU (Austria, Belgium, Bulgaria, Cyprus, Czech Republic, Germany, Denmark, Estonia, Greece, Spain, Finland, France, Hungary, Ireland, Italy, Lithuania, Luxembourg, Latvia, Malta, Netherlands, Poland, Portugal, Romania, Sweden, Slovenia, Slovakia, United Kingdom), free of charge.

It is possible to call 112 from landline and mobile phones to contact any emergency service (ambulance, fire & rescue or police).

Operators in many countries can answer the calls not only in their national language, but also in English or French. If the caller does not know where they are, the operator can identify where the person making the call is physically located which will be passed on to the emergency authorities.

112 doesn't replace the existing national emergency numbers. In most countries, it operates alongside them, but simplifies emergency contact where countries have several numbers. (Eg Spain: 062 - civil guard, 091 - police, 061 - health emergencies, 080 - fire, 092 - local police).

EUROPE AT A GLANCE
What's compulsory, what's recommended and what's banned

	Austria	Belgium	Croatia	Denmark	France	Germany
GB Sticker	C	C	C	C	C	C
Original Bike Documents	C	C	C	C	C	C
Insurance	C	C	C	C	C	C
HiVis Jackets*	C	C	C	NO	C**	NO
First Aid Kit	C	R	C	R	NO	R
Breath Test Kit	NO	NO	NO	NO	C##	NO
Beam Deflector	C	C	C	C	C	C
Bulb Kit	R	R	R	R	C	R
Daytime Lights	C	C	C	C	C	C
Motorway Tolls/Tax	TAX & TOLL	NO	TOLL	TOLL	TOLLS	NO
On The Spot Fines	YES	YES	YES	YES	YES	YES
Speed Detectors	F	F	F	F	F	F
Motorcycle Helmet	C	C	C	C	C	C
Motorway Max Speed	80mph 130kph	74mph 120kph	80mph 130kph	68mph 110kph	80mph 130kph	80mph 130kph#
Wet Weather Speed Restrictions	NO	NO	NO	NO	YES	NO

*HiVis jacket when at side of road   #130kph only suggestion – check signs
**must be worn in bad weather   ##under review

C – COMPULSORY | – RECOMMENDED | F – FORBIDDEN

EUROPE AT A GLANCE
What's compulsory, what's recommended and what's banned

	Italy	Netherlands	Portugal	Spain	Switzerland	Sweden
GB Sticker	C	C	C	C	C	C
Original Bike Documents	C	C	C	C	C	C
Insurance	C	C	C	C	C	C
HiVis Jackets*	C	NO	R	R	NO	NO
First Aid Kit	C	R	C	C	R	R
Breath Test Kit	NO	NO	NO	NO	NO	NO
Beam Deflector	C	C	C	C	C	C
Bulb Kit	R	R	R	R	R	R
Daytime Lights	C	C	C	C	C	C
Motorway Tolls/Tax	TOLL	TOLL	TOLL	TOLL	TAX ONLY	TOLL
On The Spot Fines	YES	YES	YES	YES	YES	YES
Speed Detectors	F	F	F	F	F	F
Motorcycle Helmet	C	C	C	C	C	C
Motorway Max Speed	80mph 130kph	74mph 120kph	74mph 120kph	74mph 120kph	74mph 120kph	68mph 110kph
Wet Weather Speed Restrictions	YES	NO	NO	NO	NO	NO

*HiVis jacket when at side of road All details correct at time of printing Jan 2013

C – COMPULSORY | – RECOMMENDED | F – FORBIDDEN

TOP TIPS

Just a list of some tips that might make a motorcycle camping trip run a little smoother.

Keys

Always carry a set of spare keys for the bike. Store them in a different location to the 'working' set. But don't keep them in a potentially locked pannier!

If the bike has an alarm remote fob, replace the batteries before you go; make sure the spare fob is on the spare set of keys.

Panniers

Run an Arno strap round the panniers and the frame. It should then hold it in place if a minor problem develops, and should give you time to notice it and get it sorted.

Side Stand Rest

Plastic 'puck' Top Tip - Make a small hole in the puck, and then thread some string through the hole and tie it to the puck – needs to be long enough to reach the handlebars. Tie knots in the string at intervals. (This aids with grip when wet). Now when you stop put the puck down, rest stand on the puck and tie the string to the handle bar. When you are ready to go and sat on the bike, untie the string from handlebar, pull up the puck and put it in your pocket until you are on firmer ground when you can stash it away.

Packing

If travelling in mainland Europe (or anywhere that drives on the right) try to put tools and emergency items in the right pannier – the side which will be away from the road/traffic if roadside maintenance is required. It's scary how fast and close a truck passes when the bike is parked up at the side of the road!

Getting The Tent Back In the Bag

When you first get the tent home, don't rush to get it out of the stuff sack. Carefully take it out making a note of how it comes out and is folded (take photos at different stages to refer back to).

Then after pitching lay the stuff bag near to where you are packing the tent so you have an idea of the final size it has to be.

Fold in reverse order from how it came out, and it will go back in the stuff bag easily.

Location

Get used to always putting items in the same place. For example bike keys always go in the top left pocket of trousers; money, top right trouser pocket; phone inside jacket pocket. It's a simple idea, but you will never loose your bike keys again.

Gloves

Two are warmer than one thick one

If you feel the cold then look at how skiers keep their hands warm; a thin pair of silk glove liners and then the main glove over the top. The layering system really can add extra warmth to the hands.

If your gloves leak or your hands sweat in them, a pair of tight fitting surgical style gloves under the main glove should stop the water making your hands cold and pruney and help stop the lining pulling out when you take them off.

Always take at least two pairs of gloves if touring. Basically if one pair gets a soaking they need to be allowed to dry. And some days are warmer than others so a change to lighter gloves is always nice.

Boots

To keep smooth leather boots in super tip top condition, clean the boots and then apply some Nikwax Waterproofing Wax for Leather, then buff off the excess.

For other materials like a nubuck finish use Nikwax Nubuck & Suede Proof from time to time to restore the durable water repellency (DWR)

Tents

Tent stuff sacks are light weight so can blow away. Weigh them down with unused pegs or put them in a pocket.

If strong winds are forecast, place a rock over the peg (but not touching the guy line, as the sawing motion may cut through the guy.) Or, double peg your main anchor points (guys, corners, seams etc) Place two pegs through the elastic or guy but make them cross each other at a good angle, keeping the correct angle to the guy.

Alternatively connect an 18 inch length of paracord to the anchor point and run it past the peg maintaining the same line, so if one pulls out, it's backed up by the second.

A tent is a living thing, so if the tent is to be pitched for a few days, keep checking it and adjusting the pegs and guy line tension.

To avoid tripping over guy ropes, tie a plastic bag half way up them.

Lights

If the tent has pockets along the inner, always put the torch in the same pocket last thing at night. Then if required later in the night there is no fumbling around trying to find it.

If the tent has a hook at the apex, hook an LED cluster lamp up. Then its easily found in the night

Clothes Washing

If there are no facilities for washing clothes in a sink then a good way to wash clothes is to have a medium sized waterproof stuff bag, half fill it with water, add a little bit of shampoo or shower gel. Then add the item of clothing that needs a wash. Fold over the top of the stuff bag and give it a good shake, squash down and rub about. Leave for a few minuets and repeat, then remove the clothing, rinse and dry.

Food

Riding a bike burns more calories than people think, so it's good to have some snacks and nibbles easy to hand throughout the day. Jelly Babies are a good option as they give you the sugar rush without the fat. Breakfast bars are another good snack food.

Chopping Board

Cut out a circle just a little smaller than the frying pan from a cheap plastic kitchen chopping board. Then it can fit inside the frying pan when the cook set is all packed up. Another way to save a little space.

Water Carrier

Before the first use, wash it out with warm water and baking soda! You may have to do this a couple of times, but it works! two teaspoons of baking soda, fill it up with water, give it a good shake, rinse, repeat and perfect drinking water. Otherwise the water will taste real bad.

Before moving on after breaking camp, empty and wrap in a bin bag just to be double sure no water dribbles out.

Navigation (Maps)

If you don't want to buy foldout maps, then buy a good scale road atlas of the country or countries travelling through. Then scan in the pages that the route is on and print them out (duplex if possible). That way you are not carrying a whole countries road atlas for maybe two pages of map. It's lighter and takes up much less room.

If writing routes down on paper, then hand write them, don't print them from a computer (you can read your own handwriting much better). Try to use a black pen on white card or paper.

Use Google maps and zoom into an area of interest and print out the map.

Navigation (SatNav)

What ever happens; road signs are helpful, don't become a slave to the satnav. If a sign says campsite to the left, then follow it; it might be the best campsite you stay at on the whole trip!

Mountain Pass Riding

Take things easy on the tight mountain pass roads. Uphill, you can use the rear brake during turns, that will stabilise the bike, and it allow you to keep the throttle open during the turn. But downhill, the rear brake is not so good, so go easy with it; the rear wheel carries almost no weight, which means it will stop turning very easily when you apply the rear brake. So easy front break and try to use some engine braking to slow down, break steady and in plenty of time for the corner going down hill, remembering to release the front break before starting to turn.

ROUTE IDEAS

Not everyone likes looking at maps for hours on end, so here are a few route ideas to get you started. A couple of the UK routes are great to use as a shakedown trip ready for a longer (maybe) European trip.

Obviously you will have to work out a route to and from the locations

Northumberland Round (good for a shakedown trip)

Craster > Kelso > Jedburgh > Carter Bar (border stones) > Heydon Bridge

M1(N) > A1(N) > Scotch Corner > Newcastle
at Alnwick(N) off
follow signs for Craster/Dunstan
overnight at Proctors Stead Campsite
======
Back to A1
** A1(N) > at Berwick A698 to Coldstream
A697 to Coldstream
A698 to Kelso
A698/A68 to Jedburgh
A68 – stop at border stones (Carter Bar)
A68 to R turn to Bellingham - B6320
B6320 to rbout at Humshaugh
R onto B6318
L onto B6319 to Hayden Bridge
Overnight at Poplars Campsite
======

NOTES:
** Possibility for a trip over to Holy Island if the tides are right.

Proctors Stead Campsite
Craster
NE66 3TF,
About £10/night. Pub in village

Poplars Campsite
East Land Ends
Hayden Bridge
NE47 6BY
01434 684427

About £12/night but right next to the river, nice quiet spot. Railway hotel is the pub of choice, back into town, over the old bridge and on opposite corner

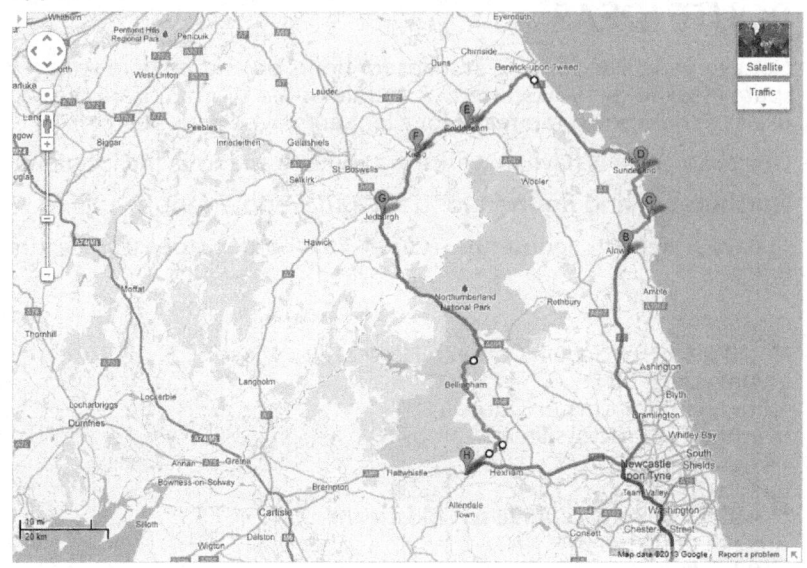

Magnificent Masham

A1 > OFF at J48
Follow signs to Ripon
A6108 TO Masham
In market place follow road to Grewelthorpe
At Grewelthorpe turn R in front of pub
At T junc turn L & follow signs for Kirkby Malzeard
In Kirkby turn R at junc signed Pateley Bridge
Head down High Street (B6265) over bridge
Turn R after bridge (signed Ramsgill/Lofthouse)
Follow to Lofthouse
(OPTION HERE TO GO TO SCAR HOUSE RESERVOIR)
Take road to Masham
After Leighton take minor road to Breary Banks
¾ mile up the road have 5mins at memorial
Backtrack & follow to Healy > Fearby > Masham
At Masham take B6267 & follow to A1

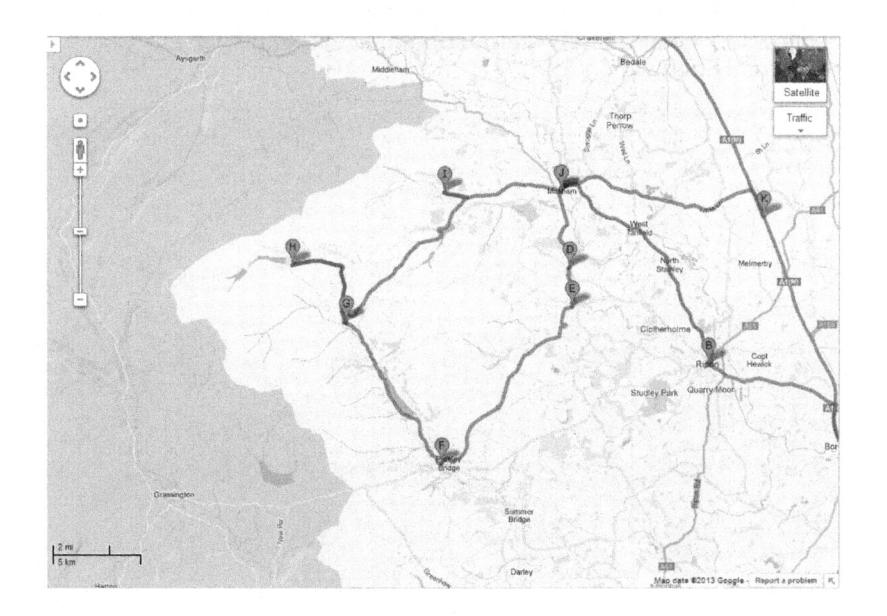

Peak Time
Sheffield / Tideswell / Millersdale / Bakewell / Leek / Buxton / Glossop

Leave Sheffield toward Hathersage (route of choice)
Follow until L turn at Travellers pub (signed Tideswell (B6049))
Follow through Brough > Bradwell
At junc with A623 go straight (staggered) to Tideswell (Nice coffee & pies available here)
Follow B6049 to Millers Dale, onto
A6 & follow to Bakewell
B5055 TO Monyash
AT A515 Turn L
After 2 miles turn R (signed Hartington (B5054))
Follow to Warslow and turn R (Leek Road)
At Y junc take L
Turn L
Mermaid pub (now not a pub) at junc
Turn L to Thorncliffe & Leek
At Leek turn R onto A53 to Buxton
At Buxton take A6 to Chapel-en-le-Frith
A624 (Hayfield/Glossop)
At Glossop turn R onto A57

Follow A57 (Snake Pass) – detour option to Fairholms
Return to Sheffield on A57

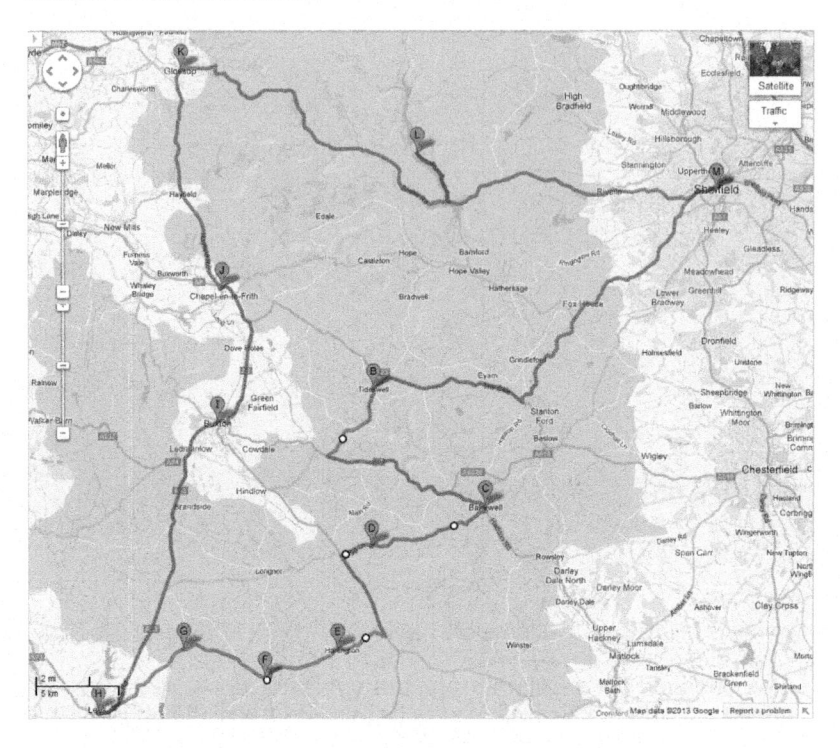

Yorkshire Loop
hawes/ribblehead/halton gill/knaresborough

A1(N) off at Leeming
onto A648 > Beedale > Layburn > Aysgarth > Hawes
B6255 TO Ribblehead & Station Pub on R for a chill
Backtrack to B6479 on R
At Stainforth turn L to Halton Gill
(NOTE: for petrol keep on for 2m, at end turn L BP station on R. Then
backtrack. At Stainforth turn R to HAlton Gill)
R at at Halton Gill
R at B6160
At Threshfield L onto B6265 to Patley Bridge
AT PB take B6165 TO Ripley
B6165 to Knaresborough > A1(S) > M1(S)

NOTES:
Great day loop. Hawes nice place for a wobble and coffee
Station pub at Ribblehead does nice pork pies and a cheeky shandy.
Very narrow single track between Stainforth and Halton Gill. After
Halton Gill single track with high built walls so not much visibility &
tricky. Nice pub at Litton on L (Queens Arms)

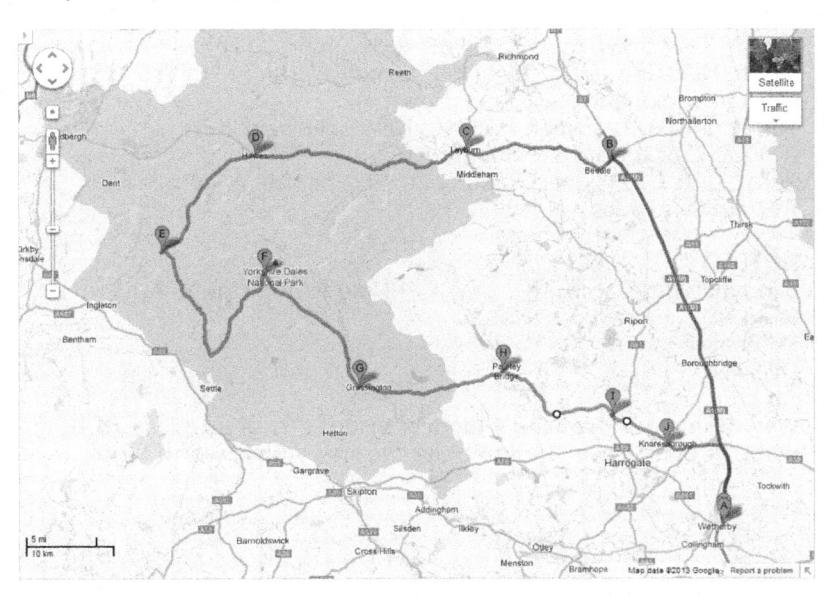

D & G Bimble
Dumfries / Wanlockhead / Sanquhr / Dalry

Leave Sandyhills Camp site A710 to Dumfries
Leave Dumfries on A76
Lurn L onto B729 (Signed Dunscore/Moniaive)
Turn L to Morrington
Follow road to Dunscore
At rbout turn L (signed Moniaive) onto B729
Follow signs to Moniaive onto A702
Car Park just before bridge on R. From CP turn L (signed Tynron)
At Tynron L over bridge
Turn L onto A702 (signed Penpoint/Thornhill)

Turn L at crossroads in Penpoint (signed Sanquhr)
Follow unclassified narrow and twisting road
Until A76 and turn R
After about ½ mile turn L and follow until A702
Follow A702 to Elvanfoot > turn L to Leadhills (B7040)
At Leadhills B797 to Wanlockhead (COFFEE AT PUB OR VISITOR CENTRE)
Follow B797 down to A76. Follow to Sanquhr
A76 to New Cumnock > B741 TO Dalmellington
A713 to Carsphairn > ST. Johns Town
Turn L onto A712 just after sign to New Galloway on R
A712 to Crocketford turn R onto A76
Turn L onto B79 (signed Haugh of Urr/Dalbeattie)
A710 to Sandyhills

NOTES:
Sandyhills Bay Campsite   £13/night, pub close by
Sandyhills
Dalbeattie
DG5 4NY

Wanlockhead – Scotland's highest village. A great place to have a wobble round. Sweetheart Abbey and New Abbey worth a look.

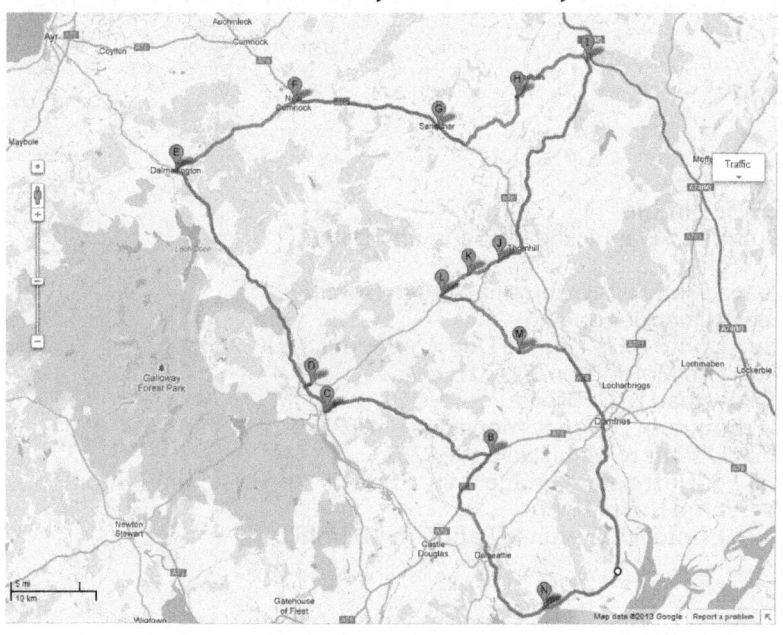

Route Napoléon, France

Route Napoléon is the route taken by Napoléon in 1815 on his return from exile in Elba. It is now a 325-km section of the Route nationale 85. The road was inaugurated in 1932, and leads from the French Riviera to the southern Pre-Alps. It is marked along the way by statues of the flying eagle symbol.

Avoid August as it's hot and busy. Early September is probably the best time, still hot (but not as hot) and the roads will be quieter.

Camping round Lake Annecy, Castellane, Camping La Viste and Les Lionnets on Lac de Serre Poncon, but most decent towns will have a municipal camp site.

On the return journey the route passes through the Gorges de Verdon, which is the Grand Canyon of France. It is about 25 km long and up to 700 metres deep. This together with Lake Sainte Croix is a nature sight not to be missed. Head towards Millau and the viaduct. Then back north the quick way on autoroutes.

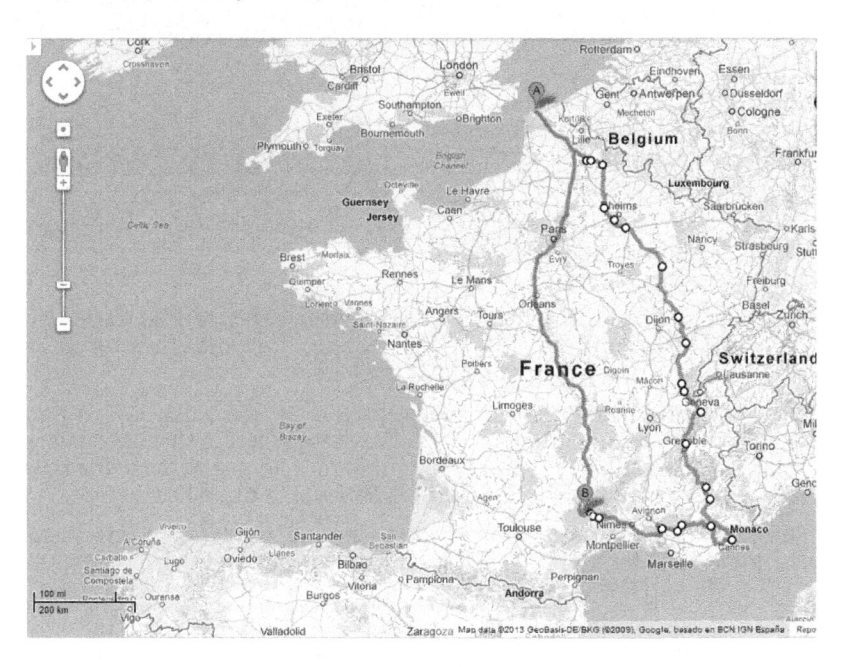

The Dolomites

The highlight of any visit to the Dolomites should be the Great Dolomites Road. The road runs through from Bolzano (Bozen) (note: most places in Südtirol/Alto Adige have two names; one Italian and one Ladin/German) to Cortina d'Ampezzo. There are very few straight roads in the Dolomites where sheer vertical rock faces tower above the roads.

Although it is possible to drive the road in a few hours, its best to take it easy with stops to admire the stunning scenery. Ideally allow at least two days to appreciate the road and more to take in the many detours.

Canazei, a town half way along the road, is a good place to spend the night. There is a good campsite at the far end of town (if arriving from Balzano).

The tour starts in Bolzano in the direction of the district of Kardaun, where the road SS241 turns off to the Eggental Valley.

Along the steep gorge of the Eggental ride to Nova Levante/Welschnofen, where there are wonderful views of the Catinaccio/Rosengarten massif.

Continue to Lagao di Carezza/Lake Karersee. This can be extremely crowded, but worth a little walk around the small lake with its magnificent mountain panorama of the Latemar.

Over Passo di Costalunga you finally reach the Fassa Valley in Trentino. In Vigo di Fassa turn left onto the SS48, where you ride through several small villages to Canazei. Camp overnight at Canazei or make it a base for a few days. Relax with a cool drink and watch the bikes go by.

From Canazei, continue on a steep winding road up to the Passo Pordoi/Pordoi Joch. It offers a beautiful view of the Marmolada, the Catinaccio and the Sassolungo.

Now ride on the SR48 through Arabba and Buchenstein to the next steep mountain pass leading up to the Passo di Falzarego: a great stop for visiting the museum and the battlefields of World War II (and a ham and cheese tostie!)

From the Passo di Falzarego finally ride down the valley to Cortina d'Ampezzo.

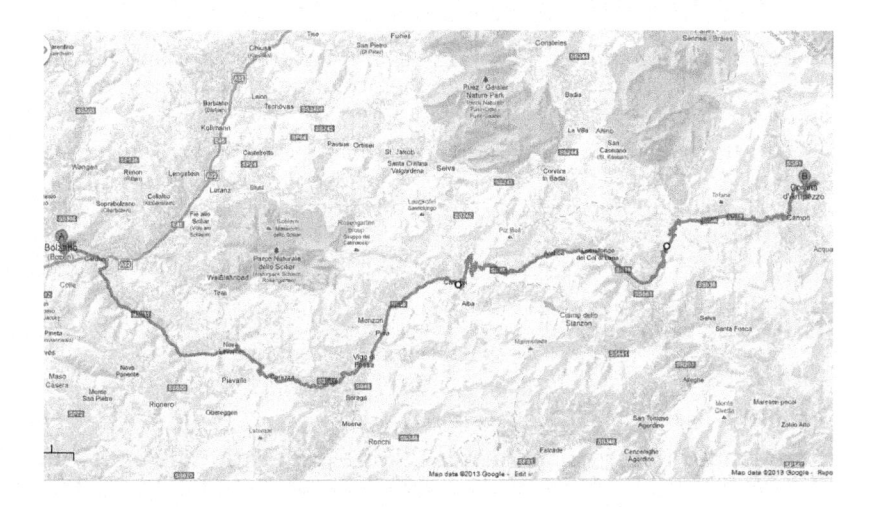

As a detour either add in the Sella Ronda circuit below, or save it for a leisurely day ride, stopping at the many refugios for coffee and to take in the vistas.

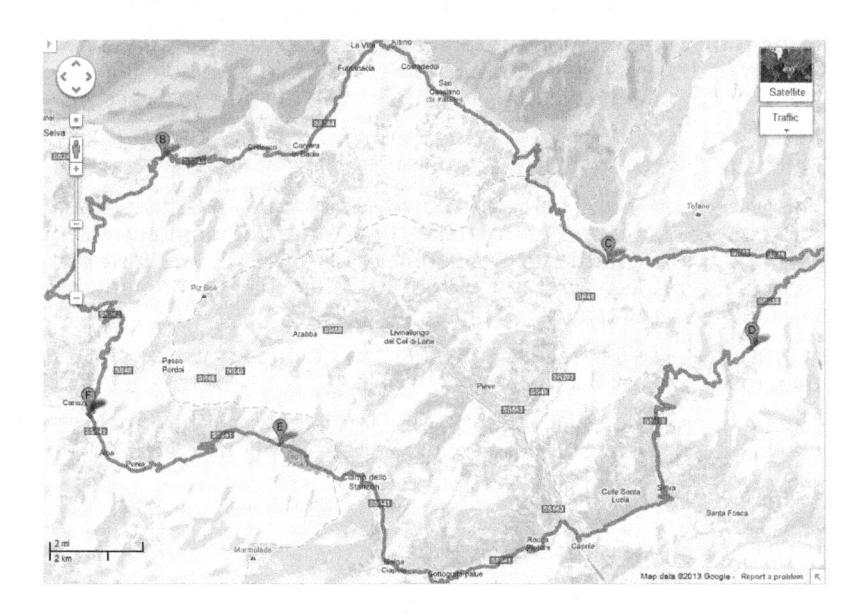

AUTHORS KIT AND PERSONAL VIEWS

Within the main body of the book everything has a for and against view to allow you the reader to see the options and make up your own mind on what is best for you.

I had to do this several years ago and after a few false starts I came up with a set of kit that works for me. Because it works for me doesn't mean it will work for you. So here is my kit and the reasons why I use it, or don't.

Bike Luggage

Kit I Use

Panniers – Hepco and Becker Gobi

At the time of purchasing them they were just a little different to the normal plastic panniers and aluminium was ruled out to due to costs. (But some aluminium panniers have come down in price as more manufacturers come on the market).

They are totally waterproof and have been with me all over the UK and Europe.

One tip that I picked up years ago and still use, is always run an Arno strap round the panniers and the frame. It should then hold it in place if a minor problem develops, and should give me time to notice it and get it sorted.

Roll bag – Overboard 50ltr black

This is my second roll bag after 'down sizing' from an 80ltr roll bag. I find it sits much better on the bike. I have the bag going across the seat and it just over hangs the panniers a little bit. The 50ltr roll bag has plenty of space for a two week trip. After that, spend a morning washing everything and start again!

My bike has a two part seat, so two straps go under the rear seat, and then round the roll bag to fasten it in place.

Then a bungee net over the top of it – yes I know, but having a net is real handy to push your gloves under at petrol stations.

Roll bag – TrekMates 20ltr

A nice small 20ltr roll bag that just sits on the pillion seat. I use this on non camping trips (eg overnight at a B&B or travel lodge) Just big enough for a change of clothes, wash bag and a pair of approach boots)

This is again tied down with some Arno style straps that run under the rear seat.

Tail pack – A 15ltr £12.95 peddle cycle rack bag farkled to fit.

I've always wondered why some manufacturers can get away with charging £120+ for a little tail bag (and still sell them). So once Id seen my need for one, I was on a mission to find one that would do the job and not cost £130! This has all my daily bits and bobs in (maps, water, jelly babies, snacks, visor cleaner etc).

Waist Pack – Hein Gericke

This is normally used on bike trips lasting 3 or more days. It's affectionately known as 'My life' as in it is everything I need to survive.

Stuff Bags – Mainly TrekMates and of several different sizes

These separately have clean clothes/dirty clothes/clean socks/dirty socks (don't know why socks are kept separate really). A nice small one acts as my wash bag.

You can never have too many stuff sacks to keep things tidy.

Straps n Stuff

2 x Arno straps round the panniers

2 x Cam buckle straps to secure the roll bag

2 x bungee straps over roll bag and tent pole bag

1 x elastic net

2x Cam buckle straps (emergency backup)

Kit I Don't Use

Tank bag – Don't use one and probably never will. I just don't like them, for me they just get in the way.

Top Box –In my opinion they move too much weight high and behind the rear axel and act as a big old sail for any cross winds.

Bike Gear

Jacket – Frank Thomas Xtreme

Fully water proof (and it's been through downpours that have lasted days), more pockets that I can find uses for and the venting is fantastic.

Trousers – Frank Thomas Xtreme

Fully water proof, four top pockets and two side leg pockets. The venting could be a lot better – well there could be some for a start!

Helmet – Arai Tour X3

In a word, fantastic – I must have an Arai shaped head

Boots – Oxtar Dunes

Comfy as slippers once the initial 'breaking in' stage passed. Far from 100% waterproof, so I'm on the look out for some new ones.

Can't stress enough the need for good protection of the feet, ankles and lower leg. – Long story short; I once had a dead cat hit me square on the leg after being hit by a car! Even with high tough bike boots on I still got some bruising.

Gloves - Spada MX1 : Frank Thomas Aqua

I used to always wear some thick FT waterproof gloves, but then I tried some thin MX gloves and for me they were the way to go. The Spada MX1s are nice and light and you can really 'feel' the bike through them. I even sometimes ride in a pair of Mountain bike gloves if it's really warm – I know they won't really protect my hands in a fall, but they feel spot on when on the bike.

Normally when on tour I take a pair of MX gloves and a pair of thicker waterproof gloves. I have been know to take three pairs of gloves when touring in September October time.

Neck Tube - TrekMates

I've got loads of neck tubes, but only ever wear the same tired looking blue one I've had for years.

Heated Items

The only item that I have used a few times are pocket hand warmers. The re-usable type where you give them a boil to re-energise. £2 from Aldi.

Kit I Don't Use

Heated Items

I tend to stay warm quite well so I don't need heated gloves, insoles or gilet – But I've never been to the Elefantentreffen!

Other Bits

Seat – Original seat

I have never had an issue with my bike seats, so no Airhawk or gel inserts have been needed. Maybe it's my bum or the well sculptured Caponord seat.

Beam Deflectors

Beam deflectors for bikes are a little overkill I think. For starters you ride more centrally in your lane, and the beam on a motorbike does not have such a drastic left side deflection as a UK car does.

I've ridden on mainland Europe a few times and have never used them and never will, but always carry a set with me just in case I come across a jobs worth police person. That way I can fit them, and they are happy (and I can take them off again round the corner).

Side Stand Extender

I still use a plastic puck that I bought about 9 or 10 years ago! Yes it can be a pain from time to time, but with the addition of the pickup string it works ok. I even carry a couple of spares for the centre stand! And yes I have had to use them a few times when camping and the ground is so soft.

I might get round to fitting one sometime soon.

Heated Grips

Now don't get me wrong – some riders swear by them, but personally I'm not a big fan of them. Yes I have a set fitted, but cant actually remember the last time they were switched on. I find that a good set of hand guards work just as well for me.

Engine Bars

Mmmm well not too much to say here apart from yes they do work! I recently had the pleasure of testing mine out on a mountain road in Italy. I believe I hit a patch of diesel and before I knew it the back of the bike was overtaking me. Long story short after sliding down the road about 50ft the bike had a scraped upper engine bar, a scraped lower bar and a scuffed end bar weight! No another mark to be seen!

So yep they work.

Puncture Repair Kit

I use an AirPro Premium Tyre Repair & Inflation Kit. Had it a few years and only had to use it once. The repair went according to plan and several hundred miles later it was still doing well and keeping the tyre inflated.

Right Angle Valve Adaptor

I have to admit this has helped me out several times. Filling station air hoses just don't fit when you have spoked wheels and a slow puncture! Screw this little fella on, add some air, remove, and you are sorted.

Food

For my on bike food I tend to have a selection of cereal bars (usually Caburys Brunch Bars and for an instant sugar rush without the fat its Jelly Babies. In Austria and Germany then Bifi snacks are always good to get hold of.

Camp Kit

Tent – Vango Spirit 200+

Id had my eye on an 'expedition' tent with a porch for some time. My original bike camping tent was a small Euro Hike tent. It was nice because it packed down small and was quite light, but after four solid days in the rain in Scotland once, I had to change it.

The Spirit 200+ has just loads of room in the porch for panniers and bike gear, leaving the living area clear for me. It's quite a long tent at 4m, but weighs in at about 3Kg, so lots of tent for not much weight.

Based on a tunnel tent with a Gothic arch pole structure. It also has the TBS (Tension Band System) which can add support and stabilisation of the pole structure to side winds, by creating an internal bracing system for each pole.

In a line, I just love this tent

Sleaping Bag – Karrimor Global900

Can't say anything about this bag apart from it packs down smaller than a kid's rugby ball! Pack size is about 26cm and weighs a whopping 850g. Just right for packing on the bike.

The down side it that it's only a 1 to 2 season bag, but I also use a liner for a little extra. It works for me though as I don't like being too warm in bed

Sleeping Bag Liner – Gelert Cotton

Keeps the bag clean and just adds a bit extra warmth if it get chilly. Its also great for sleeping in with no bag – as Ive done a few times in the south of Spain when its hotter at night than it is in the UK during the day!

Sleaping Mat – No make self inflating

It cost me £9.99 and has been fantastic – it does everything it should; it inflates, it insulates and it packs up to an ok size and weight. (Pack size could be better).

For years I used a closed cell Karrimat, so this was a step up for me, but wanted to try before I went the full distance for say a Thermarest. As it happens I never got that far.

Lighting – Petzl Head torch & a cheap and cheerful LED cluster lamp

Both have their advantages. The LED lamp is very handy for hanging up around the place while the head torch lights what you are looking at.

Seating – No make foldable stool

Again cheap and practical is much better than expensive and useless! It's just a basic three leg stool that packs down not too bad. Bad point is the feet keep coming off.

I personally can't see with the added weight and size the benefits of foldable chairs.

Stove – Trangia 27-4UL

In my mind it's the perfect setup. I've got the option of meths or gas for fuel. Everything packs into itself, even washing up liquid, scrubbie, and matches fit inside!

BBQ

Ive only ever bought disposable ones locally if staying at a site for a few days. But I was very impressed with the Grilliput that David Carson uses. And it packs down to next to nothing. Fantastic piece of kit – might have to ask Father Christmas for one!

Kitchen Roll / Self Seal Bags

Once at a camp its amazing how much kitchen roll I get through! So always have a roll or two in my panniers.

Self seal sandwich bags are an item that you want when you aint got one!

Kit I Don't Use

Air beds – Never used and never will!

Recently I've seen quite a few bikers at rallies getting out airbeds and 12v air compressors to blow them up! What's that all about? They are big, heavy, cumbersome, and don't insulate that well. I think if you need an airbed, you might as well go in a hotel.

Camp Sites

I've never pre-booked a campsite in all the years I've been camping. I always just start thinking about where to stay about 3 o'clock, which gives me plenty of time to have a ride around and find a campsite. This method has always worked and some cracking sites have been found. Park Camping at Lindau was one such place. Right on the lake front with beer on tap and great food.

It's come close once or twice. Once I finally found a site with space near Lago di Garda at about 8pm, but that was because it was the weekend and very hot so everyone was out.

Prices paid have ranged from nothing to about €22! in Europe. In the UK £3 to about £15! Sometimes there is no option but to pay the high price.

Misc Kit

Electrical Power on the road

The bike is fitted with a 12v take off, but I have to admit I only use it when really necessary.

In the past I've used a Freeloader solar charger and that kept me in power during a two week trip round Europe. But as devices now require more power this just does not cut the mustard any more. Connect a HTC smart phone to it and it buzzes like crazy, gives about a minute of charge and dies!

Now my weapon of choice is a TeckNet power bank. It's got a 12000mAh battery and can kick out 5V at 2.1A and if required charge two devices at once.

It can charge my HTC smartphone about 6 times and keep the SatNav topped up before it runs down.

Under normal conditions you do have to find a mains supply to recharge it every 5 or 6 days (depending on how much it's been used), but that's not too much of an issue at quiet campsites. Worst case, I can connect an old separate solar panel I had from the Freeloader and trickle charge it through the day.

Money

I tend to start a European trip off with a bit of cash (enough for a day or so), one credit card (for emergencies) and a Post Office travel card loaded with money for the trip. That's all I take.

I use the Post Office travel card withdraw a couple of days of money from local ATMs as and when needed and in shops as a debit card.

I was recently chatting to an English bloke in Italy who had been borrowing off his mates for a week because his bank had blocked his debit card. At this point he was getting quite concerned about how to get his hands on any money. Some simple phone calls before he had left might have been helpful.

Navigation

Maps – more than I know what to do with

Have to admit I'm a bit of a map addict. So over the years I've managed to get a good few of them.

I prefer maps to GPS/SatNav because I like to know where I'm going.

Analogue Satnav - The iPhone holder cost about £3 off ebay.

This is my preferred method of navigation when on the road. Simple, straight forward notes, usually written the night before while looking at a map over a beer.

Just remember to take a pen and a stash of pre-cut cards ready to slip in.

SatNav/GPS – TomTom Urban Rider (Europe) & RoadAngel Adventurer.

I tend to only use a satnav if I've managed to really get lost. I use the analogue satnav system and look at road signs!

These are both great at doing different things. The TomTom is great for getting me out of built up areas or when I just need to navigate to some specific coordinates.

The Adventurer is great as it can be used as a normal satnav, but it's 7also got all of the UK OS maps on as well at 1:50 000 and some 1:25 000 maps so routes can be tracked on 'actual' maps. (Shame they don't make it any more).

Security

Bike Cover

The best piece of kit I use is a black bike cover. If I'm stopping over in a motel where the car park is not barrier controlled (most are in France for example), once the bike has had time to cool down the cover goes on for the night. Watching its powers are quite funny….. Without the cover everyone who walks passed has a good look at the bike (some have even had a press of the buttons!); put the cover on and as if by magic its gone.

Security chain – Thick

One of the coil up types. Only takes up a little bit of space and just enough to make me feel better, depending on where I end up parking.

Security Chain – Thin

This is actually a laptop securing cable, but more than good enough to loop it round/through stuff and lock it up.

LIFE ON THE ROAD

The following pages show a selection of bikers and bikes on the road, loaded up for touring. This is a great example of all the different makes and models of motorcycle used, along with different types of luggage used (soft panniers, hard panniers, roll bags, top boxes etc).

It goes to show adventure bike riding is about the trip not what bike you ride!

Top - Laura Edwards & husband Phil in Morocco
Middle – 'Spud' Murphy in France
Bottom - Peter Ekins, France

Top -
Middle
Bottom – Ian Clarke

Top - John Muizelaar
Middle - John Muizelaar
Bottom – Lance Street

Top - John Bellamy, Pyrenees
Middle - Jason Robinson
Bottom – Philip Parkinson, Morocco

Top - Alistair Henderson
Middle - Phil Edwards, Morocco
Bottom – John Tinkler, Champagne region France

Top - Kelvyn Skee
Middle - Philip Parkinson, Morocco
Bottom – Andy McCowan, On the way to Piel Island

Top - Marc Harbord
Middle – Ray Skipp
Bottom – Ray Skipp

Acknowledgements & Thanks

BUSINESSES/WEBSITES/INDIVIDUALS

MEkey ICE Tags - www.mekey-icetag.co.uk

ABR Magazine/Alun Davies – for permission to use the aluminium pannier review from issue 3 of the magazine. www.adventurebikerider.com

Adventure Parts/Paul Chapman – for permission to use their photographs - www.adventureparts.co.uk

BikeVis/Dan Bailey – for permission to use HID photo & information

All the people from the ABR forum for contributing pictures to the 'Life On The Road' section – Thanks

James Davis of the Motorcycle Safety Group

Motorcycle News

Kriega

Wolfman Luggage

Editors
David Carson; Liz Mawson

EXTRAS

The term Farkle apparently originated among ST1100 riders. It is an acronym:

F.ancy
A.ccessory
R.eally
K.ool &
L.ikely
E.xpensive

From the 2 Wheel Innovations web site:

Farkle: N: An Accessory intended to improve or embellish the original system; opulent luxury item; V: to add pleasure or comfort; to strut about after adding additional items to stock unit thus improving value or performance, usually saying "whoo-hoo" loudly to yourself or your neighbours.

Farkles: As defined by the ST1100 owners' club, a farkle is:

1. (Noun) any modification to one's motorcycle.

2. (Verb) the act of modifying one's motorcycle or kit in some way.

Farkles may have functional or merely aesthetic value, or in fact no value whatsoever! To farkle is to expand one's connection to the motorcycle, to enhance its uniqueness, and provide a venue for personalization.

DIRECTORY

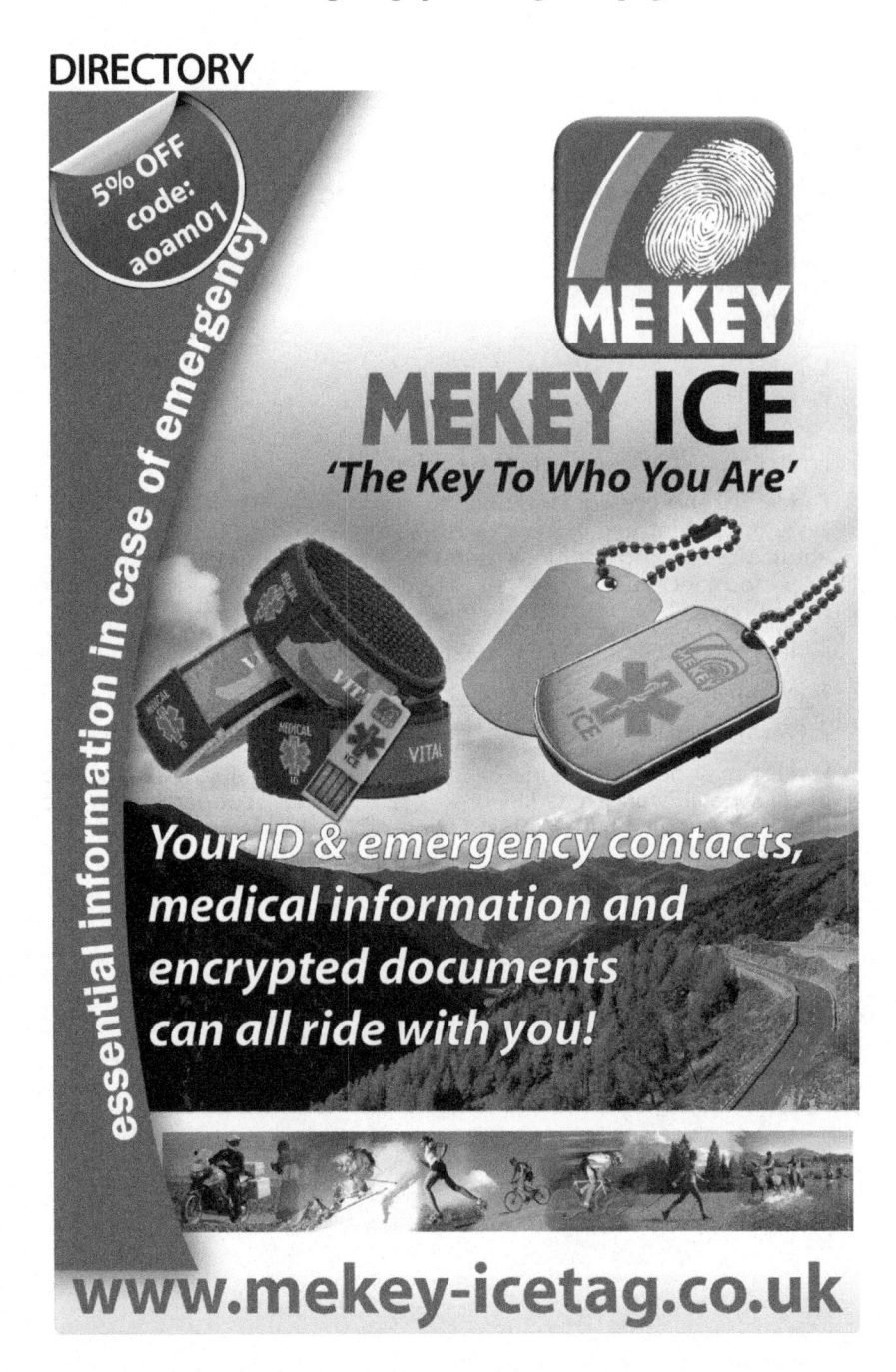

RESOURCES

LED light supplier on ebay - 2allbuyer

BikeVis - LED & HID lights – www.bikevis.com

Motorcycle seat specialist (Tony Archer) - www.tonyarcher.co.uk

Louis – www.louis.de (it's a German site, but if you use Google Chrome it will auto translate – order a free catalogue for 1080 pages of kit to look at and get ideas)

Touratech – www.touratech.co.uk (website a bit better than it used to be – easier to order a catalogue; prices only on website)

Mud Stuff – Alternative source of pannier net pockets. http://www.mudstuff.co.uk/stowage_nets.shtml

St. John Ambulance – first aid training courses - www.sja.org.uk

Helinox Chairs - www.helinox.com.au

Kermit Chairs - www.kermitchair.com

Migsel GPS mounting system - www.migsel.com

Frejus Tunnel – www.sftrf.fr

Tunnel de Puymorens - routes.wikia.com/wiki/Tunnel_de_Puymorens

Lambland - Sheepskin seat covers – www.lambland.co.uk

Scotoiler – www.scotoiler.com

Tuturo - www.tutorochainoiler.com

Made in the USA
Las Vegas, NV
28 March 2022

46463045R00154